3.95

G000160355

Speaking of
Galbraith

BOOKS BY PEGGY LAMSON

The Charmed Circle

Few Are Chosen:
American Women in Public Life Today

The Glorious Failure:
Robert Brown Elliott and the Reconstruction
in South Carolina

Roger Baldwin, Founder of the
American Civil Liberties Union:
A Portrait

In the Vanguard:
Six American Women in Public Life

Stay Tuned:
Behind the Screens at Channel 5

Speaking of Galbraith:
A Personal Portrait

SPEAKING OF GALBRAITH

A Personal Portrait

Peggy Lamson

Ticknor & Fields
New York
1991

Library of Congress Cataloging-in-Publication Data

Lamson, Peggy.
Speaking of Galbraith : a personal portrait / Peggy Lamson.
p.   cm.
Includes index.
ISBN 0-89919-913-5
1. Galbraith, John Kenneth, 1908– . 2. Economists — United
States — Biography. I. Title.
HB119.G33L36   1991
330'.092 — dc20
[B]   91-8088
CIP

Printed in the United States of America

DOH   10   9   8   7   6   5   4   3   2   1

FOR BILL FRIEDLANDER,
favorite nephew, friend, and guru

Contents

Acknowledgments

I WELCOME this opportunity to express my gratitude publicly to the many people who helped me in the preparation of this book. My first thanks go to Kitty Galbraith, who throughout this project has treated me with unfailing warmth and kindness. Sitting in on my interviews with her husband, she listened quietly much of the time but then, at strategic moments, invariably brought forth a relevant fact, a gentle correction, or a significant interpretation.

My debt to Ken's assistant, Andrea Williams, is also great. With her voluminous knowledge of the whys and wherefores of her boss, she could be counted on at all times to supply me with the background information, the pertinent document, or the apt illustration I needed, as well as with her own astute understanding of the man with whom she has worked for the past thirty-two years. Ken's sister Catherine Denholm afforded a unique perspective of his early days as well as a thoughtful, clear-eyed, and loving view of her brother today. Without the cooperation and wisdom of these three women, I have no doubt I would simply have been left at the starting line.

Notable among those who shared their insights of Ken Galbraith with me are Arthur M. Schlesinger, Jr., George W. Ball, George McGovern, Joseph L. Rauh, Jr., and Lois and Tom Eliot. From her particular vantage point, Emily Wilson contributed her colorful sentiments. So too did Ken's sons, Alan, Peter, and James. Ken's brother, William Galbraith, and his wife, Eleanore, showed me the Elgin County of Ken's boyhood. Jacqueline Kennedy Onassis responded promptly and generously to my written questions. William F. Buckley, Jr., and his staff were exceptionally helpful in providing material. Norman and Dorothy Dahl did their utmost to make India vivid for me. Frank Lindsay strove valiantly to clarify my thinking on all manner of knotty problems. Marian Schlesinger contributed especially telling recollections, as did Madeleine Gleason, Gloria Steinem, Adrian Malone, Austin Olney, and Eric and Freda Roll.

Others were generously forthcoming in answering my many questions; they include Carol Laise Bunker, David Ginsburg, Sharon King Hoge, Eugene McCarthy, Stanislav Menshikov, Jane Rumble, Henry Reuss, William vanden Heuvel, Cary Welch, Tom and Elizabeth Winship, Lochi Glazer, and the late Avis DeVoto.

Economists to whom I talked and who were kindly forebearing of my ignorance included Charles Kindleberger, Malcolm McPherson, Lester Thurow, Wassily Leontief, Robert Solow, and, with special thanks, Paul Samuelson and Henry Rosovsky.

William B. Goodman, the editor of my previous book, first suggested the idea for this one and encouraged my pursuit of it. Blair Clark and the late James D. Hart made valuable contributions. As I have in the past, I benefited immeasurably from the editorial assistance of Carol Hulsizer, who cheerfully plowed through each page with me, taking out, putting in, clarifying, reassuring, and smoothing out innumerable rough edges.

My final and most grateful thanks go to my daughter, Pat Chute, a writer of distinction. By her alert and creative chapter-by-chapter reading, she tried to ensure that I did justice to the breadth of my subject, thus saving me from costly errors of omission, as well as many others of commission.

Preface

SHORT OF HAVING the day declared a national holiday, John Kenneth Galbraith's family, friends, and colleagues (and even one or two of his closet detractors) did everything possible to ensure that his eightieth birthday would be celebrated in grand style; this he has long merited and has, in fact, come to expect.

The occasion was marked by a series of events and related tributes: three glittering parties in New York City and a fourth on the actual date, October 15, 1988, at his home in Cambridge, Massachusetts. An entire morning session of the American Economic Association's annual meeting was devoted to "the Legacy of . . ." and, in the academic tradition, a festschrift was being prepared by his peers to celebrate his contribution to one or another of his many chosen fields of endeavor.

Perhaps the high point of these festivities was the dinner held on October 13 at that mecca of intellectual achievement, New York's Century Association. On this particular evening the sound of name dropping — that is, of people saying their own names — was deafening. "A microcosm of a macrocosm," Arthur M. Schlesinger, Jr., called the gathering. And indeed the guest list — luminaries who had crossed Galbraith's path and stayed to become his friends — presented a dazzling display of his extraordinarily varied interests, accomplishments, influences, and predilections.

Ken was in his element throughout the evening. He and Kitty, his wife of fifty-one years, greeted guests in the entrance hall of the Century, in front of an imposing divided marble stairway, Ken standing tall, as people like to say about his great height (six feet eight and a half inches), and Kitty, shy, gracious as always, tiny, and enchanting in her white Indian silk dress.

Seated at dinner with Jacqueline Kennedy Onassis on his right and film star Angie Dickinson on his left, Ken could look out with benign satisfaction at the tables of eight or ten — each presided over by a family member, by Kitty, by the three Galbraith sons, by two daughters-in-law, or by Andrea Williams, Ken's long-time assistant and editor — each filled with all manner of consequential men and women; all manner, that is, except Republicans. (Only two so perceived out of the eighty-six guests.)

Present were statesmen George Ball, George Kennan, and Roy Jenkins — now Lord Jenkins — who had been Britain's chancellor of the exchequer and who flew in from London for the occasion, as well as former ambassadors (besides the guest of honor himself) Carol Laise Bunker, William Luers, now head of the Metropolitan Museum, and William Blair.

There were one-time Kennedy hands Orville Freeman, Ted Sorensen, Stephen Smith and his wife, Jean, William vanden Heuvel (chief birthday party organizer), William Walton, and, although they qualify as fellow academics as well, McGeorge Bundy and Arthur Schlesinger, Jr.

The impressive contingent of editors and publishers included Katharine Graham, of the *Washington Post;* Clay Felker, founder of *New York* magazine; James Hoge, of the New York *Daily News,* who married Sharon King in the Galbraiths' house; Harold Evans, then of *Traveler* magazine; Tina Brown, of *Vanity Fair;* Tom Winship and his wife, Elizabeth, of the *Boston Globe;* and Robert Silvers, of the *New*

York Review of Books. Writers David Halberstam, Louis Auchincloss, Tom Wicker, Gail Sheehy, Harrison Salisbury, and Richard Goodwin and his wife, Doris Kearns, were also on hand.

A small sprinkling of economists — Wassily Leontief, Lloyd Reynolds, and James K. Galbraith (youngest son), all of whom count as good friends — were joined by other good old friends David Ginsburg and Henry Reuss and their wives from OPA days and Joseph L. Rauh, Jr., and his wife from the early ADA days. Staunch liberals Lauren Bacall and Marietta Tree added to the glamor department.

Worth noting also were a few of the more prominent invitees who could not be present. Edward Kennedy was involved in his Senate re-election campaign; Gloria Steinem was barnstorming in the Midwest in support of the pro-choice movement; George McGovern was fulfilling a long-held speaking engagement he couldn't get out of; and perhaps most interesting, the two extremists from Right to Left, William F. Buckley, Jr., and Corliss Lamont, who would have neatly boxed the compass, were prevented from attending — Buckley was occupied with a new play he had written which was having out-of-town tryouts, and Lamont, no less painfully, was at home with a broken hip.

In due course the toasts began; Schlesinger's deft effort opened with the words "Thomas Carlyle, who unfortunately cannot be with us here tonight, once famously characterized economists as 'respectable professors of the Dismal Science.' " Alan Galbraith, the oldest son and a Washington lawyer, talked of the joys and pitfalls of being a Galbraith. George Ball set a pattern by toasting John Kenneth Galbraith's "humility" — for lack of which the guest of honor is justly famous.

Joe Rauh, picking up the same skein, told how when he himself had been honored by a similar party on his seventieth birthday he asked his young grandson which of the speakers he liked best. "Oh, I liked Mr. Galbraith," the boy said firmly. And when Rauh inquired why, he said, "Because all the other people talked about you and I already know all about you. But Mr. Galbraith talked about himself and I didn't know about him, so I thought he was the best."

Ken took all this in very good part, especially since he relishes jokes about his so-called arrogance. He is fond of pointing out that there are two sorts of egoists: those who are basically insecure and cover this with bombastic self-assured behavior and those who are genuinely superior. He leaves no doubt as to which category he falls into, but because he does so with such frank and endearing good humor, his vaingloriousness, which that same Thomas Carlyle called "the sixth insatiable sense," is often cheerfully accepted.

On the other hand, Ken would never think of making any reference to another of his outstanding characteristics — his enormous kindness and generosity to his friends, especially to those in trouble. Still, he must have been gratified to have this referred to by others in their tributes.

But agreeable as it may be to contemplate these birthday ceremonials, they are really just an amiable way to begin the exploration of this man of wit and irony, style and substance, contradiction and consistency, compassion and scorn, generosity and prudence. One runs out of parallels — or should. For Ken Galbraith must not be reduced to neat word pictures. He must be captured in a full-length portrait.

There is among writers of biographies a "temptation to fill up a preface with anxious statements of what a book is not about," writes Catherine Drinker Bowen in her delightful and comforting little book, *Biography: The Craft and the Calling*. She does, however, concede that at times such a confession is necessary — even imperative. Thus, I state at the outset that this is not a book about John Kenneth Galbraith's economic philosophy; rather it is a book about the man who espouses that philosophy. I have known that man over the years as a warm acquaintance and neighbor, but I have belonged nowhere near the epicenter of his wide circle of intimate friends. We've invited each other to our larger parties. I remember once asking the Galbraiths to a book-publication party, to which they were unable to come; instead, Ken sent me a funny letter. In a few pithy lines, he warned me to be wary of the sort of phony modesty that authors frequently adopt on these occasions to demonstrate how unspoiled they are by the sudden bloom of success. I recall reading his letter to the assembled multitude, saying, rather archly it seems to me as I look back on it, that I would let them guess who had written it. Several wiseacres immediately did so. The style and tone were pure Galbraith.

When people ask me, as people inevitably do, whether this is an authorized biography, I tell them that it is indeed authorized insofar as it has been written with the subject's full knowledge and cooperation. However, it is not authorized in that Ken has exercised no veto power over the manuscript and has agreed not even to read the finished product until he can read it in book form.

Introducing me to his friend and Vermont neighbor the late Robert Penn Warren, he said, "This is Peggy Lamson, she is writing a largely favorable biography of me." Since such cheery optimism is quite characteristic of Ken's general outlook, I am emboldened at this point to believe that he wants to like most of what I have written, and that he is prepared to slough off whatever he doesn't like as simply me having a bad day.

Trying to catch the essence of Galbraith the man, the writer, the social economist, the teacher, and the public servant has been a fascinating challenge; the many hours I've spent talking with Ken have been an intriguing and enlightening experience.

Still, "anxious" prefatory thoughts of a potential gap between intention and realization do tend to intrude; these have caused me to wonder from time to time if my subject ever had comparable misgivings when he embarked on one of his

twenty-seven books. Most people who know and love Ken
Galbraith would guess that he would never for a moment
have entertained such self-doubts. I, however, suspect that
they would be guessing wrong. Surely a man who devotes so
much of his intellectual energy to questioning the status quo
is bound to turn his inquiring mind inward upon himself as
well.

A NOTE ON SOURCES

QUOTES FROM John Kenneth Galbraith that are not otherwise identified in the text or in footnotes derive either from his conversations with me or from his memoirs, *A Life in Our Times*. This and all the other Galbraith books quoted from on these pages are published by Houghton Mifflin Company; I thank them for their kind permission to reproduce numerous passages.

My major source of original material was the John Kenneth Galbraith Papers at the John F. Kennedy Library in Boston. This voluminous collection, consisting of letters, memorandums, newspaper clippings, book reviews, speeches, and other writings documenting Galbraith's many-faceted career, was invaluable in the preparation of this book.

Speaking of
Galbraith

I

Determined
Overachiever

JOHN KENNETH GALBRAITH was born on a farm on the southern Ontario peninsula, in a tiny hamlet called Iona Station. The year was 1908. He was raised and worked much of the first eighteen years of his life on that farm in circumstances that made a distinct imprint on the man he was to become.

If you look at an atlas, you will see that the Ontario peninsula juts far down the banks of Lake Erie and into what we would normally think of as United States territory. At the eastern end of the lake on the United States side is Buffalo; at the western end is Detroit. In between, on the Canadian side, the lake shore is curved in an inverted U-shape, at the top of which is Elgin County, where Iona Station lies.

The shortest way between Buffalo and Detroit is across the Ontario peninsula, so when the railroads began to arrive shortly after the Civil War, they took this as-the-crow-flies route, running their lines out of the United States into Canada and back into the United States without qualm. One result was that wherever their tracks crossed a road they built a terminus of sorts. Hence Iona Station.

Doubtless if Ken had been born in rural surroundings either to the east or to the west of Iona Station, the outcome might have been quite another matter. The difference did not lie in the land itself, which was probably as variable in Lansing, Michigan, or Binghamton, New York, as in Iona Station where scrabbly, sandy, and poorly drained stretches of land mixed almost at random with splendid dark earth. The distinction was in the uniquely homogeneous Scotch-Canadian farm community in which Ken lived, surrounded there by McKillops, McPhails, Camerons, McFarlanes, McKellers, Grahams, and the like.

Here were clansmen of stern Calvinistic morals who shared a low tolerance for king and crown, for bathing, and for money loosely spent and, conversely, a high regard for honesty, for knowledge put to wise and practical use, and for money acquired and safely kept.

Ken has told delightfully of this rural settlement in his book *The Scotch*, written while he was ambassador to India, often, he claims, during boring lulls in his official routine or on occasions when waiting interminably for the conclusion of a long-winded introduction of himself as honored speaker. In this, his most endearing book — and incidentally his favorite — he invokes his neighbors with great affection and humor: "The Scotch talked constantly, clinically and unabashedly about each other," he wrote. "A man's farming methods, marketing decisions, livestock purchases, machinery acquisitions, wife, family, relatives, temperament, drinking, stomach complaints, tumors, personal expenditures, physical appearance and his political, social and economic views were dwelt on in detail by his neighbors." He also noted in passing that "to call a son something other than John was to combine mild eccentricity with unusual imagination." We thus learn a great deal that is entertaining about the Scotch of Elgin County, but almost nothing about the particular John in question.

Ken has never been especially forthcoming in fleshing out the picture of his youth, offering a bare-bones account rather than any insights that may make it easier to picture this imposing man as a small boy. "My parents were very nice people," he has said. "My mother died when I was fourteen and in high school. She was a very attractive woman, rather beautiful. My father was a former schoolteacher, a major local politician. He ran a local insurance company and was active both in the township and in county governments.[1] He was auditor of both, the job that kept people honest. In addition to that he was an active working farmer. Except that I greatly disliked farm work — not because I disliked physical labor, but because it bored me — I would say I had a happy time as a youngster."

Actually, that happy childhood seems open to question. Ken was the second in line of the four children of Catherine and William A. Galbraith, his older sister, Alice, being four years his senior, his brother, Bill, two years his junior. His favorite sibling, Catherine, is five years younger. "Catherine and I were the determined overachievers," he has noted. "Alice and Bill were committed underachievers." Well, no — he amended that slightly as not being quite fair to Alice, who was a teacher all her life (she died in 1974) and often worked with retarded children. He stood pat on brother Bill, however. "I have no real relationship with him."

Among the crosses he had to bear as a youngster, aside from his dislike of the monotony of farm work, was the polar oppositeness of Bill, who was indeed the truly happy member of the family. Gregarious, good-looking, feckless, exceedingly popular with the boys and girls of the neighborhood, carefree, and lazy, he rarely read a book, whereas Ken and Catherine and to a lesser extent Alice never did anything *but* read when they could find or steal the time. Both Ken and Catherine remember with particular joy the day that the Dutton Library rescinded its policy of lending only two books every two weeks and allowed its readers to have as many books as often

---

1. The township, called Dunwich (the *w* not silent), was bounded to the north by the Thames River and to the south by Lake Erie and included the towns of Iona, Iona Station, Wallacetown, and Dutton.

as they wished. "I devoured them," says Ken. Bill was a natural athlete; Ken an unnatural, unwilling one. Bill was always
ready to wriggle out of his farm chores to play ball or go
swimming. According to Catherine, Kenneth would then do
his own work and Bill's too.[2]

Although he is perhaps guilty of inventing his past to conform to his image of his present, Ken likes to portray himself
as an irritating, bumptious boy who read every book in the
library and frequently felt called upon to share his superior
knowledge with his elders and to look down on his ignorant
peers. Fortunately, because he was always too tall and, with
his caustic tongue, too formidable to be bullied by the other
youngsters, he was largely ignored. Sometimes he would play
a little desultory ball or swim in the gravel pit with neighborhood kids and with his cousins, of whom there were many —
both his mother and father came of large families, many of
whose members lived nearby. "We had cousins around all the
time," said Ken. "My sister Alice liked them, Bill of course
liked them too. Catherine tolerated them, and I regarded
them with high amusement." Apparently, this trait, showing
contempt by mockery, began early in his life and has persisted
through the years.

The Galbraiths' next-door neighbors — the Lyons family
and their crew of four dirty, indolent, and loutish boys and
one girl — who came regularly to invade the Galbraith precincts, were a fair subject of such ribaldry. Although they
don't appear in *The Scotch* among the more personably ec-
centric clansmen, the Lyonses deserve to be preserved for history if only because of their mother. According to legend
(much disputed as to detail) she was the fruit of a union between her father and a woman not his wife; immediately after

---

2. His wife and other family members call him Kenneth. Friends, except those
professing a greater intimacy, call him Ken. As for "John," although he abhors the
use of that name, based, he claims, on the fact that the uncle from whom it derives
was a worthless old drunk, he did name his first-born son John Alan. Alan also
eschews "John."

her birth she was placed, wrapped in a red bandanna (Ken's version), under the fence of her father's farm to be raised by him and the woman who was not her mother. She bore the unforgettable name of Etoile — pronounced *Eee* (to rhyme with bee) *toil* (as by the sweat of your brow).

Catherine Galbraith Denholm has early memories of Kenneth reading to her and substituting his own words for the ones they had both heard so often before to make it more interesting, usually to her howls of distress.

Delving even farther back, she recalled a conversation overheard between her mother and father in which they voiced concern over their Kenneth's extremes of temperament. He was so obviously bright beyond his years, yet so often moody, quick to anger and even to tears, that they feared frustration might inhibit his becoming a success in life.

Ken responded to this recollection with feigned surprise. He always thought he was most equable, he said with irony. His memory was of complete amiability. But then finally shifting slightly, he admitted, "Look. I'm sure I was often angry, but I have no recollection of it."

Did he remember feeling set apart? "Somewhat, yes. I wasn't an easy companion or a member of the community fellowship the way Bill was."

But if he sometimes felt lonely, the land in its changing seasons was a great balm to him, as least as he recalls it so lyrically in *The Scotch*.

It would be wrong to think of this as a land without beauty. On the contrary, I remember it, and quite accurately as having a breathtaking loveliness. . . . On a dozen winter mornings the snow was deep over the fields and fences and sat in great patches on the evergreens in the yard. . . . Even the steep roofs of the houses disappeared under a white mantle. . . . Sun was not good for this landscape; it brought back a certain hardness of line . . . the snow became old and used and the mud and steaming manure piles and derelict machinery showed through.

But there were other moments — one of them when the apple trees blossomed and the grass was rich and green against the newly seeded land. . . . The maples provided their special moment of grandeur in the fall . . . the spring brought thick patches of violets and forget-me-nots and a little later of wild phlox. . . . Every three or four years circumstances favored blackberries and one picked them for hours under a bright green and red canopy of sumac, encountering at intervals one's neighbors similarly engaged.

Yet in *The Scotch* a harsher reality often intrudes: "Other children of which one read had streams to patrol and mountains to climb and some natural curiosities such as caves or springs. We had none of these. A spring was only a muddy hole where the cattle watered. One brook ran in a dull way from the end of a tile drain just beyond our farm to the lake five or six miles to the south. It had water in it for only a few weeks in the spring and after especially heavy rains. . . . The only available hill could be climbed in a matter of four or five minutes."

Today, with Bill Galbraith as a guide, one can still find vestiges of the Iona Station and surrounding townships that the four Galbraiths knew as children. The Community Hall, where young people went to dance on some Saturday nights (an event drearily remembered by Ken) and where the Literary Society met, is a tumble-down, boarded-up shell. In Dutton, the McIntyre House, where in Ken's day the Scotch went to drink Scotch and make as merry as their saturnine natures permitted, is today sleazy, run-down, and depressing, the victim of one unsuccessful owner after another. The building that had once been the library so cherished by Ken and Catherine is now the town hall. What had once been the town hall is no more.

But other sturdy institutions have stood the test of time. One such hardy perennial is the Wallacetown fairground; its annual September fair was, and still is, a much anticipated event throughout the county. Even nonconformist young

John Kenneth looked forward eagerly to showing his farm's purebred Shorthorn cattle at the Wallacetown Fair, competing each year with Duncan Brown, a neighboring farmer who also had purebred Shorthorns. One year first prize would go to the Brown farm and second to the Galbraiths, the next year it was vice versa, and they would divide the prize money — usually forty or fifty dollars — between them. "My pets were really those cattle. I was always quite involved with them and gave them a lot of attention," said Ken.

Bill Galbraith and his wife, Eleanore, have lived on and off in Wallacetown through the years. Bill is exactly as tall as Kenneth and bears a strong family resemblance in other ways, especially in his voice, which if one were blindfolded would be quite indistinguishable from Ken's, except that there is often a marked difference in what he has to say. He likes to look on himself as a sort of perpetual Peck's bad boy, but in the 1980s he began to refer to himself, quite aptly, as Ken's Billy Carter. Bill is fond of spinning tales about his Elgin County neighbors; he also delights in showing off the old haunts of his and his siblings' childhood.

"Now here's the McKillip house, and over across there that used to be the store — it's been boarded up like that for years. . . . Now we're on Starvation Street. . . . Just turned off Back Street. . . . Right here is the Catholic church. . . . Over there was the McPhail place, and it still is the McPhail place, the only one that has prospered. . . . And here! Now here is Old School Baptist Church."

If Ken, Bill, and Catherine are, or ever were, united on any one subject about their early days, it is in their shared horror of the tedium they had to endure in that Old School Baptist Church.

Catherine: "Once a month our father took us there. He didn't belong but he preferred it to the regular Baptist church where Mother belonged and went every Sunday. At the Old School Baptist, elder somebody would take the sermon and preach hell and damnation. Father went to sleep."

Ken: "How this creed got into rural Canada I do not know, but there is no doubt as to its hold on the affections of the rural Scotch. It completely accommodated their culture. This became evident the moment one stepped inside the church. For it contained nothing, literally nothing, but square oaken pews and a plain wooden pulpit."

Bill: "Whoever preached there never changed the tone of his voice; he just droned on the same way for two hours. There was no choir; somebody might start up the singing. There was no collection except maybe some groceries for the preacher. And once a year at the May Meeting, they took up a collection for him and the dish would be overflowing."

Catherine: "It's funny that Father, who was such a socialist, would go to this fundamentalist Baptist church."

Ken: "Central to the creed of the church was an uncompromising predestination. A man was born saved or he was born damned."

Bill: "Everything was foreordained. You didn't have to worry about anything. It was foreordained, whatever was going to happen."

On Willey's Sideroad stands a small, square, yellow-brick, peaked-roof building, unadorned — with two windows, one on each side of a projecting doorway with triangular lintel — plain but not uninviting; this was, and is, Willey's Corner School. Here in the one-room schoolhouse all four Galbraiths received their first eight years of education, Ken making the passage in five years, thus readying himself technically for high school at the age of ten. But as he points out with uncharacteristic modesty, his "greatly accelerated rate of movement was the result less of academic merit than academic convenience." With only one or two children in each of eight different classes, the teacher found it more practical to move a bright child from junior first to join another, perhaps not quite so bright child from junior second.

The little Galbraiths did not have far to walk to school;

Hogg Street was just a half mile north of Willey's Sideroad, and on Hogg Street is the one-time Galbraith farm.[3]

Today it looks gentrified; its tree-lined driveway leads to an expansive white frame house with green trim, complete with a covered breezeway, an attached two-car garage, and carefully tended shrubbery. The original homestead had a verandah going all the way around it; the garage for the Model-T Ford was one of several green frame outhouses, next to one just like it, only considerably larger than the one that housed the Galbraith pigs. Very little of today's *House and Garden* look bears any relation to the rough-and-tumble setting and the boisterous vitality of earlier years when squabbles and laughter, bicycles strewn all over the lawn, and kids everywhere dominated the scene.

Bill seems to scorn the current tidied-up, button-down feel of his boyhood home and to note that a major difference between then and now is the almost complete absence of any movement, of anybody's doing anything — even the animals are notable by their absence. "That's because all the farmers around here work someplace else," he says. "They just put in their crops in the spring with big machinery so it's all done in a day, then somebody comes along with a harvester and harvests it. There's no real farmers left anywhere around here. I was the first that went broke," he adds.

When William Galbraith the elder died unexpectedly in 1938, he left the farm to Bill, since his older children were embarked on lives of their own elsewhere. Ken had just married Kitty and was by then well launched on his career. Alice, who never married (she was as tall as her siblings, but unlike them she was shy about her height), had a job teaching at a school north of Toronto, and Catherine, who was doing a year of postgraduate work at Ontario Agricultural College, was engaged to be married to Jack Denholm.

---

3. So named because at one time hogs did indeed feed there. The extra g was added for nicety's sake, by the local Dutton *Advance*.

Bill lasted about four years on the farm, when, to nobody's surprise, he had to sell it. He attributes his failure to changing times that brought with them a preference for single crops — mostly the soybeans that were everywhere, with maybe some corn — instead of the wide diversification in both crops and animal husbandry which prevailed when he and his brother were growing up.

And indeed, as far as Ken was concerned, this diversification made farming, at least in retrospect, not only bearable, but often a fascinating exercise in cyclical management. He greatly admired what he called

> an arrangement of tasks which, while avoiding peaks and valleys in the need for labor, kept one man reasonably employed the year around. This was accomplished by a combination of livestock and field husbandry which spread the demand for labor very adequately over the year. The animals required a good deal of attention through the Canadian winter but could do very well by themselves on the summer pasture. The field crops confined their demands to the summer and these, in turn, had their own well-considered sequence. Oats . . . were in the ground and growing before the corn land needed to be prepared. . . . Equally important were the tasks such as cutting wood, taking grain to the gristmill, putting the manure on the land (hauling shit in the brief language of the average clansman) which were undemanding as to time. These filled up the space between the jobs that could not be postponed.[4]

When Ken finished Willey's Corner School at the age of ten, his parents decided that he was too young to fit in comfortably at the high school in Dutton, the largest of the Dunwich townships (population 980), and elected to keep him back on the farm for a year. Ken claims the decision was also made because of "some foot trouble" he was having. (Catherine says this was simply a euphemism for flat feet.) In any case, this would prove to the first of four extra years he took to com-

---

4. *The Scotch* (Boston: Houghton Mifflin, 1964), p. 35.

plete his academic life, a practice common enough today, when students often take at least one leave of absence from high school or college, but certainly less so in the 1920s and 1930s. As wildly precocious as he was, Ken surely benefited from this deceleration and despite the delays wound up completing his Ph.D. at the age of twenty-six — certainly par if not above par for the course.

More than any other, the circumstance that had a truly profound effect on Ken Galbraith's young life was the death of his mother, when he was only fourteen years old. "We all had a feeling of dispossession," he says.

His use of that word is significant; dispossessed was indeed what the four Galbraith youngsters and their father were when Catherine Galbraith, after having been in poor health for six months, finally died of a heart attack. Alice, at age eighteen, had to give up her first job teaching school in a town far north of Elgin County to come home and assume responsibility for her younger brothers and sister. William Galbraith was so distrait that he was incapable of resuming his rightful place as the idolized head of the family who had always guided his children's well-being with a firm but loving hand. His disorientation was such that even when Christmas came along a few months after his wife's death, he eschewed any celebration for his family; there were no presents, no tree, no cheer of any sort. Nor would he permit his many relatives to step in and try to help him bring back some sense of normality into their lives.

Interestingly, Catherine is able to speak freely and vividly of this very troubling period, while Ken seems almost wordless, constrained from expressing his most deeply felt emotions. Catherine says that even as adults, she and Kenneth have never talked together of this dismal time, which as she recalls lasted for nearly a year. Fortunately, William Galbraith then regained his equilibrium and once again became the compelling force in his children's destinies.

Much of what Ken was to become can be traced directly to

his father's influence, beginning with his liberalism, often referred to (as in the case of his son) as his socialism. He was the leader of the tiny Liberal party in the township of Dunwich, a party almost universally supported by the Scotch in the township (and equally scorned by the merchants in the various towns, particularly in Dutton). Clansmen and others in pursuit of their common interest regularly visited William Galbraith at his farm — especially on Sunday afternoons — to talk politics, and young Ken was always present, listening, noting, absorbing, and as time went on, one cannot doubt, holding forth. Moreover, even as a little boy, he seized every opportunity to accompany his father when he went to speak at political meetings, and early became a keen appreciator of his father's humor. Once, notably, when his father "mounted a large manure pile to speak to the assembled crowd, he apologized with ill-concealed sincerity for speaking from the Tory platform." And afterward when Ken congratulated his father on his witticism, the elder Galbraith observed dryly, "Yes, it was good, but it didn't change any votes."[5]

In common with many young people raised on a farm, the Galbraiths, with the exception of Bill, tended to feel ill at ease when they were thrown into social contact with the more "urban" types in Dutton. Their clothes, Catherine believed, had a homemade look that never seemed quite right. And Ken maintains that instinctively during much of his youth he felt himself as a farm boy to be an outsider looking in — a feeling, he insists, rather incongruously, that often persists to this day. "There's still a slight flavor of manure," he has said more than once, always with obvious relish. In fact, the insider-outsider theme has played out in a variety of ways throughout his life.

Such misgivings as the Galbraith children may have had were more than compensated for by their father's uncanny ability to make them feel — without ever putting it into

5. Ibid., p. 75.

words — that they were a lot smarter than everybody else, that they could do things the others couldn't, that they were just plain better than their cousins, their neighbors, or anybody else they associated with. To be sure, Ken probably always believed this, and in the fullness of time Catherine says she did too.

Furthermore, their father's prominence, his secure position in the community as a "man of standing" (to quote from a chapter title in *The Scotch*), tended to give his children a strong sense of their own worth. "My father was once a schoolteacher and he never gave up," Ken said. "He was always somehow engaged in instruction of his family and his neighbors. It was never didactic; he would just talk. I can see him now at the Wallacetown Fair, sitting with his hands on his knees, talking, telling people what they should believe. There must have been — and I'm not exaggerating — a hundred or even two hundred people around who didn't have views on *any* subject until they got them from my father, who had views on *every* subject. And I paid close attention to that, with, I suspect, a certain independence that allowed me to differ with my father from time to time." The picture of William Galbraith, sitting, talking uninterruptedly, enlightening the uninformed, could have a certain ring of familiarity to his son's many admirers.

Ken tends to think in terms of what he calls "break points" — certain memorable moments in his life when he has had a clear, sharp sense that his future was either at risk or was hovering on the brink of a sea change. One such watershed occurred just as he was finishing his fourth year at the Dutton High School, years that had not been altogether fulfilling for him. It had been a hard day on the farm; Ken, unglamorously, had again been having trouble with his feet. He and his father were working together on the granary in the barn, when suddenly, without breaking stride and apropos of nothing they had been talking about, his father said, "I think you'd better decide to go on to college at Guelph."

By Guelph he meant the Ontario Agricultural College (OAC), then a branch of the University of Toronto, located at Guelph about eighty-five miles northwest of Iona Station. The Galbraiths had a white bull servicing their heifers named OAC Pride because William Galbraith had bought him at auction there. This gives rise to one of Ken's nicest little conceits, an apocryphal story, surely, in which he delights. One fine spring day, as he tells it, Ken was strolling with a young girl — the object of his love, he claims — through the orchard toward the land that separated the Galbraith farm from that of the McCallums. As he and his "compact young girl" — her name was May Cameron — stood leaning against the fence looking at the cows pasturing in the field below them, OAC Pride dutifully went to work on one of the heifers then in season. Noting that the girl was watching this procedure with evident interest, Ken ventured, "I think it would be fun to do that."

To which young May replied succinctly, "Well, it's your cow."

But at the time that his father made his pronouncement in the barn, Ken's thoughts were not on OAC the white bull, but rather on OAC the avenue of his liberation from farm work. He believes that for as long as he can remember he had plotted his escape, and, although he thinks his father was probably aware of this, the day in the barn, the break point, was the first time the word *college* had been uttered in connection with his future.

Still, there were some roadblocks. First there was the matter of money. Although OAC offered the least expensive opportunity, it still cost more than William Galbraith could afford. So ultimately an arrangement was struck whereby Alice, who was then back teaching school away from home and earning a salary, would lend Ken five hundred dollars and as it worked out he would repay Alice's investment in his education by giving the money to Catherine when it became time for her to go to OAC. (There was apparently never any question of Bill's going to college.)

The further problem, difficult as it may be to credit, is that Ken Galbraith at the age of sixteen was really not academically strong enough to be admitted even to Ontario Agricultural College. As he puts it, "I had a couple of courses to make up, which either I hadn't taken at all or my grades weren't good enough. I don't remember which." In any case, he did the necessary work by repeating his senior year in high school, not at Dutton but at St. Thomas, which was the county seat of Elgin County, but not in the Dunwich township.

The change of locale was deliberate. St. Thomas was farther away, but in St. Thomas Ken did not have to deal with that scourge of his young life, "Old Tommy," principal of the Dutton High School, a man of "remarkable ignorance" whose primary skill was his ability to exploit the instinctive mistrust between the merchants of Dutton (who tended to be the Tories) and the rural Scotch (the Liberals) — always to the advantage of the merchants, who, incidentally, controlled the purse strings of the high school.

Of course, there is nothing unusual about a malevolent, spiteful, and cranky teacher or principal, someone theoretically charged with guiding our schooling and expanding our horizons. More often than not, though, time softens the harshest memories, and we tend to look back on a hated tormentor with amused tolerance, even grateful to him or her for having taught us a useful gem or two. Not so Ken. He found no mitigating circumstance in his four-year-long affliction with Old Tommy.

There was first the matter of getting to school on time in order not to run afoul of Old Tommy's obsessional preoccupation with promptness. Along with other farm children from Iona and Iona Station, Ken had to get up very early on school days to help feed the cattle and then to groom and harness the horse, have breakfast, hitch the horse to the buggy, and set off for school, some six miles away, first with his sister Alice and in later years with his brother, Bill. With their fate at the mercy of an often cantankerous horse, a rickety buggy, and snowy, rutty roads, the Galbraiths and other farm youngsters were apt to run into transportation difficulties that made them a few moments late.

The stress of anticipating the punishment that surely awaited them, coupled with their close contact with their recalcitrant horses, often caused a malodorousness in these unfortunate children which further offended Old Tommy's already aroused sensibilities. No matter how cold the weather, he would force the miscreants to put their heads and shoulders under the icy stream of the school pump — a practice that only exacerbated matters; the one thing worse than a sweaty, horsy stink is a *wet,* sweaty, horsy stink.

A further and even more devastating menace was Old Tommy and his Dutton High School Cadet Corps. This relic of World War I was clung to tenaciously by the penurious principal because the school received a small subsidy for each cadet. Accordingly, every boy, from the littlest twelve-year-old to the gawkiest seventeen-year-old, was subjected to the rigors of a twice-a-week close-order drill. It is hard to imagine a less suitable endeavor for Ken Galbraith to engage in. Footwork had never been his strong suit, and used as he was to strolling along beside his Shorthorn cattle, he simply could not seem to master a brisk military stride forward, let alone contrive to stay in step. His clumsiness strained even the bullying instincts of Old Tommy, who devised, for Ken and other farm boys similarly afflicted, a special "Awkward Squad" and reduced them to writing five hundred times a day the words "My left foot is not my right foot!" One need look no further for the roots of Ken's lifelong mistrust of the military.

All this belittling, coupled with the necessity of having to repeat a year at school, might have broken the spirit of even a would-be "determined overachiever" like Ken. That it didn't is attributable both to his inherent belief in himself and to the wise, steadying, and supportive hand of his father. For his son, he was, and would remain, a matchless role model.

2

Escape from Tedium

No trumpets sounded on the day in September 1926 that Ken Galbraith set out to conquer a new world. Outwardly, it was all quite ordinary. He drove his father's car, with his father beside him, a half mile to the Iona Station station. When the train for Guelph approached, he shook his father's hand, picked up his valise, and hopped on the train.

On board he met two other young men also headed for OAC, and they talked during the two-and-a-half-hour journey. He had never been to Guelph and knew no one except for his two newfound acquaintances.

In Guelph, the about-to-be students took the trolley car from the station up to the campus, which sits on a high hill above the city. "It was a lovely autumn day, the campus was extremely beautiful, the football team was practicing, I was shown to my room and" — here his voice betrays a hint of emotion — "I felt I had arrived."

In point of fact he had not — not quite. His opening days were disappointing. He had trouble with roommates; the first one assigned to him, an apparently agreeable man, slightly older, requested a transfer after only one evening of listening to Ken, and Ken himself moved off to a single room after only a few months with his second roommate, Jack McCalla (who would resurface briefly in Ken's life some thirty-six years later).

Of more concern, the course of study at OAC was so rigidly farm oriented that Ken might have wondered just how much of an escape he had actually made from tedium. At first, however, that did not appear to bother him. He entered with a certain enthusiasm into his fixed curriculum (no electives) of animal husbandry, field husbandry, poultry husbandry, horticulture, agricultural engineering, and apiculture. Because his father was a "minor but known livestock breeder," Ken gravitated naturally to animal husbandry as his major — called his "option" at OAC — and for the same reason, he says, was treated with respect by the faculty.

But after a year or so he stopped returning that respect and began complaining that the only people at the college who were more anti-intellectual than the students were the faculty.

Still, much as he might dislike having it said, in the beginning of his student career Ken Galbraith could almost have been called gung ho. He, whose abomination of sports is matched only by his inability to perform on any playing field, actually admits to going out in his freshman and sophomore years for various teams. "I even turned out for football one autumn," he conceded, and then, hastily explaining this lapse, added, "My class team, that is, because we were all encouraged to take part, but no one recalls my having any competence whatsoever." The same could also be said of his contribution to Canada's national sport, hockey, where he claimed his only distinction was slipping the puck by accident into his own net. Here again no one appeared to have urged his further participation, although his class yearbook did record his feat.

Not surprisingly, basketball gave him the most trouble. His six-foot, eight-inch frame was actively sought after, and for two years he succumbed to the importunings of the coach, who was also his professor of entomology. But he hated basketball most intensely, perhaps because he felt trapped by it and also because he may have been embarrassed that given his natural endowment he was so bad at playing it. "I was awkward. A fellow a foot shorter than I would take the ball away from me at center. My coordination was extremely poor, and the crowd would react with contempt to my playing."

In his junior year he decided to stand firm against all blandishments, until finally, when the frustrated coach asked him why he was refusing to come for practice, Ken alleges that in his exasperation he answered, "Because I hate the fucking game." An unlikely reply, but whatever word he used worked. He was never bothered to play basketball again, and he believes that this proves his point that if you take a strong position in slightly intolerable language, you can bring a whole problem to an end in much less time than if you tactfully negotiate your way out of it.

Ken had considerably more success in various other, non-athletic extracurricular activities. As "Spike" Galbraith he was well known among the students for his very considerable part in starting a college newspaper, in naming it the *OACIS,* and in editing this lively publication in a manner, he says with pride, "that gave maximum offense to the faculty."

There were ample reasons for his growing skepticism about much of that faculty. "I think it's fair to say that almost nobody at this institution had an advanced degree," he said. "People held their positions by right of having been given the job early in life and nobody ever changed them. The teaching was very superficial and some of it was ill directed. For instance, in my major — animal husbandry — you judged animals by their shape rather than by their possibility of productivity."

Fortunately for Ken, two exceptions to the rule of faculty mediocrity happened to be his two English teachers, "well-known Canadian literary figures, of the secondary sort, named O. J. Stevenson and E. C. McLean. They were meticulous; you had to write weekly compositions and they were corrected very carefully. I became one of their favorite students in my junior year and that was where I first became involved in writing."

Ken is generous about spreading the credit for his literary

success among numerous other writing mentors who encouraged his unswerving belief in himself as a writer. They range from Henry Luce at *Fortune* magazine to an English teacher at Dutton High who paid him the dubious compliment of passing off his youthful essay on Shakespeare's sonnets as her own work, albeit with his full concurrence, and submitting it to a contest of work by high school English teachers. There is no evidence that it won the prize. If it had, we would surely know of it.

Although not quite in this elevated category, at this time the editors of two small western Ontario newspapers, the St. Thomas *Times Journal* and the Stratford *Beacon Herald,* commissioned the aspiring young writer to a weekly column on agriculture for which they paid five dollars — "an enormous sum," Ken noted. "It paid for all my forms of recreation."

Indeed it may well have done, since recreational opportunities at Guelph were severely limited. Ken recalled only one woman in his entire class, and a very small number in any of the other classes. (His memory may well be flawed here, however, since his sister Catherine, who went there for four years, did not feel set apart.) It is doubtful whether he greatly mourned the absence of young women at this stage in his life. All evidence suggests that where women were concerned he was both shy and inexperienced. "We were brought up — all of us — with a rigorous commitment to the notion that sex was dangerous because you might get somebody pregnant, and that sex was not only extremely unwise, but even wicked. That was a dominant theme."

Even allowing for Ken's strong tendency toward hyperbole, it is doubtless true that his stern Calvinistic-Scotch upbringing contributed to his early lack of ease with the opposite sex — a lack that he was to make up for in later years when he greatly enjoyed and even preferred the company of women.

Still, life at OAC was not all work and no play. Much of the work, in fact, *was* play. Animal-husbandry students got to travel around to all sorts of fairs judging livestock. Ken was selected to be on the team that went to the Chicago International Live Stock Exhibition, which he found most exciting, though he continued to believe that animals were being judged according to a prearranged design of what good livestock should be, rather than by their proven productivity. He also invented a specialty for himself as a designer of the OAC exhibition booths at county fairs throughout Canada.

He is fond of remembering Henry H. Dean, professor of dairy husbandry, known to his students as Henry "Holstein" Dean, who was famous for such earth-shaking pronouncements as "The dairy cow is the foster mother of the human race" and who taught him how to make cheese and butter.

One has to wonder just where Ken and other students of these various "husbandries" thought their not-too-challenging curriculum would lead them after college.

"I didn't have any long-range view and neither did my colleagues," said Ken. "We all lived in the present. [The present, it must be remembered, was the Great Depression.] But there were various possibilities. If you were good you might get taken on as a county agent, advising farmers on how to improve their agriculture. That was a very attractive job. Or there were other quite good 'escapes.' Some of the boys went on to take a year at the University of Toronto School of Education and then to teach agriculture in high school. Others got good jobs grading livestock in the stockyards of Toronto, or being hog graders."

Luckily, Ken did not have to consider any of these options because by then he had begun to think in terms of agricultural economy. Since he took five years to finish OAC (necessitated, he contends, by an incipient tuberculosis, which is a familial weakness, plus the residual effects of his inadequate high school education), this change in his thinking occurred in what should have been his final but was actually his second-to-last year.

"I became aware that there was something wrong with a system where you could produce excellent livestock and excellent crops and fruit and couldn't sell them," he explained. "The problem was in the market rather than in the technique for production. So I shifted my attention over to agricultural economics, which was not a very rewarding field at OAC. It was not a major and I soon discovered, not to my surprise, that the professors didn't know any more than I did. But they were rather respectful of me, and in the summer before my last year they gave me an automobile and the task of going out and investigating the conditions of tenant farmers."

Ken found this an agreeable summer job; he enjoyed traveling all over Ontario, visiting poor farmers and filling in long questionnaires about how they survived as tenants, what the nature of their lease was, and what protection they had from their landlords. Then he wrote "a definitive treatise" on tenancy which became his undergraduate thesis.

The shift from animal husbandry to agricultural economics would have consequences much more far-reaching than even he, who tended to think in boundless terms, could have imagined.

His career took a decided upward tick on a day in 1931 as he was standing in the OAC administration building, idly looking at the bulletin board. A notice that hadn't been there a few days before caught his eye — a notice announcing a scholarship for the Giannini Foundation of Agricultural Economics, newly created at the University of California by Amadeo Peter Giannini, founder of the Bank of America.

He applied promptly with a carefully worded letter and shortly after received a letter from Professor of Agricultural Economics George Peterson, accepting him at a stipend of sixty dollars a month. "I cherished that acceptance," he said, "but I was not wholly surprised by it because I was after all editor of the newspaper and very near the top of my class. I recognized this as the ideal opportunity. In fact, next to meeting Kitty it was the most important thing that I ever did."

·   ·   ·

Almost thirty-five years later Ken had an altogether different encounter with his alma mater. In 1965 OAC was reconstituted and became reborn as a brand-new entity — the University of Guelph — a step that Ken and many of the more enlightened graduates had long advocated.

On the occasion of the first convocation of the University of Guelph in May 1965, John Kenneth Galbraith '31, formally cited as "the greatest living graduate of Ontario Agricultural College, a great American and a distinguished citizen of our world," was awarded a Doctor of Laws, *honoris causa*, the first to be so honored by the new institution. Good will and warm collegial feelings abounded at this happy event.

Three years later the much exalted Galbraith became, at least for a brief time, a much vilified pariah. What prompted this change of heart was a February 16, 1968, cover story in *Time* magazine titled "John Kenneth Galbraith, the All-Purpose Critic," which was favorable in the main, portraying Ken as the "current cynosure of the Eastern intellectual set, [who] has long been a purveyor of predictions."

Buried deep in the piece, which concentrated largely on Galbraith's dedicated efforts first to avoid and then to get the United States out of Vietnam, was a paragraph dealing with the subject's earlier days. He was quoted as cheerfully referring to Ontario Agricultural College as "not only the cheapest but probably the worst college in the English-speaking world."

Loyal OAC alumni reacted with outrage. Their varying degrees of anger were exacerbated by a rumor that a building on the University of Guelph campus either had been or was about to be named Galbraith Hall.

J. W. McCalla, Ken's former roommate, wrote to the university's president, railing against the remarks of a "professional spreader of a material well known in agricultural circles," and warning that "I will not contribute one further penny until such time as a Galbraith Hall is re-named and if you have conferred an honorary degree on him, it is rescinded."[1] To this, W. C. Winegard, president and vice-chancellor, responded that while he could not stoop so low as to take back the honorary degree, he could assure Mr. Mc-Calla that "no building on this campus has been named after Galbraith and none will be."

Thomas H. Jukes, a brilliant fellow student of Ken's who went on to become an important biochemist at the University of California, wrote directly to *Time,* pointing out that Galbraith's resentment "may well stem from the fact that O.A.C.'s scholastic requirements severely taxed his abilities. His high school grades were so low that the college admitted him under condition that he spend five years to complete the four year curriculum, in which he opted for majoring in animal husbandry (livestock judging), this being the gut subject of its day at O.A.C."

And finally, Ken waded into these very turbulent waters with a response that could hardly have been calculated to calm them. His letter was addressed to President Winegard.

February 21, 1968

Dear Mr. President:

Even at this distance I have heard some slight static over my recent observation, in *Time,* that OAC some forty years ago was "not only the cheapest but possibly the worst" institution of higher learning in the English-speaking world. I suppose the objection is to my making it the cheapest for, I believe, no thoughtful historian has doubted that it was the worst except only for Arkansas A. and M. where there is some doubt that they spoke English.

But do, on my behalf, remind everyone that this was forty years ago. I do not for a moment doubt the relentless improvement ever since or that the Lord's preference for a reformed sinner is matched only by His affection for a rejuvenated academy.

---

1. All the material surrounding this controversy is contained in the Archival Collections, University of Guelph Library, in a restricted file designated not to be opened during the lifetime of J. K. Galbraith. However, through Galbraith's good offices, the contents of the file were made available to me.

Robert Kerr, one of Galbraith's more sympathetic classmates, commented to the university, "I suspect that Ken by now inwardly regrets the pronouncements concerning OAC. The oracle having spoken, however, he feels that he can only remain an oracle by defending himself with further brilliance."

And in fact, the oracle did speak again a few months later, sending a considerably more measured and balanced — and perhaps less "brilliant" — letter, written not to President Winegard (with whom relations had doubtless gotten sticky) but to the director of alumni affairs at Guelph, in which he suggested gently that "in my time at OAC criticism of the college was considered to violate some intangible value called college spirit. I doubt that this is ever in the best intellectual tradition. . . . But surely we can agree to accept past shortcomings and rejoice in their correction and the prospect of greater advances in the future."

The next leg of Galbraith's journey was galvanic, taking him from a paucity and mediocrity of ideas to an exhilarating richness. "Berkeley in those days was an enormously exciting place," he says. "And to go there from the dreariest of colleges in Canada was like a great flash of light. At Berkeley you took classes all day and sat up all night discussing the state of the world. Faculty members joined in — it was a wonderful example of what a university should be." This heady atmosphere set Ken on the path that would lead him toward the distinction, acclaim, and celebrity he was eventually to achieve.

But before he could set foot on that path, he had to solve the more mundane problem of how to *get* to Berkeley, how to make the continental crossing from Iona Station in the shortest time and for the fewest dollars.

The cash-flow situation was acute. Although his promised scholarship of sixty dollars a month seemed to him untold riches, there was no money on hand for the journey. Eventually a fond and generous aunt stepped in to fill this void with a loan, and shortly thereafter another of his endless stream of relatives learned that a jeweler-oculist in Dutton had a nephew living in Cleveland who had also won a scholarship to the University of California and was proposing to buy a second-hand car and drive out there, and why didn't Ken hook up with him and share expenses?

As Ken puts it in "Berkeley in the Thirties,"[2] his loving essay about those halcyon days, he set sail for California in July 1931, on a vessel that took him from Port Stanley on the north shore of Lake Erie to Cleveland. The following day the two travelers set out at 5:30 A.M. in a 1926 Oakland recently procured by the jeweler's nephew. (For some reason, this young man has never acquired a name, either in conversations with Ken or in any of his written recollections of that period.)

The car, a decrepit old jalopy, was a disaster; since among other things its gasoline gauge was broken, the jeweler's nephew had prudently bought a jerry can of gas and a one-quart can of oil in case of emergency. As it turned out, the entire trip was nothing but an emergency. The Oakland, they discovered to their horror, was a gasaholic, swallowing a gallon of gasoline and a half pint of oil every four miles, which amounts to, according to a crude reckoning, 625 gallons of gasoline and 415 pints of oil, at a cost that cut deeply into Ken's aunt's loan. The trip took eleven days, including a twenty-four-hour stopover in Casey, Iowa, to deal with a broken connecting rod, also at hideous expense.

But all their horrors and financial woes faded into insignificance when they finally reached their destination. Ken, always inclined to be lyrical about his moments of arrival at pivotal points in his life, glowingly describes how in the early evening "the low sun glistened on the live oaks" as they drove up Bancroft Way to the imposing mission-style International

---

2. *Economics, Peace and Laughter* (Boston: Houghton Mifflin, 1971), pp. 344–60.

House. "I thought it a place of unimaginable splendor," he wrote.[3]

Although Ken is quick to acknowledge that his academic record at OAC was mediocre at best, he points out that this applies only to his record in animal husbandry. When he changed to agricultural economics, he entered a whole new learning phase. Certainly, the twenty-two-year-old who arrived in Berkeley in August 1931 was contemplative, speculative, and poised to absorb a wide range of knowledge and new ideas.

Berkeley remains sharply focused in Ken's mind as a place where professors knew their subjects but were willing to learn more about them from lowly graduate students, who, by the way, weren't treated as lowly but were encouraged to challenge the faculty as together they grappled with the great economic problems of the day.

Even in his unwavering euphoria about Berkeley in the thirties, Ken clings to another idée fixe — namely, that agricultural economists were regarded as second-class citizens.

There was ample reason to believe that such a prejudice existed and was in fact sharpened during the 1930s at Berkeley because of the radical persuasion of many of the graduate students. "The most distinguished were Communists," Ken points out. "I listened to them eagerly and would have liked to join both the conversation and the Party but here my agricultural background was a real handicap. It meant that as a matter of formal Marxian doctrine, I was politically immature. . . . [Marx had referred to the 'idiocy of rural life.'] I sensed this bar and I knew also that my pride would be deeply hurt by rejection. So I kept outside."[4]

Furthermore, agricultural economists were suspect because of the notoriously applied nature of their work. While the Giannini Foundation was dedicated to mitigating the vast pri-

---

3. Ibid.
4. Ibid.

vations resulting from the terrible farm depression in California and beyond, many of the teaching assistants earned their stipends by doing research about specific farm-related problems such as the appallingly high price of cling peaches, the chronically indigent prune industry, and in Ken's case, the marketing of different kinds of honey — sage, orange blossom, clover — an arcane subject on which he wrote a paper, one of three he published while at Berkeley.

Such work, he suggests, was not well regarded by nonagricultural or pure economists. It was considered "exoteric." He cites a distinction that his role model and hero Thorstein Veblen made between *exoteric* and *esoteric*. "Esoteric knowledge is by and large respectable and reputable in Veblen's phrase, and its application is of university stature. Exoteric is merely useful knowledge and thus obviously of a lower order." "We were second-class citizens," he wrote, "but we protected the first-class citizens and never ceased to wish that we were better appreciated."[5]

This uncharacteristically humble approach notwithstanding, Ken lost little time in establishing himself at the University of California as a comer, thanks, at least initially, to his promptly noted fluency as a writer. Before too many months had passed he found himself called upon to be the scribe for a number of his professors' research works. He was more than equal to these tasks, doubtless well aware that he wrote better than any of his professors. Nonetheless, he held them in high esteem and still retains his warm regard for those early mentors: Howard Tolley, an "exoteric" who was head of the Giannini Foundation and who later left to join the New Deal, becoming head of the Agricultural Adjustment Administration; Leo Rogin, a brilliant teacher of critical economics who first introduced Ken to John Maynard Keynes, before the Keynesian revolution had actually hit with full force. But probably the most important professor for him in those Cali-

---

5. *A Life in Our Times* (Boston: Houghton Mifflin, 1981), p. 25.

fornia days was Ewald T. Grether, who taught him economics proper, that is to say, classical economics, especially as preached by its chief exponent, British economist Alfred Marshall.

Grether drilled his graduate students with stern diligence, making them read and fully absorb the 871 pages of Marshall's great *Principles of Economics*. Marshall believed that the sole function of the entrepreneur was to maximize the firm's profits, while the state, recognizing the pre-eminent role of the market, modestly confined itself to such services as education, sanitation, and defense. It was a watershed moment for Ken when he realized that although he fully grasped Marshall's received principles, he did not agree with them. Their conclusions, he believed, were reached not from what existed but from what was assumed, a distinction between fact and supposition which was to color much of his own economic writing. But he was grateful for his mastery of the Marshall orthodoxy, for as he has pointed out, "To know what is right, one must have a firm grasp on what is wrong."

Marshall was the lineal descendent of the other great British economists, Adam Smith, David Ricardo, and John Stuart Mill, to whose work Galbraith was introduced in his Berkeley days. But after Marshall, the economist who was the major influence on him in those years and beyond was Thorstein Veblen.

The two had much in common: Both had intelligent, cultivated parents and both were raised on a farm, Galbraith in Ontario, Veblen in Minnesota. Both used ridicule as a tool to excoriate the pretensions of the rich, Galbraith in his *Affluent Society,* Veblen in his *Theory of the Leisure Class.* Both added phrases to English usage, Veblen "conspicuous consumption," and Galbraith "conventional wisdom." Both were articulate in expressing trenchant, significant ideas, although Veblen's writing was denser and often more obscure. Both deprecated mainstream economic thought, yet neither is associated with constructive reform.

Veblen died in 1929 while Ken was still mired at OAC. It is too bad the two men never met. Together they would have found much to be skeptical and ironic about, including, perhaps from force of habit, each other.

Although Ken would have us believe that he spent all his waking hours at Berkeley talking about Marx and the state of the world, there were some diversions. At least he is on the record in "Berkeley in the Thirties" about his relationship with a bizarre young woman — a slim, well-tanned "anthropologist" with an aversion to wearing clothes — with whom he claimed to have fallen "deeply in love." It seems that the object of his affection had been in the South Seas — Tahiti and Bora Bora — for several months living without clothes and therefore had developed the habit, continued at Berkeley, of going out into the great court at International House naked in order to make her obeisance to the Polynesian gods. She also alleged to have been in the chorus of the noted Tex Guinan before taking up her elevated anthropological calling.

Miss X — Ken claims to have forgotten her name — left Berkeley before he did. The next thing he heard about her was that she had gone to Haiti (not Tahiti) and married a Pan Am airline pilot.

This encounter, mythical or not, took place during the year that Ken, after having studied two years at Berkeley, was sent as an instructor to the university's campus at Davis, near Sacramento. There, in a curriculum reminiscent of OAC, he constituted practically the entire Department of Agricultural Economics and taught several sections of the obligatory course in that discipline. Along with his teaching he also found time to return to Berkeley every weekend (to see the Love Goddess?) and to write his Ph.D. thesis on the Structure of County Government in California — hardly a pure economics subject, but obviously one chosen for convenience rather than posterity. The work of some hundred pages still exists in the Bancroft Library at Berkeley, where it does not appear to be much dog-eared by repeated usage.

During all his time in California Ken could not afford to go back East to see his family. But he did keep in very close touch with them by mail. Of particular interest is a letter to his older sister, Alice, written near the end of his second academic year in California, in which he expresses his concern for the higher education of his younger sister, Catherine. He tells Alice in strictest confidence that he has heard rumors that he might be added to the University of California teaching staff at Davis, and after many protestations of how this probably will never happen, he says that if by some remote chance it should, he will be in a position to make some provision for Catherine's college education. He then goes on to suggest the arrangement that ultimately prevailed: half of the money he gave to Catherine for her education would be applied to his debt to Alice for the money she had lent him for his education. "In that way we could share the matter without any expenditure on your part which I know you can ill-afford."

The manifest decency and sense of family responsibility notwithstanding, Ken's letter is surprisingly dull, pedantic, and quite devoid of humor. He admits to having been "very earnest, very serious, very hard working. You have no idea what a grim, committed student I was."

Could that have been because he didn't have a whipping boy at Berkeley as he had had in the faculty at OAC? Could that have made him more somber than sardonic? Perhaps. At least it seems to suggest that the wit of Ken Galbraith which had popped up briefly at OAC had yet to resurface.

3

Off and Running

IN MANY WAYS Harvard was inevitable for Ken, although he likes to claim that if all things had been equal (that is, salary) he would have preferred to remain at Berkeley. In fact, sometimes listening to him one might think that Harvard was some mere way station on the road to glory, instead of being, as he clearly believed in his heart it was, the ultimate glory itself.

But as he loves to tell it, he looked up from his desk in the library one day in the spring of 1934 — his third year in California — and saw a Western Union messenger holding a telegram containing the offer of an instructorship at Harvard for the following academic year, at a salary of $2,400, as opposed to the $1,800 he was making at Davis.

"I had not the slightest intention of accepting it, for I was totally happy at California," Ken insists, and then goes on with feigned innocence to explain that since he had heard that the way to win advancement in academia was to brandish offers from other universities, he let it be known at Berkeley that Harvard was "after" him. The astute dean of the School of Agriculture, however, took that information in his stride and let it be known right back to Galbraith that he had best take the Harvard offer, since he probably wasn't worth that much money to Berkeley anyway.

And so, nonplused but trapped, poor Ken had no choice.

He *had* to go to Harvard, or so the legend goes. What isn't revealed in any version of this fanciful tale is just how Harvard happened to make a job offer in the first place. Did it come completely out of the blue? Probably not. Jobs in academic institutions, like jobs everywhere, are usually obtained by the careful cultivation of those in a position to offer them. In this case that was Professor John D. Black. John D. was a noted professor of agricultural economics at Harvard, where agricultural economics was hardly looked upon as a top-level discipline but where its principal disciple was widely admired.

But how was John D. made aware that 2,500 miles across the continent was the very man he was seeking to be his acolyte? Certainly Ken, never one to be shy, was not loath to bring himself to Professor Black's attention. But at that point in his career he'd barely had time to establish an outstandingly promising reputation. Nor did the corpus of his published works set him apart,[1] although Ken does imply, mockingly, that since printed pages were counted rather than read, it was his reputation as a "prolific scholar" that brought him to Harvard.

In fact, it almost certainly was not. John D. Black heard about Galbraith in January 1933. Ken was in his second year of graduate study at Berkeley when he applied to the Royal Society of Canada for a fellowship they were sponsoring at Harvard. The plan was for him to spend a year carrying out a research project on the agricultural economics of Canada under the guidance of John D. Black. Howard Tolley, head of the Giannini Foundation, wrote personally to Black, extolling Ken's virtues, as did numerous of his other professors at Berkeley, and even his old professor of English at Guelph. Yet

---

1. Besides his thesis, this consisted of a paper for *Scientific Agriculture* titled "Some Aspects of Overseas Markets for Canadian Honey," and two for the *Journal of Farm Economics* — one "The Concept of Marginal Land" (written with one of his professors) and the other "Branch Banking and Its Bearing upon Agricultural Credit."

despite all the laudatory backing, Ken did not get the fellowship.

Today he insists he has no memory whatsoever of the entire
episode. He dismisses copies of both Tolley's letter to Black
and his actual fellowship application with an airy "If it had
been important I certainly would have remembered it."[2]

At the end of 1933 Ken went back East — the first time
he could afford to do so since he had gone to California —
to spend Christmas with his family in Ontario. Afterward
he went on to Philadelphia for the annual meeting of the
American Economic Association, knowing that this yearly
get-together was where department chairmen and other job
dispensers went to look for young talent. Ken doesn't recall
meeting John D. at that time, but in view of his selective memory about this entire sequence of events, this is hardly surprising. However, he doesn't deny that he might have met
Professor Black. In any case, it seems safe to assume that Galbraith, given his predilection for setting wheels in motion,
tried at Philadelphia to strengthen his ties either with John D.
Black or with someone else from the economics department at
Harvard, and that the subsequent offer of an instructorship
came, not as a bolt out of the blue, but as an outcome he had
eagerly anticipated and had no intention of refusing.

Before he ever got to Harvard in the fall of 1934, he made
a stopover in Washington that would prove symbolic as well
as propitious. Never one to fail to improve a shining hour, he
reflected, on leaving Berkeley, that he might well profit by
looking in on his old mentor Howard Tolley, who was then
working in the Agricultural Adjustment Administration. Tolley was glad to see his former student, of whom he obviously
thought well, and asked him what he planned to do during
the summer before taking up his duties at Harvard. When
Ken said he had no plans, Tolley at once offered him a summer job and said he could start the very next day.

His duties were concerned with the enormous amounts of

2. John Kenneth Galbraith Papers, John Fitzgerald Kennedy Library, Boston.

land, particularly in the South and in the Midwestern lake states, that were in default because of nonpayment of local taxes. Ken's job was to study the feasibility of having the federal government pay the delinquent taxes, thus getting the local governments off the hook and at the same time acquiring huge new acreage that would be added to the public domain.

Ken strongly recommended that such a course be followed, but his words fell on deaf, or at least skeptical, perhaps even the wrong, ears. "I was too young and probably too casual to be an effective lobbyist," he recalls. One may wonder why it wasn't his boss, Tolley, or even Tolley's boss who was doing the lobbying, rather than a twenty-five-year-old economist who had never worked in Washington before. Skeptics may also doubt that Ken was all that casual about it.

The summer job, which continued for numerous weekends into the fall, had two distinct long-range benefits: it served as a good foot in the door that led to a dramatic and even a dominant role for Galbraith in the nation's capital a few years later. Before he could be hired, he was required, for reasons of patronage, to swear that he was a bona fide Democrat, although at that time he was not even a U.S. citizen.

Following his penchant for traveling by water to significant junctures along his career route, Ken took the steamer from Baltimore to Boston. It was the first time he had seen the Atlantic Ocean and he was suitably impressed, although on a stopover at Virginia Beach he quickly developed an unwavering prejudice against sitting in the sand, especially in the hot sun and even more so while eating a hamburger. He has, he insists, sternly rebuffed all offers made by those he calls the "weary literate" to entice him to such favorite watering places as Martha's Vineyard, Wellfleet, or Block Island.

Finally arrived at Harvard, Ken launched his teaching career there somewhat inauspiciously. As assistant to John D. Black he was assigned to give the undergraduate course in agricultural economics. Never a very popular subject at Harvard, the course had been taught for years with "considerable indifference" by Thomas Nixon Carver, an older member of the economics faculty. By the time Ken inherited the course, there were, he maintains, only three students — one quite bright, one Japanese, with only limited English, and a third who constantly struggled, usually without success, to ward off sleep. Even allowing for his habitual hyperbole, something clearly had to be done to brighten up this situation before the next year.

Ken laid his plans and began his proselytizing early, at least well before fall registration. Drawing on his somewhat minimal Washington experience, he buttonholed his fellow economics instructors, telling them all the wonderful plans he had for introducing a lot about the New Deal's agricultural legislation — "inside" stuff, he doubtless implied — into the syllabus for the tired old Agricultural Economics course. Apparently he did such an effective job of selling himself (he would, with much practice, become quite expert at this) that by the time of registration forty students had signed up for the course. Forty! An unheard-of number, and, it was quickly decided by the higher-ups, far too many for a mere instructor to teach. The course was turned over to Ken's boss, the ever popular John D. Black.

Once again this entire recollection, suggesting a certain dash and offhandedness on his part, demonstrates Ken's strong tendency to conjure up a picture of himself as an insouciant young man — a picture consistent with his image of himself today. This is especially marked in view of other people's remembrance of him in those days as sober, serious, polite, and almost entirely lacking in the irony for which he would become so famous. To be sure, he was very bright and receptive to new ideas. The habit of mind acquired at Berkeley, the need to stretch the limits of his knowledge and understanding, stood him in good stead in the heady intellectual atmosphere of Harvard in the 1930s.

In the economics department two new waves of thought were being bruited about. One stemmed from the publication in England of John Maynard Keynes's *General Theory of Employment, Interest, and Money,* which led to the so-called Keynesian revolution, in which Galbraith became a significant player. And the other was the rebirth of mathematical economics, of which a fellow Harvard instructor, Paul Samuelson, was to become a leading exponent. Since Ken Galbraith already had his Ph.D. from California, he needed no further course work for credit. But he sat in on a number of classes anyway, not wanting to miss out on such experiences as Frank Taussig's sweeping graduate course in economic principles which he calls unquestionably the most famous economics course in the country, or Don Williams's almost as notable course in modern banking, or Alvin Hansen's seminal course on Keynes.

Toward the end of his first academic year at Harvard, an opportunity came his way to work during the summer for a remarkable man. His name, Henry Dennison, was and is a household word known to anyone who has ever used the red-bordered gummed labels, the wide spectrum of Dennison colored crepe papers, or any of the other dozens of products made at his factory in Framingham, Massachusetts. Dennison was a rarity among his peers, a successful businessman who not only admired Franklin D. Roosevelt but had worked for the New Deal as a member of the Business Advisory Council. This connection had stimulated his interest in the economy and had led him, along with a few kindred souls — notably Edward and Lincoln Filene, of department store fame, and Ralph Flanders, a Vermont machine-tool manufacturer — to undertake a book proclaiming the virtues of Roosevelt and the New Deal to the business world. For this project Dennison needed an economist who could write, and Ken was duly installed in his delightful house in Framingham as the man who filled this bill.

There was a slight hitch at the outset, however. Dennison had a clear idea of what was wrong with the economy — and so did Galbraith. Although Keynes's *General Theory* had recently been published in the United States, Ken had not yet become a celebrant. As he describes it in *A Life in Our Times,* he was still influenced by vestiges of the classical orthodoxy of Alfred Marshall, particularly as modified by the published works of Joan Robinson, the British economist, and Edward Chamberlain, of Harvard. He thus believed that monopoly, which meant too few sellers, dominated the market. And the remedy he arrived at, in the first draft of a paper prepared for Dennison, was more free competition.

Dennison, however, had come to a different conclusion. He believed that both a "spending stream and a saving stream" existed, people of modest income being more likely to spend and affluent business people more likely to save. And since he also believed that depression was caused by the nonspending of income, the remedy he proposed was "to tax the money that was going to be saved — income tax — rather than the money that was going to be spent — sales tax."

To Ken, still clinging a bit to Ewald Grether's teachings at Berkeley, this was heresy, until he had read and absorbed Keynes and discovered to his chagrin that the great man was on Dennison's side rather than on Grether's, Marshall's, and his. At that time he was living in Dennison's house and working in his library, so he felt especially compelled to confess to his host that although Dennison did not have Galbraith's support for his heretical ideas, he did have Keynes's. After that, it did not take long for Keynes to hit Ken Galbraith with "tidal force."

The resulting book by Dennison and Galbraith was published by the Oxford University Press as *Modern Competition and Business Policy.* Today Ken tends to disavow it as a very bad book, but it apparently found some favor with others. (In the same year Dennison and Ralph Flanders put together a second book, called *Toward Full Employment;* Ken says he wrote this one too, but he is neither credited nor even mentioned by the authors.)

Paul Samuelson has this to say about the Ken of this period:

"When he started at Harvard, there were two Kens. There was the conventional Kenneth Galbraith, who was an agricultural economist, went to a jerkwater college and then to Berkeley — but in the Giannini Foundation — then came to Harvard as John D. Black's boy. But the first sign of the new Ken was when he teamed up with Dennison and wrote that book."

By autumn 1935 there were further signs of the new Ken's emerging. Socially his life took a distinct upward turn when he was invited to become a resident tutor at one of Harvard's then seven Houses. He was thus able to exchange his comparatively humble lodgings on Irving Street in Cambridge (just around the corner from where he would eventually live permanently) for the grand luxury of a tutor's suite at Winthrop House, complete with living room, fireplace, bedroom, bath, and, to his particular satisfaction, even a telephone. All his meals were provided, along with an opportunity for interesting and stimulating conversation with his peers and his elders, which he took full advantage of. His duties were to meet once or twice a week one-on-one with the "tutees," economics majors assigned to him. His mission was to fill in the cracks left by their courses, to enlarge their perceptions of their chosen field, and generally to impart a potpourri of related wisdom. It was a natural milieu for Galbraith, and as he puts it, "I prospered."

He soon fell in the habit of such Harvard-like recreations as rowing on the Charles River; "rushing," as it was termed in those days, attractive Radcliffe graduate students; and having coffee at various times of day at the Merle, a restaurant across from Widener Library frequented by economists, where the famous Professor Joseph Alois Schumpeter held forth. All three of these particular activities were to have certain long-range consequences.

Schumpeter, a notable conservative, thrived on being controversial, now offending the capitalists and reactionaries who were his natural constituency by praising Karl Marx, now shocking his poor graduate students by telling them that a gentleman could not possibly live on less that fifty thousand dollars a year. He was something of a role model for Galbraith, who, while not endorsing his ideas, liked him and admired his potential as a cult figure, an image Ken may have had an eye on for himself.

One of the graduate students that he was most attracted to was Maxine Yalpe, a beautiful, glamorous, and popular young economist. (It has been said that Maxine Yalpe was everybody's first love in those days.) One afternoon Ken waited for her to come out of a class to ask if she could come to dinner with him that night. No, she said kindly, she was afraid not. She had just agreed to marry Paul Sweezy, also a very bright young economist (he was for a time Schumpeter's assistant), whom Ken knew and very much liked. End of that romance. But another, which was indirectly related to Ken's rowing on the Charles, was soon to follow.

An incident occurred one fine spring day when he was still in the wherry stage of his maturation as a rower, roughly the equivalent of still using training wheels to ride a two-wheeler. Bearing this in mind, imagine Galbraith contriving somehow to tip over his wherry, and picture him extricating himself, all six feet eight and a half inches of him, from the oars, the overturned boat, and the water and coming ashore dripping with water and self-disgust.

Standing on the dock and getting ready to go out in a single scull (rowing's most advanced stage) was Madeleine Rowse, an engaging Radcliffe graduate student in German literature, who has been accused of laughing at the miserable picture presented by this very tall man whom she had not yet met. But today she vigorously denies that she would have reacted so meanly, particularly since she herself had tipped over in the so-called untippable wherry during her early rowing days. Doubtless, they both commiserated a bit and then, to the best of anyone's recollection, Ken asked her for a date. Madeleine Rowse (later Gleason) became a good friend rather than a serious girl of Ken's. In her down-to-earth way she is well aware that her importance to this story is not who she was but who her roommate was.

Catherine Atwater was very appealing; shy, graceful, and gentle, she was a gifted student, a junior Phi Beta Kappa at Smith, and at the time she met John Kenneth Galbraith, was studying for her graduate degree in Romance languages (she was equally at home in German and in French). She was also a wonderful dancer, which coupled with her charming good looks attracted numerous beaus. But she was essentially a very private person — sensitive, thoughtful, intellectually eager — and, to quote her husband of fifty-three years, she "had a complete embrace of life."

Kitty was fortunate in her fine, classically simple, and sturdy Yankee background. Her father and mother were born within one block of each other in Middletown, Connecticut; her mother, Alice Merriam, graduated from Smith in 1908 and her father from his hometown Wesleyan College in 1906 and from Harvard Law School.

Kitty, the oldest of the three Atwater children and the only girl, grew up in Plandome, Long Island, and walked a mile each day to the Manhasset public school from which she graduated in 1928 at the age of sixteen. She took a year off to teach at the Friends School in Locust Valley before going on to Smith College, where she was admitted with advanced standing in most of her courses.

Although Kitty Atwater and Madeleine Rowse were in the same class at Smith and both took their junior years abroad — Kitty in France, Madeleine in Germany — their paths did not cross until they met for the first time on shipboard, returning from that year abroad. They quickly became friends and decided to room together after graduation when both would be in Cambridge getting graduate degrees. As it turned out, Kitty decided to take another year abroad, this time in Munich, before starting graduate work at Radcliffe, so Madeleine settled in Cambridge without her, and it was

during this year that she first met Ken Galbraith walking out
of the water.

Not long after Kitty's return, she and Madeleine were having lunch in Hayes Bickford, the once-celebrated all-day-
and-all-night cafeteria in Harvard Square, when Kitty heard
Madeleine say hello to someone who was standing behind her
chair. As Madeleine introduced her, Kitty turned and, as she
says, "looked up and up and up!"

Ken was galvanized. Before long he had maneuvered a date
with Madeleine that was to include Kitty and her date — a
young man whose identity is in dispute. Each of the three has
a different recollection, but the best version has it that Kitty's
date was Fred Skinner — the late B. F. Skinner, a world-
famous behavioral psychologist — who was quite smitten
with her. Kitty, however, denies that he was on hand that evening. In any case, whoever it was, was rather promptly eradicated as a suitor by Ken.

Although, apart perhaps from Maxine Yalpe, he had not
had much experience (if any) with serious affairs of the heart,
he seems to have acted with great resolve and gallantry toward Kitty. "I was never in doubt," he said. But to convince
Kitty, he needed every bit of persuasiveness he could command. "She wasn't at all sure she wanted to get married," he
said, "but still she was certain she wanted us to stick together."

Making decisions has always been a rather vexing exercise
for Kitty, and making this one was the hardest she had ever
faced. "I thought he was very supportive and very amusing,
though I wasn't sure I wanted to marry him." Part of her dilemma was that although she was intrigued by Ken and by
what she rightly guessed her life with him might be, she was
also afraid of being engulfed by his oversize personality. She
wanted to make her own mark, not live in the shadow of his.
And in a sense she has never fully resolved this conflict. She
has never quite accepted her role as the indispensable companion and helpmeet of a celebrated, complex, compelling,

and much-in-demand man, although that is what she is, what she has clearly chosen to be, and what she mostly enjoys being. Yet some part of her still occasionally rebels when she thinks of accomplishments and gratifications that might have been, solely on her own merits and on her own agenda.

They saw each other constantly during the academic year 1936–1937, Kitty continuing to vacillate, although less so. Perhaps, as Madeleine Gleason has suggested, "even when she's made a decision, Kitty is still making up her mind." By the summer of that year they were both in Washington, Ken hired to do a study of the new farm credit agency ("a dreary job of no consequence") and Kitty at her first paid job in the catalogue department of the Library of Congress.

Ken had his car and on weekends they explored the Virginia and the West Virginia countryside — Charlottesville, Monticello, the Blue Ridge Mountains, the Shenandoah Valley, the Civil War battlefields, all of which was to be a preview of a life of continual travel and, spearheaded always by Kitty, intense sightseeing.

Meanwhile, Ken had been granted a Social Science Research Council fellowship in England for a year's study under John Maynard Keynes at Cambridge. He was thus able to tighten the vise on his sometimes elusive bride-to-be by convincing her that he would be too much of an innocent abroad without her knowledge of foreign lands and tongues, her supply of Baedeker guidebooks, and her inexhaustible commitment to seeing every cathedral, museum, castle, ruin, monument, stately home, and historical site in every country he promised to visit with her.

And as she was to tell her Smith classmates at her fifty-fifth reunion, "He promised me that though we were married we would not settle down, and on that part he kept his word."

Indeed, Ken, who had never before his marriage been abroad, has almost never stopped being there since. To illustrate this point, Kitty told this little story to her fifty-fifth reunion class: "Many years later at a Harvard faculty meeting someone asked, 'Where's Ken?' and someone answered, 'He's at a meeting in Rhode Island.' Then someone else said, 'Ken doesn't go to meetings in Rhode Island. He must be at a meeting on the Island of Rhodes.' "

They were married on September 17, 1937, at the Presbyterian Church in Plandome, with the reception at Kitty's parents' house. Three days earlier, John Kenneth Galbraith had become a United States citizen, and although he says it was an event without emotional impact, it was surely part of an emotional week.

By every account the wedding was a total success for one and all. Catherine Denholm recalls that when she and her father and her sister, Alice, arrived at the house for the beginning of the festivities, Kitty's mother, Alice, came hurrying out, smiling, arms extended in welcome. For William Galbraith it was a moment of joy and satisfaction to know, as he at once did, that son Kenneth was casting his lot with a warm, loving family. He was rhapsodic about the beauty and kindness of the bride, and sister Alice told Ken quite prophetically, "You know, the great advantage you have in Kitty is that she'll be like her mother and won't ever look old."

For all his awesome presence, Ken is still something of a soft touch, a sentimentalist. He was devoted to Kitty's family; he found her mother "young and vital, entertaining and kind — a wonderfully attractive person." Her father, too, delighted him, a progressive, "intellectually enthusiastic" man who enjoyed the sport of sitting at the table after Sunday lunch, arguing with his accomplished, opinionated, and amusing son-in-law.

With his fondness for anyone who has achieved eminence, Ken likes to boast about Kitty's grandfather Wilbur Olin Atwater, a brilliant professor of chemistry at Wesleyan who made a significant contribution to calorimetry — the methods and machinery used to measure the energy various kinds of foods produce when they are oxidized in the body. He was one of three founding members of the Department of Agricul-

Year one.

Alice, Mr. Galbraith, Ken, Bill, Catherine, Mrs. Galbraith.

Lecturing.

Writing.

Contemplating.

Arrival in New Delhi.
Every inch an ambassador.

Open diplomacy, with Jawaharlal Nehru and Kitty.

Kitty, Jamie, Ken, Alan, Peter.

Left: Escorting Jackie Kennedy. *Right:* Debating Bill Buckley.

Above: The quintessential academic.

Left: Namaste to Mother Teresa at Harvard Commencement. Harvard President Derek Bok is at far left.

Above: The farm. *Below:* 30 Francis Avenue.

Above: "An Evening with Champions," with figure
skating champion John Petkevich and partner.
Below: Secret diplomacy with grandson Douglas.

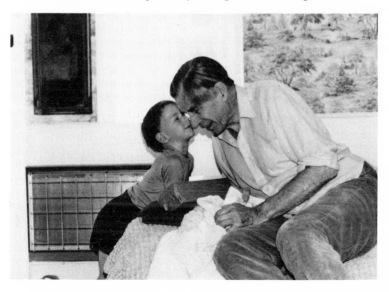

Strolling in Paris.

Bernard Charlo

ture, and his portrait still hangs in the anteroom just outside
the secretary's office.

Paul Samuelson has noted that in and around the Harvard
economics department most people thought that Ken had
married rather above himself. Ken graciously agrees — or
pretends to.

The day after their wedding, Ken and Kitty Galbraith sailed
for Southampton on board the SS *Britannic*. Practically everyone from the wedding party came to see them off, as people
tended to do in those days of ship crossings, usually bringing
with them books or a steamer basket (fruits, candies, pro-
cessed cheese, and sometimes a tiny jar of caviar, all packed in
masses of shredded green tissue paper). In pictures taken at
the time, Kitty looks slender and spirited, and Ken — tower-
ing over her, bespectacled, genial, and less sharp featured —
looks somehow more forebearing than he has in the last
twenty-five years or so.

Ken has called Cambridge, England, the Jerusalem of economics and has referred to his traveling there to study with
Keynes as "going to the temple." But when he and Kitty arrived in London and went to their temporary quarters in
Bloomsbury (where else would a Harvard graduate and instructor have dreamed of staying in those days?), they learned
that Keynes had had a heart attack and would not be in Cambridge during that term.

Ken was disappointed but not devastated; the temple in Jerusalem, even without its high god, was full of bright apostles
eager to carry forth his message. "It would have been pleasant," he says, "to have said I had been a student of Keynes
and been in his seminar, but actually the seminar we conducted all that year was almost in the presence of Keynes." It
clearly did not take long for Ken to consider himself one of
the chosen disciples.

Of the others he speaks with his habitual trenchancy. Piero
Sraffa, fellow of Trinity College, an Italian escapee from Mussolini, had spent his whole career developing and editing the

works of David Ricardo. He was, according to Ken, "one of the most lovable and certainly the laziest economist I've ever known. But because of all the books he edited, he was regarded as incredibly industrious."

Joan Robinson was a strong, critical personality who became Ken's good friend. "She could see no professionally popular figure, no popular idea, or idea agreeable to the establishment without expecting to attack it." R. J. Kahn succeeded Keynes as bursar of King's College and had "one of the great analytical minds I've known." Michal Kalecki, sitting out the dictatorship in Poland, also had an enormously analytical mind. "We all got ideas from him, but he was not tolerant of people who disagreed with him." When the Communist party came to power in Poland, he went back to a high position, which did not long endure because "the only party Michal could be a member of was one in which he was the sole member."

That year did much to establish Galbraith's credentials as a leading Keynesian. Few, after all, could lay claim to having been a member of such a stimulating economic community. "I don't know," says Ken, "but I suspect that when I came to express myself on the subject, I was very arrogant about it."

Galbraith's about-face from his early Dennison days, before he had been to the temple or had even read Keynes with absorption, was now complete. He continued to believe in the market but he did not believe, as did most conservative and many mainstream economists, that the market was infallible or even self-regulatory. He stood strongly with Keynes in his forthright advocacy of deficit spending by the state, or, as Keynes himself had put it more elegantly in a December 1933 letter to the *New York Times*, "I lay overwhelming emphasis on the increase of national purchasing power resulting from government expenditure which is financed by loans."[3]

Furthermore, the fact that Ken instinctively empathized

---

3. Quoted in Galbraith, *Economics, Peace and Laughter*, p. 47.

with Keynes is evidenced by this Galbraithian sentence in *Life in Our Times:* "Keynes himself had made his career by attacking men in high positions who join comfortably to reassure each other in their mutual commitment to error."[4]

Through the good offices of Piero Sraffa, Ken was accorded the privileges and perks of Trinity College, including, of course, the famed High Table where fellows of the college, dressed in worn black academic robes, convened in the sixteenth-century Great Hall for good meals, fine wines, and stimulating, perhaps even memorable conversation. He loved it all extravagantly. There was still something of the farm boy in him, but here he was dazzled, not by the lights of the big city, but by the grandeur of these stately rituals.

For his wife, however, it was another story. While Ken reveled in the splendors from which women were rigorously excluded, Kitty sat at home in their rather dingy little council-type house, angry because no one treated her as if she had a brain at all, because her husband was insensitively neglecting her, and worst of all, because she was so cold that she had to huddle by a gas stove that offered no comfort. To this day, Ken takes a rather hard line about her miseries: "After all, she was very much in love and she was busy learning Italian, so she was not without some advantages." But Kitty remains unconvinced. "If I had had any money I would have left him — especially when it got really cold."

Luckily, the long Christmas vacation came just in time to rescue them from themselves, and they set off in good spirits for a month's holiday and sightseeing on the Continent. They left Cambridge with Ken at the wheel of his Ford roadster (it had crossed the Atlantic with them on the *Britannic* at a cost of $150) and traveled from Ostend to Bruges, to Gent, to Brussels, crossed into Germany at Aachen, on to Cologne, Hamburg, Flensburg, then across Denmark to Copenhagen, arriving there on Christmas Eve.

---

4. Ibid., p. 68.

Throughout this and their subsequent trips that year, Kitty's linguistic ability stood her in good stead, the more so perhaps because Ken was already beginning, with his newfound and ever growing sophistication and self-confidence, to take charge. Speaking her fluent French and German and some of her recently acquired Italian, she managed a degree of one-upmanship, an advantage she pressed in order to get her way about sightseeing. "A castle an hour," Ken sighed and went on to tell how Kitty, her Baedeker always at hand, would carefully check off each cathedral, et cetera, before leaving the town or city they were in.

Dreadful and foreboding events were happening all around them in those months (they also returned for much of the summer of 1938 to Germany), which they, like many others — tourists and natives alike — saw and noted with fleeting horror but did not fully grasp.

Hitler and the evil Nazi regime were fast picking up momentum. The military restrictions of the Versailles treaty had been breached, universal military service was established, and more than half a million men were in uniform by the Christmas of 1937. This small force had already moved to militarize the Rhineland without a shot being fired and without any protest or move being made to stop them by the British and French. By March 1938 the Anschluss was complete; Austria had been joined to the German Reich and Hitler had made his triumphal entry into Vienna. And worse, there were abundant signs that Poland and Czechoslovakia would be next.

Even with such compelling evidence, the preponderance of British and French people so recoiled — and who can blame them — from accepting the dreadful inevitability of war that many of them convinced themselves that it would never happen. Meanwhile, the all too many Germans who fell prey to Hitler's hypnotic madness also believed that his master plan for the master race could be accomplished without a war.

Nevertheless, there were many visible signs for the Galbraiths during their German visits; they had seen their share of goose-stepping, swastika-waving, Heil-Hitlering troops and "Juden Verboten" signs to have reacted strongly against the relentless Nazi rise to power.

Yet somehow Ken did not reflect a genuine sense of outrage in recalling these days, as he himself conceded. "When I was in Europe that year I wasn't nearly as involved with the evils of fascism as I had been here at Harvard. And I'd have to say it was partly the result of my upbringing in Canada. I was raised to view Europe with detachment. My family and the Scotch in general saw World War I as the particular insanity of a Europe in which we had no part. As I have written in *The Scotch,* we didn't think slaughter ennobling or especially necessary and we had instinctive misgivings about the men who were in charge. My father, for example, got himself made head of the draft board and exempted everybody. That's the sort of mild form of protest — the sane form — that always appealed very strongly to the Galbraiths."

After their giddy month on the Continent, Ken and Kitty returned in mid-January to their house at 21 Leys Road, Cambridge. A few days later — it happened to be Kitty's birthday — a terrible telegram came from Catherine Denholm. William Galbraith, Ken's beloved father, had been killed at a grade crossing when a train crashed into the automobile in which he and another man were riding. It was a devastating blow to Ken, who greatly revered, loved, and counted on his father; he is quite unable to talk about it, however, just as he is incapable of expressing his feelings about any of the sorrows that have affected him deeply.

In May the Galbraiths took another lengthy trip, fine-toothcombing France and hitting the highlights of Italy as well. Ken, naturally, fell in love with Paris, which pretty well completed his cosmopolitanization.

While in that beautiful city he had one duty to perform that he rather dreaded. He was required to appear before the head of the Rockefeller Foundation, financial sponsors of the So-

cial Science Research fellowship, on which he had been galli-
vanting all around Europe, to report on the mind-improving
activities he had been engaged in during the year. A touch
uneasily, since he really hadn't accomplished anything scholarly or even very concrete, he went all out to describe his vivid
impressions of each of the places he had visited (many of them
blessedly not included in this account).

The head of the Rockefeller Foundation listened to his recital gravely. Then he said, "Young man, I have some advice
for you." Ken braced. "I suggest you now take a couple of
months off and get a good rest."

They sailed for home in mid-September, just as Neville
Chamberlain was going to Berchtesgaden to confer with
Adolf Hitler. As they neared New York, they learned of the
Munich compromise and the resultant sacrifice of Czechoslo-
vakia. Peace with Honor was proclaimed.

Eleven months later came the Nazi invasion of Poland and
the start of World War II.

4

We Need a Good
Keynesian

A HIGH HURDLE at Harvard faced Ken Galbraith when he returned to teach there in the fall of 1939. He was beginning the third year of his three-year appointment as instructor (following two one-year appointments), and at this juncture it was up or out — up to assistant professor and the tenure route or out and "find yourself another job."

To make matters worse, there was a glut of brilliant young economists, all in their early thirties, lined up for the one or two available "up" slots. Many of these, who would subsequently be among the country's most distinguished economists, were squeezed out, some allegedly given an extra push, because of their too liberal views. Prominent among this group were Ray Walsh and Alan Sweezy, who had the honor of being referred to as a case. The Walsh-Sweezy case was for a number of years synonymous with beleaguered young academics who stood boldly for their strongly held beliefs. Both Walsh and Sweezy moved on to Williams College.

Ken, who would probably have relished having a case named after him too, went on to Princeton as an assistant professor. Reflecting on this move in later years, he once again went through the routine of how he talked to the powers that be at Princeton only in the hope of improving his bargaining position at Harvard and how, as before with California, he "had no intention of taking the job." However, the motivation was quite different because this time he really did want to stay at Harvard and really did not want to go to Princeton.

Not surprisingly, he didn't like it when he got there, although he rather enjoyed their pleasant apartment on Palmer Square. He found the social structure of the university offensive and the economics faculty rooted in pre-Keynesian dedication to realities of the past. He has called Princeton "one of the great cul-de-sacs in history," and he was no sooner there than he began to lay plans for his escape. His avenue came once again through the good offices of his old mentor Howard Tolley, by then very high up in the Department of Agriculture, who recommended Ken to the powerful American Farm Bureau Federation as the perfect man for instituting their new economic research department. Princeton appeared quite willing to grant him a year's leave of absence (perhaps the coolness was mutual), and so in May 1940 Ken set off to take up his new duties in Chicago; Kitty would follow a few months later, having stayed behind to visit family and friends and to disassemble the Princeton household.

The Farm Bureau, which was not in the least hard up for funds, affected dingy offices in a seedy section of Chicago to keep its image pure from any taint of association with the federal government. The head man in this unlikely setting was Edward A. O'Neal, a well-born Southerner, a graduate of Washington and Lee University, and an urbane, much traveled man who was an Anglophile and wore Savile Row suits. Ken greatly liked and admired him, more so because, in common with the other Southern members of the Farm Bureau, he was a liberal who supported Roosevelt and the New Deal. (The Midwestern members, on the other hand, were almost entirely Republican and many were also isolationists.)

As it turned out, Ken had little opportunity to get started on the research for which he had been hired because O'Neal and his associates quickly discovered his writing skills and put him to work on speeches, memorandums, and the like. But even this activity was short-lived.

On June 25, 1940, Ken was walking down State Street in Chicago when he saw the headlines proclaiming the fall of France. It was, as he observes in *Life in Our Times*, "the last of a terrible sequence — the invasion and fall of Poland, the invasion of Denmark and Norway, then of Holland, Belgium and France, the evacuation at Dunkirk and now the end."

Two days later he received a summons from Lauchlin Currie, a highly placed economic adviser at the White House; they needed a good Keynesian, Currie said urgently, to join Leon Henderson and a few others already gearing up under the umbrella of the newly formed National Defense Advisory Council (NDAC) in order to consider how to control inflation in the now very likely event of the United States' being drawn into the war. In World War I prices had more than doubled and because the terrible social consequences of such rampant inflation were still a vivid memory, prudent and far-sighted planning on this score was deemed essential.

Filled with patriotic zeal and a sense of mission, Ken promptly caught the B and O's *Capital Limited* for Washington.

Leon Henderson, then forty-five years old, was already something of a fixture in the nation's capital. A graduate of Swarthmore College and the University of Pennsylvania's Wharton School, he had been economics adviser to the Senate Commerce Committee, the Democratic National Committee, the National Recovery Act (NRA), and the Works Progress Administration (WPA), and at that time was a commissioner at the Securities and Exchange Commission (SEC) and the designated member for prices on the NDAC. It was to his office next to the White House that Ken reported.

Recalling that moment, which should have been a heady one, he notes with a degree of sophistication he probably didn't have at the time, that within a few days it was obvious to him that there was no job there, primarily because there really weren't any prices to fix, at least not yet.

Ken has spoken and written eloquently about this particular form of "unemployment" which prevailed widely in the war years. Eager men and women, stirred by their country's call for action, would drop important, well-paying jobs in their native heaths to hurry to Washington and share significantly in the war effort. Once they arrived, the most deflating situation often awaited them. The job that sounded so vital and full of responsibility had not yet been created or had been created but put indefinitely on hold, so nobody expected them and nobody knew what to do with them. They had no office, no secretary — not even a shared one — and usually not so much as a desk to sit at and read their newspaper while they waited for some function, any function, to materialize which would justify their existence. This disease would later flourish with particular virulence at the Pentagon, where it was known as Pentagonorrhea.

When Galbraith arrived in Washington that summer of 1940, the NDAC was divided into three equal parts, Henderson concerned with prices, William Knudsen with defense production, and Chester Davis with agricultural matters — all acting in an advisory capacity in these pre-Pearl Harbor days. Fortunately for Ken, who was, as he put it, "just short of desperation," he was rescued by a call from Paul Porter, Chester Davis's only staff member at the time, who had more work than he could handle and could offer a definite job that needed doing at once. Accordingly, although the same agency paid his salary, Ken moved over to the Davis offices in the Federal Reserve Building. He was put in charge of a committee that was spotting locations for defense plants all over the country — important especially because with massive unemployment there was hardly a community anywhere that didn't want a defense plant — and he had the pleasure of being sought after and importuned by various high members of Congress, Chambers of Commerce, and other distinguished people, all seeking defense plants.

This activity led him to become much involved with the ongoing struggle over whether the Tennesee Valley Authority (TVA) or two other chemical company bidders should win the

right to build a new nitrogen plant at Muscle Shoals, Alabama. The endless dispute, which Ken professes to have
stage-managed for a time on Davis's behalf, is, he says, still
looked upon as a model of how far the ills of bureaucratic in-
fighting can be carried.

All during the summer and early fall, he continued his initial association with the Farm Bureau, going out to Chicago
from time to time for meetings or to whip together a quick
speech for Ed O'Neal. His status was labyrinthian; he was on
leave from Princeton, on leave from the Farm Bureau, on loan
more or less to Davis, who in turn lent him in October to
the Department of Commerce, where a group of economists
was being assembled, as the Roosevelt-Wilkie election approached, to write speeches for the president. Ken never saw
Roosevelt during this period. His efforts and those of his two
or three colleagues were sent up to Harry Hopkins or play-
wright Robert Sherwood at the White House; their ideas were
distilled and their choice phrases tucked in wherever needed
in upcoming presidential speeches. "Without taking undue
credit," says the ever modest Ken, "I think it's fair to say that
I was the most facile writer of that group. I had a certain in-
sidious competence with words."

Meanwhile, Kitty had been having a terrible time trying to
keep pace with her husband's fast-changing place of employment. The furniture from the Princeton apartment was
packed and ready, but she didn't know whether to ship it to
Chicago or to Washington. They wound up putting it in stor-
age and taking a furnished apartment by the month in Washington at the Marlyn, near the intersection of Wisconsin and
Massachusetts avenues.

At Christmas time they managed to touch all of Ken's various bases, going first to the Farm Bureau's convention in
Chicago (the British ambassador was the featured speaker,
thereby establishing the bureau's drift away from the isola-
tionist leanings prevalent among many of its members). They
then went on to the American Economic Association's an-

nual job-seeking jamboree in New Orleans, stopping en route to look over potential defense-plant locations in nearby Arkansas (thus probably getting that part of the trip paid for by Uncle Sam). They wound up with a brief vacation in Mexico City where they enjoyed a happy reunion with their good British friend, economic historian Eric Roll, and his wife, Freda. Before getting back to Washington they made one more stop so that Ken could have a thorough checkup at Johns Hopkins Hospital in Baltimore; the verdict was that he was pressing too hard and should ease up. He complied reluctantly by finally resigning from his Farm Bureau connection.

He did, however, keep another option wide open. On February 14, 1941, he wrote an apple-polishing letter to Stanley E. Howard, chairman of the Department of Economics at Princeton, assuring him of his firm intention of returning to Princeton the following September. "Academic work is my life and I look forward to getting back to it with more anticipation that you can guess." He pointed out that he was subject to a draft by the selective service, but that apart from such an enforced intervention he could "promise that I will not be seeking non-academic work next year of my own accord." In fact, the work sought him out; it is, however, fair to say he did not strongly resist.

As 1941 wore on the National Defense Advisory Council, perhaps because of its emphasis on the passive word *advisory* rather than on a more active one, was being phased out. It was replaced by both the Office of Production Management (OPM), which absorbed William Knudsen, and the Office of Price Administration and Civilian Supply (OPACS), which took care of Leon Henderson but left no place for Chester Davis and hence none for Ken. With the threat of another bout of enforced idleness facing him, Ken quickly turned his gaze back to Henderson, who was after all the man he had originally come to Washington to work for. Fortunately, he had been riding to work with David Ginsburg, Henderson's legal counsel, and with John Hamm, his general assistant, so he was au courant on their hopes and plans for managing the wartime economy and only too glad to offer a number of pithy suggestions on how their goals could be realized. Also important was the fact that he had good farm connections inasmuch as the farm lobby was seen as militantly opposed to price controls.

But the key to his future wartime role was a paper he prepared in which he articulated his conviction that it was desirable to allocate or to ration goods only as they became scarce. He believed at that time that overall we should practice Keynesian restraint on aggregate income, by increased taxation if necessary, to keep a general equilibrium in the economy. We should certainly not depend on an across-the-board ceiling on prices. His treatise on this subject, which he called "The Selection and Timing of Inflation Controls," was widely read in Washington and with particular interest, apparently, by Leon Henderson. The results exceeded even Ken's most dazzling expectations.

On April 29, he was called to the Blaine Mansion, just off Dupont Circle, where OPACS was then housed, and asked by Henderson to take full charge of the control of prices in the United States — perhaps the most powerful civilian post in the wartime economy, second only to Henderson's. (And sometimes listening to Ken one wonders whether there was really very much left for Henderson to do.) The fact that Henderson candidly told him that he had not been his first choice — Isador Lubin, a more senior New Deal figure had been — did not in the least dim Ken's enthusiasm. Lubin's unavailability was his good fortune — and perhaps also the good fortune of the country, Ken wrote in *A Life in Our Times* and with admirable candor went on to explain why.

> Truth is not always coordinate with modesty. The job required one to envisage the structure of the wartime economy in the largest terms and then to translate this into extremely specific lines of action. That, better than most economists I could do. It also required a truly extraordinary capacity to adjust one's

views and actions when the initial conception or some details were shown to be inadequate or wrong. Economics is not durable truth; it requires continuous revision and accommodation. Nearly all its error is from those who cannot change. This too I had begun to see. Finally, as the other side of confidence, one had to believe that one's critics were ill-motivated, uninformed, unintelligent or instinctively wrong. This also was my tendency. These qualities are not wholly endearing. To the sensitive they could suggest an insufferable sense of superiority. But, on balance, they were probably right for the job.

The enormity of the task facing Ken Galbraith would surely have daunted a lesser man. To begin with, almost everyone, no matter of what political hue, had some objections to the idea of price control. The very term — especially when it was called price fixing — had a pejorative, Big-Brother, antilibertarian ring to it that sounded threatening to basic freedoms.

Every eighth-grade student knows about the law of supply and demand; those with a slightly greater degree of economic sophistication may also know that freely moving prices — the function of the market — communicate wants to production and keep the demand for goods equal to what is available. Therefore, to freeze prices seemed to rob our economic system of one of its important links. Furthermore, economists (including Galbraith) pointed out that previous efforts at price (and wage) control, notably in World War I, had been not only ineffective but seriously counterproductive.

But as his words above demonstrate, Ken had a particular talent for adjusting to or, if necessary, rejecting received truths. In the circumstance in which he found himself on that day in April, prices *had* to be controlled to prevent the terrible inflation of World War I and goods *had* to flow to meet the insistent — the life-and-death — needs of a country mobilizing for war.

Galbraith was thirty-two years old. Today he says, "If I were president, I would have the greatest difficulty putting anyone thirty-two years old into that job. And maybe wisely."

His first act as price czar, predictably enough, was to go into one of the bedrooms at the Blaine Mansion which had been assigned to him as an office and call his wife to tell her his extraordinarily good news. Her response, not predictably, was to burst into tears. "But then you won't be able to help me move," she sobbed. "And what about all those books to pack up?"

"Most wives," Ken told her wistfully, "would have been proud."

Kitty laughs, recalling that scene. "I *was* proud. But I was also seven months pregnant and we were moving in a couple of days." (They were moving for the summer to Seminary Hill in Alexandria before settling into their house at 3207 P Street in Washington where they would be rejoined with their furniture from Princeton.)

Ken next sent a wire to his friend and fellow sufferer at Princeton, James A. Perkins (later vice-president of the Carnegie Corporation and still later president of Cornell), with whom he had made a pact that the first one to escape from Princeton would rescue the other. For the first time in his life Ken was in a position to offer someone else a job, in fact, to offer hundreds of people jobs.

To that end, he at once decided to divide American industry according to Department of Commerce classifications — textiles, steel, nonferrous metals, apparel, rubber, fuel, and so forth. He invented the title "price executive" for those who would head these departments, and then started sending out telegrams and letters, calling up all the people — mostly from academia — he thought would be suitable and eager to come to Washington and head those departments. All of them came, turning up promptly on OPACS's doorstep within the first few weeks.

From TVA he snagged Robert Sessions, who was the assistant to the general manager, to take care of his burgeoning administrative problems, and from Chester Davis's fading staff a superb secretary/assistant named Mary Jones, who performed the indispensable role of protector, booster, scolder, advocate, and mainstay that was later played in his Harvard office by Andrea Williams.

Meanwhile, David Ginsburg was bringing in a large number of lawyers, one assigned to each price executive.[1] Ken is always generous in his praise of this colleague. "In a very substantial manner, David was the person who envisaged the structure of the organization — I envisaged the economics."

Ginsburg also has handsome things to say about Ken. "He was a marvelous expositor with a fine sense of history and politics. He was willing to take bold positions and he could make clear the likely consequences of his actions. He made egoism his symbol, but always leavened it with humor, which was very ingratiating. But on the other hand," he adds, "he was not easy to work with. He was not a person who understood the meaning of compromise in his day-to-day relations. I often had the feeling it was more difficult than necessary to work things out with him."

To which Ken noted, "I think it's fair to say I didn't waste a great deal of time improving the feelings of my colleagues."

When Roosevelt created OPACS, his executive order gave the office power to ensure an adequate supply of essential civilian commodities and to "prevent price spiralling, rising cost of living, profiteering and inflation."[2] An executive order alone could not provide the power to impose penalties for noncompliance. This required legislation by Congress, and as early as February 1941 Ginsburg had already drafted for transmission to the Hill the first versions of the Emergency

---

1. Among them was a young lawyer named Richard Milhous Nixon. While Ken has had obvious pleasure in lightly tossing off "when Richard Nixon worked for me at OPA," Nixon has found his association with that largely New Deal–dominated office to be an embarrassment. He has avoided this by referring to his wartime occupation before the navy as having been with the Office of Emergency Management. The OEM, according to Galbraith, was an umbrella organization for all the war agencies. "It was much as though a Marine had said that he worked for the public sector," he has pointed out.

2. Office of Price Administration, *First Quarterly Report* (Washington, D.C.: U.S. Government Printing Office, 1942), p. 7.

Price Control Act of 1941, designed to put teeth in the original executive order. By the time Ken came aboard in late April, the bill had already gone through many substantive changes and petty revisions.

The president was ready to do anything he could to speed its progress. During the summer Henderson and his top staff — Ginsburg, Galbraith, and John Hamm — sent the White House extensive briefs on all the important aspects of the legislation. As Ken tells it in *A Life in Our Times*, Roosevelt finally called a meeting to consider their proposals. Answering each question that the president asked — the effect on labor, on the farmers, on the courts — Henderson kept telling him, "We've sent you a memorandum on that, Mr. President." After about the third or fourth time, the president looked at him thoughtfully and said, "Leon, are you under the impression that I read those documents of yours? I couldn't even lift them."[3]

Roosevelt sent his message to Congress on July 30. The House hearings on the bill began a few days later and were, Ken says, "a marathon." Henderson appeared daily, Ginsburg rose occasionally to speak, and so did Ken. But concerns lingered over the vast powers they were asking, until finally, on November 28, 1941, the Emergency Price Control Act was passed. Nine days later came the attack on Pearl Harbor.

Meanwhile, during the summer prices had begun to rise — lumber, scrap metal, and textiles were of particular importance. When these prices seemed to be moving up too rapidly, the price fixer's job was to determine a ceiling — a maximum permissible level. Under pressure of wartime need this ceiling was usually respected, even then, before the power of enforcement had been granted. By that time Ken and his staff of several hundred and growing had already moved twice, first to a large apartment house at 2500 Q Street and then to Temporary D on the Mall.

John Alan Galbraith was born on July 3. Ken took Kitty to

---

3. P. 140.

the Columbia Hospital in the morning but didn't get back to
see her and his son until late that evening. As he walked into
his wife's room, her phone was ringing: It was Robert Ten-
Broeck Stevens (later a key figure in the army-McCarthy hearings), to continue the argument he had been having with Ken
all day. Ken had ruled against the excessive prices J. P. Stevens
and Company were charging for the cloth out of which the
army's summer uniforms were being made, and Stevens was
still pleading for a more lenient finding. Ken yielded nothing,
but Stevens kept him on the line for what must have seemed
like an hour to Kitty, who was doubtless hoping for a few
words herself with her husband.

And that was one of Ken's good days. At least he had managed to *get* to the hospital; he was not able to do so again for
the next three days.

"It was a job of the most intense pressure," he says. "You'd
hope to get a few hours' rest on Sundays so you'd have the
energy to start another week. And there were months when
you'd read about the war only for a little while in the newspapers and then get back to fighting the war in Washington,
which was the struggle between the businessmen and the government agencies. The businessmen had spent the previous
eight years in antipathy and antagonism to Roosevelt. So they
had a predictable ambivalence. On the one hand, they wanted
to work for the war effort and increase war production; on
the other hand they were deeply disturbed about the extension of government wartime authority."

After Pearl Harbor the pace intensified as commodities and
services became increasingly scarce. When the OPA was given
the power to ration, Galbraith assumed, perhaps logically
and not without considerable satisfaction, that the huge administrative task of setting up rationing boards all over the
country would fall to him. Henderson, however, assumed
otherwise. The nationwide rationing authority involved a
huge number of political appointments which Henderson,
who relished such maneuvering, chose to oversee himself. He

therefore decided it was much better to separate rationing (and rent control) from the price fixer's job.

Like any self-respecting empire builder, Ken was reluctant to see all that power slip away from his grasp, but he soon became reconciled, particularly since rent control went to his good friend Paul Porter, and the day-by-day administration of rationing to another good friend, Paul O'Leary, whom Ken called the ablest of his subordinates.

So all was relatively harmonious except that there remained a certain turf battle with the Office of Production Management. One of the first staples that threatened to turn into a dangerous shortage was rubber tires. Until synthetic rubber, which was in the works, became available, the war effort would have had to make do with the inventories of rubber tires then on hand. The OPM had the power to stop sales of civilian products; the OPA did not. The OPA had the power to ration, but what good would that be for the rubber stocks they believed could be dissipated in a matter of days?

Inaction seemed intolerable; one of the lawyers, Harold Leventhal, a favorite ally of Ken's, came to him on the day before Christmas to propose that they act on their own, an idea entirely consonant with Galbraith's nimble modus operandi. Together they drafted an order of "draconian simplicity" forbidding the sale of tires anywhere in the United States and requiring manufacturers and dealers to make an inventory of their current stocks. They then made a list of the dozen or so names in the OPM whose initials were required on such a directive. Ingenuously, Leventhal then took it around to the OPM, where no one knew that he didn't belong (Ken would have been too noticeable), and presented it to each signer with a casual but firm "Here's the new rubber order. It has to go out tonight."

Forty-eight hours later, on the day after Christmas, the order prohibiting the sale of tires to civilians went into effect. "It was, in a small way, one of the most important acts of the war," says Ken. "Without it I don't know how we could have spanned the gap until synthetic rubber came in."

To prevent hoarding, it was necessary to act in complete secrecy about which scarce products were about to be rationed. Operation Oyster was created as a code word for whatever favorite commodity — aluminum foil, for example — was soon to be unbuyable. Ken, of course, was privy to, was in fact the instigator of, all such privileged information; Kitty remembers how frustrated she was when shoes, for which she had a weakness, were rationed without even a hint of forewarning to her from her husband.

During one three-day period in November 1942 Ken wrote memorandums to Leon Henderson about such goods as cigars, cigarettes, beer, used passenger cars, paper towels, toilet paper (this memo was full of gentle double-entendres), sponges, beef, and pork. On the day following the beef and pork memo, he sent his boss the following:

> From time to time we have been criticized for the complexity of our schedules [that is, orders]. It has occasionally been said it would be simpler if they were written in Chinese. You can imagine my astonishment when I discovered that our Legal Department — composed, of course, of literal-minded gentlemen — has taken the criticism to heart and actually produced a schedule in Chinese. I understand it has been widely circulated as the most lucid document the OPA has yet put out. I trust that it will have your earnest attention. Attachment: Chinese Schedule.[4]

All these months Ken had been operating with selective controls — prices fixed on an item-by-item basis. The mechanics of considering each case on its merits was cumbersome and uneven; some price executives and their teams were slower or more deliberate than others, resulting in the office's "moving vigorously on pepper and not at all on bread." Yet

---

4. Unfortunately, the Chinese schedule that Ken says really did exist was not preserved with the memo among the Galbraith papers at the John F. Kennedy Library in Boston.

he had clung to this one-by-one concept because of his previously stated belief in the Keynesian balance between goods produced and purchasing power.

But then, about March 1942, when much of the war was going badly — serious reverses in the Pacific at Bataan and Corregidor, the sinking of the *Repulse* and the *Prince of Wales* — Ken Galbraith began to be uncomfortably aware that he was wrong, disastrously wrong. ("A salutory experience no economist should be denied," he has said, "and not many are.") Heavy wartime demand was relentlessly driving up all prices; a ceiling would therefore have to be put on all prices.

With this conclusion Ken finally came around to the strong views held on this subject by Bernard Baruch, doyen of price management during World War I and in World War II still a considerable figure. Appearing before a congressional committee in 1941 Baruch, then in his seventies, stated, "I do not believe in piecemeal price fixing. I think you have first to put a ceiling over the whole price structure, including wages, rents and farm prices up to parity level — and no higher — and then adjust separate price schedules upward or downward, if necessary, where justice or governmental policy requires."[5]

Ken, who tended to mock the pompous, self-important Baruch and to treat his economic views lightly, now faced up bravely to his own slightly embarrassing 180-degree turnabout. To implement his reluctant but now firm ceiling-over-all-prices policy, he held a series of meetings with his most resourceful colleagues, notably two men: the wise, perceptive Donald Wallace (one of the few economists chosen to remain at Harvard at the time of the Walsh-Sweezy case) and the ever responsive Harold Leventhal. The omnipresent Howard Tolley, Ken's former mentor and now a member of his staff, also chipped in here and there with sound advice, as, of course, did countless others.

It seemed to them all easy enough — easy, that is, consid-

---

5. Quoted in *A Life in Our Times*, p. 133.

ering the monumentally disruptive step they were about to take: to write the order fixing prices. They decided to decree that prices would be frozen at the highest level they had reached in the month just preceding the issuance of the order.

But what caused them sleepless nights was the thought of how they were going to settle the inequities and deal fairly with the outcries they knew they would hear — often justifiably — once their order became law. And this it did on April 28, 1942, with the passage of the General Maximum Price Regulation.

General Max, as it was immediately called, proved as cumbersome to administer as its creators had anticipated. The prices charged in March were now the upper level at which these prices would remain for the duration of the war. Inevitably, as with any previous month anytime, March had caught some companies with prices at an abnormally low level. Then the screams for mercy began. On principle, Ken says he and his staff would automatically delay for a few weeks because one of the strategies of price control, they believed, was never to act promptly. But if companies were really suffering, the OPA would sometimes give them relief, and sometimes not.

A great part of Ken's day was taken up by hearings; although his staff handled many of the hundreds of requests, the urgent ones — for example, steel, petroleum, or other commodities produced by large firms — would come to Galbraith.

"Some of these pleas for relief were from firms that were actually doing very well," he explained. "A person from the steel industry, for instance, would tell us at endless length how we were impoverishing them. And we, of course, knew that we weren't. So then I would look down the table at my staff and some of them would be wagging their index and third fingers back and forth like this. And that was the signal to remember the ants.

"It seems," he went on with obvious enjoyment, "there was

an ant colony on the side of a very steep hill that was having a
great famine. Then one day one of the ants was out scouting
and found a wonderful large piece of horse manure up on top
of the hill. So he hurried back and told the queen ant, who
quickly mobilized the ant colony and sent them out to shove
this wonderful food down the hill. But when it got rolling, she
had to take the ants from behind the pile and move them in
front of it to keep the pile from rolling right past them down
the hill and away. And still she needed more and more troops
to hold the pile back. First she got out a battalion and then a
division and then a whole army corps of ants to hold against
it. And to keep them all motivated, the queen ant went up and
down among her troops, encouraging them to hold tight. And
as she did so her antennae were going like this [wagging third
and index fingers], which in ant language means 'hold the
shit.' "

Early in their Washington days an event took place which was
to have a profound effect on every member of the Galbraith
family. Kitty has never made a secret of the fact that she
abhors cooking and that when she is forced into the kitchen
the results are usually less than satisfactory. To counteract
this, Ken and Kitty let it be noised about that they were looking for part-time help, and one day, while they were still living
at the Marlyn, Emily Wilson walked into their life and at once
set about to facilitate it. She stayed on as a dominant member
of the family for the next thirty-seven years, a resolute,
fiercely loyal, tough-talking dynamo.

The disparity between her tiny stature and Ken's prodigious height must be more than twenty-five inches and has always been a source of the greatest merriment to them both.
"When I first went to work for them," says Emily, "I thought
he was crazy. He would stand right beside me — *right* beside
me — and yell, 'Where's Emily? Kitty, have you seen that new
girl?' And sometimes she'd go along with it — she called him
Johnny in those days. 'No, Johnny, I haven't.' And he'd keep

yelling for me and then all of a sudden he would look down at me and say, 'Aha, there she is, way down there. Now Emily, don't walk under any tables.' "

Clearly relishing this recital of Galbraith's antics, Emily warmed to her theme. "He'd put all the glasses up on the highest shelf where I couldn't reach them, except by standing on a high ladder, and then just extracasually ask me for a glass of water."

It's hard to imagine when Ken found time in those incredibly busy days to play tricks. Usually it would be over weekends, Emily explained, when she didn't go to work and when he did most of the cooking. "But then I would fight fire with fire," Emily said. "I would put all the pots and pans and utensils I knew he used on the lowest shelf, so he'd have to crawl on the floor to get them."

When Alan was born, the Galbraiths hired a nursemaid to help take care of him since Emily was working only part-time. It was a mistake, they soon found out. Emily, convinced that every time the nursemaid had a fight with her boyfriend she took it out on the baby, went to Ken and Kitty with a predictable either-she-goes-or-I-go edict. "She," of course, went and since then Emily has referred to the Galbraith boys as "my children." Should anyone venture to suggest that Mrs. Galbraith had been very generous in sharing her babies, she bristles. "There was nothing to share," she snaps. "They were my children; they called me Mummy."

Kitty has always been clear-sighted and forebearing about this situation, which was similar to that of some families in this country and more prevalent in England and on the Continent, where many children were brought up largely by loving and exceedingly competent nannies. And Emily was certainly that. Kitty had made a choice, whether consciously or not, fully to share Kenneth's life, and if that meant, as his life became more far-reaching and complex, that she had to cede some of the day-to-day responsibility for her children to Emily, what better person could she possibly have found? Indeed, as Jamie Galbraith, the youngest son, has pointed out, "We had the advantage of having *three* extraordinarily intelligent and loving people looking after us."

Emily understood all that too. "It didn't bother Mrs. Galbraith because she knew they were her children no matter what I called them or they called me."

A notable feature of those war years was that during the summers of 1941, 1942, and 1943 the Galbraiths moved out of the heat of the city to nearby Seminary Hill, a reasonable commute for Ken and a remarkable compound on the grounds of the Episcopal Seminary in Alexandria, Virginia. Here they joined a lively group of liberal intellectuals, most of whom would become friends for life — people like Tom and Lois Eliot (Tom, then a congressman from Massachusetts, was the grandson of Harvard's famed president Charles W. Eliot and was to be a distinguished chancellor of Washington University in St. Louis); Charles and Janey Siepmann (Charles, formerly of the British Broadcasting Corporation [BBC], was then a lecturer at the Phillips Gallery); fellow economists Charles Kindleberger and Emile Despres and their wives; news commentator Eric Sevareid; writer Jessica Mitford (Decca) and her husband, Bob Treuhaft; and Clifford and Virginia Durr, liberals from Alabama who introduced the Galbraiths to a young congressman from Texas named Lyndon Baines Johnson, for whom they were raising money.

Returning to P Street somewhat refreshed in the fall of 1942, Ken needed every bit of his reserve strength to cope with the next eight or ten months.

As the deep ideological differences between New Dealers and the businessmen began to crystallize, specific resistance to price control grew more determined. After all, price control denied people profit; the New Deal was denying businessmen income to which they believed they were entitled. The epitome of this conflict and at its fulcrum was John Kenneth Galbraith. "I must say that on the whole I enjoyed it," he says now.

Perhaps. Except that at the time, with Fulton Lewis, Jr., blasting him two or three times a week on his radio program, with various congressional committees calling him and others of the OPA's top echelon to account, and with some New Dealers seeming to regard his operations as unfeeling and without sufficient political deftness, he felt more bruised than he was willing to admit. On the whole, Ken does not respond lightheartedly to such negative criticism. "Looking back, I think I was fairly thin-skinned," he admits. "Certainly criticism doesn't just roll off my back. But I function at two levels; I know that a critic only has satisfaction if he thinks he's hit home. So I have always carried around a protective shield to show that I have certainly *not* given the critic that satisfaction." One thing is certain; this shield is made up in large part of his carefully cultivated ego.

Leon Henderson was forced out of his job by increasing pressure from the business community and was allowed to resign for reasons of health in December 1942. Unfortunately, his health really was bad, grew worse, and his lifestyle became increasingly chaotic. In 1966 Ken stepped into the breach and rallied about twenty-five of the old OPA group to contribute to a fund that Ken euphemistically dubbed the Leon Henderson Papers Project. The hope was that if they could assure Leon five hundred dollars a month for a few years, it would put him back on his feet and permit him to write what should have been his fascinating memoirs, and this would give him a new lease on life. Altogether Ken raised around twelve thousand dollars, giving a considerable part of this himself, but the salutory effects fell far short of expectations. Henderson lived with an increasingly debilitating illness and without ever regaining his true zest for a useful life. When he died, in 1986, Ken wrote an appreciation of him for the *Washington Post,* in which the tone in general was admiring.

At the time of Henderson's "resignation," Ken was both regretful and apprehensive. "The pressures had been enormous on Henderson," he notes. "And then they shifted to me."

Ken Galbraith lasted for another six months; by May 1943,

many of his favorite colleagues — David Ginsburg, John Hamm, Harold Leventhal, and Henry Reuss — were gone too, and Ken was seen in many eyes as a pariah. In that month Kitty had their second son, Douglas, and Ken noted that in contrast to the flowers that had made her hospital room look like the last rites of a Chicago gangster when Alan was born two years earlier, this time the only flowers were those he had brought in from the garden.

Like Leon Henderson, Ken too was finally asked to resign for reasons of health; he refused. A noisy public fight ensued between Ken and a man named Lou Maxon, brought in by OPA chief Prentiss Brown to try to improve the agency's image, so noisy that Roosevelt intervened and sent word through Harry Hopkins that another post was to be found for Galbraith.

Ken left the Office of Price Administration on May 31. Two days later he collapsed from exhaustion on the floor of his living room. "It was awful," Kitty recalled with a shudder. "I don't think I've ever been more frightened. Emily and I tried to lift him up onto the couch and loosen his collar. We managed to get a doctor to come; he said Kenneth's blood pressure was terribly low and we just had to get him out of town to someplace he could get a complete rest. I wasn't in that great shape either," she added. "Douglas was just two weeks old. But the doctor was insistent. 'It's terribly important,' he kept saying, and then he told us, 'I'll give you a medical request for extra gasoline for your car so you can get him away.' "

The patient gave a hollow little laugh at this. "My whole physical being had just given out," he says. "But even so, I knew I couldn't possibly go to the OPA and ask for extra gas."

They tried to get on a bus to take them to White Sulphur Springs, a most suitable spot for R and R, but were told it was standing room all the way for four hours. Desperate, they ultimately managed reserved seats on a B and O train to take them to Kitty's family, and from there they were able to go on to a quiet little inn in Connecticut, where they got a bit of rest but not quite enough to eat.

The job that was offered to Ken as a sop was not even that; it was ludicrous. He was to be the Lend-Lease administrator for South Africa, which, not surprisingly, turned out to be a nonjob with no discernible function. Furthermore, it was under the direction of the man to whom Ken always referred, with high sarcasm, as "the beautiful Edward Stettinius."

Meanwhile, since he was at least under- if not quite unemployed he became a fair target for the draft. To forestall this dreadful possibility, he decided to volunteer, having first obtained his wife's necessary permission to do so and, second, having ascertained that since his height — six feet eight and a half inches — was two inches over the maximum, he would probably be rejected as unclothable and, had they but known, also unmanageable. ("My left foot is not my right foot.")

So he was left to decompress gloomily for a month or so at the State Department, doing nothing. It was not a time he looks back on fondly.

Running price control during World War II had put Ken into an entirely different orbit from the one he had been spinning around in. He had gone to OPA as a young man — a Keynesian — seeking power and eager to prove his worth; he came out still a young man, but now a personage to be reckoned with. His accomplishments in the public arena had brought him great renown and many rewarding acquaintances. In his private life he had developed warm and enduring friendships, as with the Seminary Hill group, for instance, and with his close colleagues at the OPA.

In the future all other positions he held would be measured against his job as price controller. Never would he work harder; never would he have so much power or put it to use in a way so vital to the national interest. He left it with reluctance, but without regret. He had acquired a taste for being a public figure that he knew he would never lose.

5

At the Cutting Edge

To be a successful writer," Ken pronounced one day, "you first of all need to have somebody looking over your shoulder. In my case when I went to *Fortune* it was Henry Luce — constantly asking, 'Are you wasting words?' 'Can you put that more concisely?' or simply with a slash of his blue pencil, 'This can go.'"

Ken has called such instruction from the founder and editor in chief of *Time* and its progenies *Life* and *Fortune* a lifetime gift. For his part, Henry Luce, a man of generous impulse but conservative inclination, was once heard to remark to President John F. Kennedy, "I taught Kenneth Galbraith to write. And I can tell you I've certainly regretted it."

Joining *Fortune* turned out to be another of Ken's famous "break points." After his brief few months "working" as Lend-Lease administrator for South Africa, he had tried a stint with Governor Herbert H. Lehman, planning for the agency that was to become the United Nations Relief and Rehabilitation Administration (UNRRA), a job that he found worthy but far too "lacking in active participation" to suit his jaded post-OPA taste.

He was by then bewitched by the big time, and in its way *Fortune* fulfilled that need for him. In the thirteenth year of its existence, it was a big-business-oriented, glamorous, and brilliantly written publication, informative to many and a coffee-table status symbol to others. The magazine was handsomely printed on heavy, expensive-looking matte stock, rather than on the glossy paper common to chic, upscale monthlies. Everything about *Fortune* was restrained and opulent, bespeaking old money rather than flashy new.

Galbraith's first contact with *Fortune* had been at the height of his price-czar days, when he had a meeting in New York with two or three of the editors, including managing editor Ralph Delahaye Paine, to talk over the many concerns of wartime mobilization that were central to their journalistic efforts. Not surprisingly, he acquitted himself well on this occasion. ("I think it's fair to say that I was more helpful to them than anybody else they had encountered.") At the end of the dinner Del Paine had told him, "If you ever get out of the job you're doing in Washington, come and work for *Fortune*." And so in the autumn of 1943 he did.

It was a rash move for Ken. "*Fortune* was the big league in New York writing," he said. "At that time it was next to being on *The New Yorker* or perhaps even more than *The New Yorker* in some respects." Certainly he had never before written for so elevated a publication or one with such a large readership. Yet he had gone ahead and uprooted Kitty, their two little boys — Alan, two, and Douglas, six months — and Emily and installed them in an apartment on Riverside Drive. Despite his outward bravado there was, he admits, a certain nervousness in the Galbraith household as to whether he was going to make it.

He started at *Fortune* in late October, and shortly thereafter he was assigned to work on a major piece predicting, recommending, and spelling out in some detail what shape the postwar economy should and could take — this, of course, while the war was still going on — and how the transition to a peacetime economy would be achieved. Not without interest at this writing, in the 1990s, are the headlines over his article:

THE JOB BEFORE US
TRANSITION TO PEACE: BUSINESS IN A.D. 194Q [*sic*]
Its goal: A job for nearly everyone.
An average wage of $2,200.
Profits fortified by performance
To be achieved by strong incentives, not directives.

As anyone who has ever written or worked for a magazine knows, the magic words that finally assure you that
your piece is going to see the light of day are: "It has
been scheduled." But when Ken got this good news, it was
even better than he could have imagined. Not only was his
piece scheduled, but because the editors deemed it so important, they were going to take apart the already made-up
issue of January 1944 to make Ken's the lead article. Once
again he had arrived. And once again he phoned Kitty to
tell her so.

They went out that evening to celebrate. Kitty, whose recall is flawless, said they went to an inexpensive little Mexi-
can restaurant (Ken, who today drinks only wine and little
enough of that, still likes to have an occasional margarita),
and then on to a twenty-five-cent movie. "But," she added
nostalgically, "we did enjoy that evening so."

"There was no way to spend money in those days," Ken
noted. And that, of course, is nonsense; there have always
been ample ways to spend money if one is so inclined, as the
Galbraiths clearly were not and are not. While both give extremely generously of themselves — their hospitality, for example, is boundless — and support many worthy causes, they
are restrained when it comes to parting with actual cash, especially to spend on themselves. And, considering the gad-
about lives they have always lived, they part with it relatively
infrequently. Ken always tries and usually manages to get out
of paying for his trip (or Kitty's) to Europe, Japan, India, Aus-
tralia, California, Toronto, or Austin, Texas. He goes only
when invited to give a prestigious lecture, attend a conference,

take part in a high-flown colloquium, or receive a notable award.

And if such an event should not be available at the precise time or place to suit his purposes, he can always engineer a book-promotion trip — there being always another book to promote — to pick up the slack. Even when going to New York City for his own grand eightieth birthday party, he managed to squeeze in a talk at the Manhattan YMHA to pay for his and Kitty's shuttle trip and other incidental expenses. Before a Thanksgiving that the Galbraiths were planning to spend in Washington, D.C., with their son Alan and his family, Ken was called by the *New York Review of Books,* just in the nick of time, wanting a review on short notice at a stipend that would take care of the Washington trip. He was enchanted. "Do you know," he demanded, "what two Boston-to-Washington airfares *cost* these days?"

A related facet is Ken's lifelong habit of recycling for a second appearance in print — and payment — every one of the hundreds of pieces he has written for magazines and newspapers. However, he follows this practice not entirely because of its monetary advantages. He also feels that he should not allow his words to melt into oblivion without giving them a second exposure between hard covers, so that a different and perhaps wider (and younger) readership may benefit from them.

Hence there are on the Galbraith five-foot shelf three volumes of collected essays: *Economics, Peace and Laughter* (1971), *Annals of an Abiding Liberal* (1979), and *A View from the Stands* (1986), all edited by Andrea Williams.[1]

Ken has been known to plagiarize from himself. In 1980 he

---

1. When *A View from the Stands* was being prepared Ken and Andrea referred to it as "Galbraith light." Another volume, currently under way, is "Galbraith heavy," its contents being considered somewhat weightier, but, we are assured, not discouragingly so.

contributed a piece to *Fortune*'s fortieth anniversary volume: "Writing for Fortune." It was duly reprinted in his 1986 *A View from the Stands* — a warm and evocative piece on Henry Luce — in the section called "Portraits and Remembrances." This, however, represented its third printing; Ken had already given it its second airing, albeit in abbreviated form, in *A Life in Our Times*. But even at the risk of venturing into yet another — a fourth — exposure, herewith a passage to demonstrate that Ken's fondness for Henry Luce stems in part from a trait they have in common: "In speech he [Luce] had an unparalleled talent for parentheses. When he spoke at company gatherings, there would sometimes be bets as to whether he could unravel a particular sentence and come back to his original subject and verb. Often he could." And often, in fact most of the time, Ken can too. It seems that the "talent" the two men shared derived from their desire, when expounding on a subject, to pack all pertinent information into one meticulously constructed sentence. But then as they spoke, extra facts or ideas kept creeping into their thoughts, so they had to take little detours via parentheses before they could get everything squared away into that one, sometimes not so meticulously constructed, sentence.

Ken was made a member of *Fortune*'s board of editors in time to get on the masthead as such in the June 1944 issue of the magazine. While not quite unparalleled, it was still a very quick rise to the top, a perch to which Ken would thereafter aspire in all of his numerous subsequent posts.

There was a collegiality among the members of the board of editors that he welcomed; he even claimed not to have minded the anonymity that the magazine's no-by-line policy forced on its staff. "It didn't make any difference," he said. "You were engulfed by the enterprise." In addition to Del Paine, among the editors he particularly admired were Gilbert Burck, Herbert Solow, and two "diligent connoisseurs of corporate absurdity," Eric Hodgins and Wilder Hobson. Hodgins in particular delighted Ken with his marvelous range of imagination and a wonderful sense of humor, gifts that were to remain unknown until he burst on the public consciousness as the author of the famous *Mr. Blandings Builds His Dream House* and subsequent related catastrophic happenings.

Ten months after his name appeared on *Fortune*'s masthead, Ken took another of what were beginning to be routine leaves of absence. There was nothing in the least routine about the reason for this particular leave, however; it was to prove a once-in-a-lifetime experience for him. In April 1945 the war was fast drawing to a close. He was to go to Germany, and at that critical moment in the ebbing life of the Third Reich, he was to help conduct an economic assessment of the effects of the U.S. air attacks on Germany's war mobilization.

The idea originated in part with George Ball, who had been general counsel to the Lend-Lease program in Ken's brief stint there; he was a dynamic, witty, and mischievous kindred spirit who was to play an increasingly vital role in Ken's life. Ball, along with what he terms "a small handful of medium-grade officers in the Pentagon who had come up with the same possibility," generated enough support to have the plan cleared by Secretary of War Henry L. Stimson and ultimately by President Roosevelt. The result was the creation of the United States Strategic Bombing Survey (USSBS). Ball recruited two men — Paul Nitze and Ken Galbraith — to be among the eleven directors of the USSBS. The survey members were to be a civilian and military group independent of the air force command structure. To permit them freedom in making their judgments, the survey teams would report directly to Secretary of War Stimson.

An amiable but ill-qualified figurehead, Franklin D'Olier, was made chairman, but fortunately he had enough sense to appoint as his deputy Henry Alexander, a man of rare competence, according to Ball, and a lawyer who had been a J. P. Morgan partner, which somehow seems to have given him the clout to stand up to the air force. The secretary to the directorate was Charles C. Cabot ("a Cabot," Ken characterized him succinctly), who was a considerable thorn in Galbraith's side, then and later.

Commenting on his choice of Ken to be director of the economic team, Ball says, "I thought in the first place that this was a man who was a highly competent economist, but who wasn't bound by the rigid and rather hoary traditions of that trade. And what the enterprise we were engaged on needed was a very fresh look. And Kenneth, I was convinced, would be able to provide that, which he indeed did."

For his part Ken was positively entranced by his assignment. Even when talking of it today, his voice takes on an animation that his long years of studied casualness have almost completely eradicated from his habitual manner of speaking. "I don't know of a higher pace than that time in Germany or of a greater sense of excitement than I had during that spring and summer. History developed a manic taste in those months. Mussolini was killed, Hitler committed suicide, the war came to an end in Europe, the atomic bomb . . . and we were there at the very center of it with Ribbentrop, Göring, Jodl, Frisch, and especially Albert Speer coming into our hands for interrogation. It was just incredible."

The survey personnel — over one thousand civilian officers and enlisted men — were based in London, where Ken went on April 14, two days after Franklin D. Roosevelt died, in Warm Springs, Georgia. For his new assignment, he had the simulated rank of colonel and wore a paramilitary uniform, which he had made for himself, since there was no standard issue that would fit him. In an incredibly short time he put together an "economics faculty," as he called it — the finest team of statistical economists that could be found — to grapple with the question of what verifiable results the U.S. bombing had on the German wartime economy.

There were ten men besides Ken, including his deputy, Air Force Major Burton Klein, who after the war became a professor at the California Institute of Technology; Nicholas Kaldor, a noted (and absent-minded) British economist, later to become Lord Kaldor; and Edward Dennison (no relation to Ken's early mentor), who became a leading statistical analyst. Most of these exceptionally able people had just been released from jobs in the United States relating to the U.S. wartime economy. Some had been working with Simon Kuznets, the noted economist who first gave form and statistical values to the concepts of a gross national product and national income.

To be nearer to the source of all their information, Ken's team, called the Overall Economic Effects Division, along with numerous other teams, moved to Bad Nauheim, northeast of Frankfurt. From here the "economic warriors" fanned out to follow the German armies in their last days, to inspect battered and burned-out factories, and to look for production records that would yield them figures and solid information as to how much German war production had been curtailed by Allied bombers.[2]

The team concluded in their report that "prior to the summer of 1943, the air raids had no appreciable effect on German munitions production." This is not to say that the air offensive didn't do great damage to civilian morale, as well as cause bottlenecks that affected armament output.

After August 1943 and until near the end of the war, only 5 percent of the damage inflicted on tank, aircraft, and ball-bearing production could be credited to the air raids. "We established irrefutably," Ken said, "that the strategic bombing air attacks were a major failure considering all the lives and the costs that had gone into them."

Aware of his inbred mistrust of the military, one might suspect that he had gone to Germany with a preconceived notion. He denies this vigorously and with just the barest twinkle. "My confident expectation was that the bombing had been extremely successful." And with evident satisfaction, he added that the air force has been struggling ever since

---

2. Four survey men were killed during this part of the operation.

to downplay the USSBS report, if not to eliminate it altogether.

Albert Speer begins his memoirs *Inside the Third Reich* with these words: " 'I suppose you'll be writing your memoirs now,' said one of the first Americans I met in Flensburg in May, 1945." That first American may well have been Ken Galbraith, although he doesn't remember whether he uttered that unmemorable conjecture. But one thing is certain: Ken was and has remained the American who best understood and wrote most decisively about the role of Albert Speer in Germany's war effort. Along with Ball, Nitze, Col. Alexander, Major Klein, and two other army lieutenants, he conducted a seven-day interrogation of Speer. He also wrote two important articles — widely spaced in time — on the subject.

The first was a contemporary account, "The Interrogation of Albert Speer," which appeared in *Life* magazine on December 17, 1945, and was signed by Ken and George Ball. "I wrote it all," said Ken, "but I brought George in because I was a little hesitant about taking full responsibility for what may have been a breach of decorum."

The survey teams were quartered in Bad Nauheim in May 1945, as the war was drawing to a close. Hitler took his own life (and that of Eva Braun) on April 30, having sent word to Admiral Karl Doenitz to assume command, if such a word can be used to describe the death rattle that was then the Third Reich. By May 7 Doenitz had set up his provisional headquarters at Flensburg, near the Danish border; American and British forces kept a close watch on their activities. As Ken tells it in the *Life* piece, two alert American soldiers, Lt. George Sklarz and T. Sgt. Harold Fassberg, were poking around a makeshift office building in Flensburg, when they spotted the name Albert Speer on a door. They went inside and waited. Speer could not be questioned as a prisoner of war because he still enjoyed immunity as a minister in the

Doenitz government. However, he agreed at once to be interviewed as a Nazi official.

Ken and other staff members were flown from Bad Nauheim to the northern tip of Germany at Flensburg. George Ball was in London when word of Speer's availability reached him. "He was the man we were most interested in," Ball said. "Because he operated the whole war economy, he knew where all the bodies were buried, what the history had been, and what failures and successes they had had. So I laid on an airplane and we took a fair number of clerical people from London to transcribe and a couple of interpreters because neither Ken nor I spoke German, although Paul Nitze did speak a little."

Ken's recollection of that support staff is quite different. Never one to miss a chance for a gratuitous jab at the military, he says, "Of course the United States Army couldn't provide any assistance except a typewriter and maybe one secretary, so we recruited Speer's own secretary to take it all down in shorthand."

The setting in which this drama took place could not have been more appropriate. Speer had been lent a sixteenth-century castle overlooking the sea at Glücksburg — some ten miles east of Flensburg — by his friend the duke of Holstein, and it was here that the interrogations took place for seven afternoons and most of one night.

Ken describes the Schloss in Glücksburg as complete with towers, turrets, and a moat, and the room where the interviews took place as having low ceilings and being filled with red and gold brocade furniture. Speer, who "sat on a low settee, with arms locked around his knees, leaned forward a bit as he listened to questions, then rocked gently back and forth as he answered. He wore his military uniform the first day and looked like a Nazi, but thereafter — in civilian clothes, with his high forehead, scraggly black hair, and easy smile — he looked more like a casual young college professor. It soon developed that, like any professor, he enjoyed an audience."

Speer, writing of the same days, said, "I sat in the sixteenth-century castle built out into the water, with several civilians of my age belonging to the USSBS. . . . We went systematically through the various aspects of the war in the air [with] Chairman Franklin D'Olier, along with his vice chairman, Henry C. Alexander, and his assistants, Dr. Galbraith, Paul Nitze, George Ball. . . . During the next several days an almost comradely tone prevailed in our 'university of bombing.' "

Lest Ken be thought in his *Life* piece to have been too companionable with the charming and highly intelligent Speer — an architect by profession — he observed that Speer was an egoist who, caught up in his own ambitions, had sold himself out to the prospect of power. Furthermore, at the time of the "university of bombing" he wanted the world to know what a good job he had done against the formidable odds presented by many of the misguided members of the Third Reich high command.

A fundamental fallacy in our thinking about the Third Reich came to light during the Speer interviews. From the moment Mussolini had Italy's trains run on time, these dictators had been perceived as, if nothing else, efficient. It was not so. According to Speer's testimony, mistakes abounded; overconfidence in the early days of the war, after the quick trampling over Poland and France, allowed production to remain at comparatively low levels. The attack on Russia was unquestionably the most costly mistake the Germans had made, the more so because, with confusion and cross-purposes rife in the top echelons of the army, navy, and air force, by the time the miscalculation was acknowledged it was too late to cut losses.

In war production far too much reliance was placed on handcrafting rather than on more modern assembly-line techniques. And only a very few high-priority industries ever worked multiple shifts, let alone the around-the-clock shifts that were common in the Allied countries. Worse, complete manpower mobilization was never realized or even attempted

since women were not recruited to work in wartime industries. In fact, Speer pointed out, fewer women worked in
World War II than did in World War I.

Moral corruption was an incalculable factor. Ken, in his
Life article, quotes Speer characterizing "Goering as a dis-
honest, sensual and stupid traitor. Goebbels as an empty
headed fool; his propaganda succeeded only in convincing
German leaders that they could win the war without exerting
themselves. Bormann was a vicious gutter politician, Ribbentrop a clown, Himmler a monster and Sauckel a beast." And
because power had come to these and other men in high
places late in life, they were trying to crowd as much sybaritic
pleasure as they could into the remaining years. Many simply
turned to drink. In the last months of the war alcoholism was
rampant.

All this evidence of miscalculation, misjudgment, and
moral decay contributed to Germany's ultimate defeat far
more decisively than did the air attacks. Such was the belief of
the USSBS teams — Paul Nitze excepted — and the production figures available to them amply sustain their conclusions.

Galbraith's account of a second Speer interrogation was
not published for thirty-seven years — a record for one accustomed to having his words printed still warm from his pen.
This piece covers the final late-night interview with Speer,
who was aware that on the following morning the Doenitz
government would be dissolved and that he would become a
prisoner of war. Under these circumstances he was willing —
perhaps he even offered — to submit to questioning, not on
bombing-related matters, but on the last days of Hitler's life
and how they were spent, along with some of his still loyal
spear carriers, in a bunker with no windows and with air
pumped in, underneath the garden of the chancellery in Berlin.

On this historic occasion there was no secretarial help; Ken
took all the notes. After the session, which started in the late
afternoon and ended five hours later, he sat up the rest of the

night, getting his notes into usable form. The result may well be the earliest account by a high Nazi official of what was going on in the minds of Hitler and his top command during the closing days of the war. It is called the United States Strategic Bombing Survey Special Document. The reason it took Ken so long to publish the document, which is in effect his own handiwork, is that he claims it got lost. Although it had a wide circulation in typescript at the time it was released in 1945, he couldn't find a copy of it until thirty-four years later when one of his assistants stumbled on it.[3]

Much salient and chilling information emerged from this final Speer session as he described the bunker mentality that prevailed in those last days of the Third Reich — "fantastic plans in isolated air," as he put it. Unleashing chemical warfare, for example, was discussed repeatedly, as was delivering the so-called nodding donkeys — such yes men as Keitel and Himmler — to the enemy side in the hope that this offering would appease the Allied armies and make them take a gentler view of the German people.

Toward the end, a major controversy developed over the scorched-earth policy; factories, farms, livestock, communications were all to be obliterated to leave nothing but rubble for the conquerors. A large group of leaders believed that the German people could not survive defeat and hence there was no reason to leave them the means for survival. Speer claimed to have been instrumental in derailing this suicidal plan, by vigorously arguing, and quite speciously, as he must have known, that if the earth were indeed scorched, it would leave nothing for the Germans to come back to when they reconquered the territory, as inevitably they would. Apparently this was the view that finally prevailed.

Before Speer left the bunker at 4 A.M., he expressed his belief that Hitler had made up his mind to stay. He was, how-

---

3. The Special Document, along with a brief contemporary introduction by Galbraith, was first published in the July 1979 issue of the *Atlantic Monthly*.

ever, much concerned over what would happen to his corpse. "He knew what had happened to Mussolini's body and was agitated lest something similar happen to his. Accordingly, he had decided if the end came to commit suicide instead. He had given firm instructions that his body was to be cremated. Speer does not doubt that this is what happened."

Albert Speer and the Special Document in particular were milestones for Ken. Given the fact that he was called upon to reconstruct history so soon after it had happened — only eighteen days after hostilities had ceased — he did a brilliant job.

After the arrest of Speer and the fall of the Doenitz provisional government, things started to wind down for the survey teams. George Ball stepped in to fill a vacuum he saw looming by suggesting that he and Ken get themselves over to East Germany where Truman, Stalin, and Churchill (replaced during the sessions by Clement Attlee) and their staffs were meeting at what was to become the famous Potsdam Conference. Because, Ball said, he usually found himself in fundamental agreement with Ken "about all sorts of mischievous things," he was surprised when Ken demurred on the "flimsy" grounds that they had not been invited to attend. Ball pooh-poohed this scruple, saying that if they allowed hurt feelings to govern their actions they would only compound their error. So they "laid on" another airplane and, along with Paul Nitze, went blithely off to Babelsberg, outside Berlin, where the summit was being held. Telling the military guard at the gates that they had come for the conference, they were promptly admitted, welcomed by various friends they encountered, invited to lunch, and Ken was even asked by Isador Lubin to take part in an ongoing meeting on reparations.

Meanwhile, Ken's Overall Economic Effects Division was coming to the end of its closely reasoned treatise, *The Effects of Strategic Bombing on the German War Economy*.[4] When

---

4. It was one of two hundred detailed reports prepared by the various survey teams.

finally it was completed, Ken, Ball, and company shut up shop in Bad Nauheim and flew home in the miserable discomfort that military air travel afforded in those days of eighteen hours in the air huddled in bucket seats, with no heating and many stops.

Back in Washington they discovered to their distress that the secretariat of the survey, spearheaded by an air force general and egged on by Charles C. Cabot, had already written a preliminary paper on the effects of strategic bombing, calling it a *Summary Report*. Their account was clearly designed to head off Ken's team's painstakingly arrived-at conclusions and come up with a judgment much more favorable to the U.S. Air Force, which, if their version were to be believed, had won the war for the Allies.

Galbraith and Ball vigorously protested such a whitewash, and in a sense were backed by Deputy Chief Henry Alexander, who, Ken said, was less distressed by the conclusions of the *Summary Report* than by its "abysmal level of literacy." Ken, as the in-house writer, was called upon to repair to the Cosmos Club in Washington, to barricade himself and his typewriter behind stately doors, and to come up with a more acceptable draft. "By giving way on nonessentials," Ken wrote in his memoirs, "we kept the basic case. . . . Strategic bombing had not won the war. At most, it had eased somewhat the task of the ground troops who did."

The *Summary Report* (published on September 30, 1945) bore the mark of this controversy. If it still seemed tilted toward the success of U.S. strategic bombing rather than toward its shortcomings, Ken's fine hand was clearly evident, counterpunching whenever possible.

One month after the *Summary Report,* the full-length *Effects of Strategic Bombing on the German War Economy* was published exactly as written by Ken and his Overall Economic Effects Division, with no censorship of any sort. However, since this version was hard going with all those weighty statistics, it was less read than the *Summary Report*. But between the two versions, the case made by Ken and his colleagues was loud and clear enough to win him a fair number of enemies and detractors, adding to those he had garnered from his OPA days.

Fortunately, the reverse was also true. He had rallied many friends and admirers to his side. Moreover, the entire experience of those four months with the USSBS in Germany was key to putting Ken at the cutting edge of international events. He was now in a position to tell the world, as he did in an article for *Fortune* published not long after his return, that "Germany Was Badly Run," and to back his title with facts and figures gleaned from a firsthand experience that few had shared.

6

The Harvard Matter

AFTER HIS RETURN from Germany, Ken had hoped to stay
put for a while, working at *Fortune,* living with Kitty, Alan,
Douglas, and Emily at 450 Riverside Drive, and enjoying
New York, which he believes was at its best in those days. But
the hope was vain, because by that time his life had become
chronically peripatetic.

In the fall of 1945 he went off to Japan to have a look at
how strategic bombing had affected Japan's war mobilization. His not surprising conclusion was that, even though the
Japanese economy was less resilient and its plants were not
put back into operation nearly as soon as plants had been in
Germany, Japan had lost the war not because of the U.S.
bombing, but because of the "luminous insanity of her military leaders." He also believed that these considerations were
almost irrelevant in dealing with Japan, where such thoughts
would always be concentrated not on the effects of strategic
bombing, but on the atomic bomb.

Spring and summer of 1946 found him back in Washington
for another stint at the State Department, this time as director
of the Office of Economic Security Policy. (Inclusion of the
word *security,* he notes, was thought to confer cachet.) Since
the job dealt with economic affairs in Germany and Austria,
Japan and Korea, Ken appeared on paper to be well quali-

fied — uniquely so, he suggests in *A Life in Our Times*. "It is possible that I knew more about the drained and shattered economies of both Germany and Japan than anyone alive." Unfortunately, he was unable to put his expertise to good use, as he himself vaguely concedes. One of his Seminary Hill neighbors, economic historian Charles P. Kindleberger, who worked in the Economic Security Policy office, unambiguously confirms this. "Ken was not a success," he says. "But the guy before him was awful. Real trouble. Ken wasn't trouble; he would do what we told him because we were all so immersed in the details. But he didn't know what to do himself. He never got hold of it, probably because he wasn't that interested in the job. I don't know why he even took it."

He took it because to him the prestige of public service was very high. But even as he went to Washington, he and Kitty hedged their bets, hanging on to their New York apartment, exchanging it for a time with Abe Feller, who was coming to the UN, for Feller's house in Washington.

It seems that Ken and the State Department simply were not made for each other. Writing about his second tour of duty there (the first having been the Lend-Lease miniperiod), Ken seized the opportunity to air some of his mordant views about the "secular priesthood," as he obviously relished calling it, that traditionally dominated the higher echelons of the Department of State.

"[This] small group of well connected, upper income Americans, [was] selected for their task by family membership and attendance at Groton, Exeter, Andover or St. Paul's, Princeton, Harvard or Yale. They were attracted to the State Department because manner there was as important as knowledge, and more easily acquired, and because it was the one government department where a true-blue gentleman could work. No Groton man could serve in the General Accounting Office, the Bureau of Labor Statistics or the Department of Agriculture."[1]

---

1. *A Life in Our Times*, pp. 242–44.

He had many more caustic observations about the "priest-hood." It looked on American democracy, as evidenced by Congress or other branches of the executive, as being filled with "decidedly vulgar people." It abhorred Communists, the Soviet Union, and Jews, and "for many the three were roughly identical."

As for his own relations to the "priestly group," he conceded that from his boyhood days he had felt required to be "compulsively against any self-satisfied elite. One never joined, and one never overlooked any righteous opportunity to oppose or, if opportunity presented, to infuriate."

Some Galbraith watchers may ponder this rather frenetic attempt to distance himself from the elite of the Department of State. Was it to gloss over what had not been a significantly successful, albeit short, period in his career? Or were these admonitions laid out to remind himself — subliminally, at least — that come what may this farm boy was not going to be taken into camp by this or any other branch of the establishment?

Yet to many minds he was not only taken in but by the early 1950s had practically become a bona fide member of the establishment. Even Ken admits to having been on the fringe. "If you consider Averell Harriman, John McCloy, and McGeorge Bundy as the quintessential figures in the establishment, then yes, I was there. But I always kept myself a little outside because when the establishment enunciated ideas that I thought were nonsense or worse I wanted to be in a position to say, 'Oh, that's just a lot of — that's ridiculous.' "

Back at *Fortune,* where they had been exceedingly forebearing about Ken's comings and goings, he was conscious of "the embarrassing fact that I have undertaken a considerable number of projects in recent years. Now, with the peace I must settle down lest I earn the reputation of being a bird that flits from branch to branch."

These lines were written in April 1946 to David Rockefeller, who was then exploring the idea of having Ken come to work for the Rockefeller brothers. Ken explained why he thought he ought to remove himself from serious consideration. He further noted that "there is the Harvard matter of which I spoke. If that appointment is made — which I think is still a fairly long shot — I intend to accept. I have indicated my availability to the University and have mentally committed myself."

Two years later, in 1948, the long shot paid off and the Harvard appointment was made — another one of those "out of the blue sky" affairs that Galbraith is so fond of citing. "It was summer of 1948 when John D. Black phoned me and asked me to come back to take over a new operation studying agricultural marketing. A big federal grant had just been made to Harvard for such a study on the assumption that maybe the farm program could be made cheaper — price controls diminished, that sort of thing — if there were a better, more efficient marketing system."

"Mentally committed" as Ken and Kitty were when they drove up to Cambridge in July, they had two distinct worries. First, they had no idea where they were going to find a place to live at this late date. Second, Ken was not happy that he had been offered only a lectureship as his re-entry rank. A lectureship was a catchall for persons considered not quite ready for the professorial rank; Ken knew beyond question that he was ready and fully qualified.

Although their first fear proved quite justified, the second — the lectureship — was taken care of in a matter of weeks; whether it was reactively or proactively orchestrated by Galbraith remains, as always, open to question. Ken swears he had nothing to do with the fact that his friend Howard Bowen, then dean of the College of Commerce and Business Administration at the University of Illinois, stepped into the breach early in September to offer Ken the chairmanship of the Department of Economics at his university. The Galbraiths dutifully journeyed to the Urbana, Illinois, campus, making certain that those in Cambridge who might be thought to care knew where they were going and why.

The desired result followed. The Harvard economics department voted, with only one dissenter, to change Galbraith's appointment from lecturer on economics and director of Agricultural and Marketing Research to simply professor of economics. The appointment was subject, as a matter of course, to confirmation by Harvard's board of overseers. That should have been the end of it, the overseers' approval being considered nothing more than pro forma.

In the case of John Kenneth Galbraith, however, and, probably for the first time in fifty years, it was not. At the heart of the matter was Ken's old Bombing Survey antagonist Charles C. Cabot, then sitting, as Cabots inevitably must, on the Harvard board of overseers. It was he who provided the initial impetus that stopped Galbraith's appointment to full professor and put it on hold for almost a year. Still smarting, apparently, from the near black eye he considered Ken to have given the U.S. Air Force, Cabot must have been determined that this provocateur of the Bombing Survey would not be rewarded anywhere for his pains, least of all at Harvard, where he had something to say about it.

But one man's voice, even that particular man's, would not have been enough. Cabot was joined, albeit for other reasons, by three others: Sinclair Weeks, a former U.S. senator who became secretary of commerce under Eisenhower; Clarence Randall, chairman of the board of Inland Steel; and Thomas Lamont, of J. P. Morgan. One may think that these three captains of industry and finance based their objections to Galbraith on the rigors he had imposed on the business world during his days as price czar. Apparently this wasn't the case. "If they had known more about some of my OPA decisions, they might have made a case there too," said Ken, and then, demonstrating that the years had not made him feel more magnanimous toward these antagonists, added, "But these were men of very limited knowledge."

Their objection to Galbraith's appointment it seems was to the fact that he was a major Keynesian in a department that, they felt, was already too full of persons of this virulent stripe.

"Keynes was regarded as a much more real and present danger even than Marx," Ken noted.

There are thirty members on the board of overseers. (Harvard clings to its particular nomenclature; every other university has trustees; Harvard has overseers; to refer to the Harvard "campus" instead of the Harvard Yard signifies the basest country-bumpkin ignorance.) Obviously, they couldn't all devote themselves to the fate of one economics professor, even a larger-than-life one like Galbraith. A special committee was formed to look into the matter; Ken has called their findings "deeply adverse." Fortunately, he was not without his friends at court, notably Charles E. Wyzanski, a federal judge — liberal, erudite, and a savant — who was then chairman of the board of overseers. Although the opposite in physical stature, Wyzanski had much in common with Galbraith, up to and including his complete intellectual courage and a self-assurance that was often referred to as arrogant.

Fortunately, too, James Bryant Conant was president of Harvard at the time, and he strongly supported Galbraith's appointment, first for reasons of academic freedom, and second because the economics department had recommended him and Conant was committed to the autonomy of the university's departments. If Conant's successor, Nathan Marsh Pusey, had been president, Ken, who did not admire Pusey, was convinced the outcome would have been quite different, and he and Kitty might well have wound up in Urbana, Illinois. Pusey had once committed the unpardonable by calling him John. Whether President Pusey knew better or not, Ken loves to retaliate by referring to him as Marsh Pusey.

Strength also came from outside the university, particularly from George Ball, who has a habit of coming forward at critical times in Ken's career and changing the outcome — always, it seems, for the better. "Ken knew this was the kind of injustice that would appeal to me and that I would be activated by," Ball said. Like Galbraith, Ball knew Cabot well from the Bombing Survey, and he was convinced that Cabot, being a Cabot, looked at — or down on — Ken as a brash young man of the sort he was reluctant to see on the Harvard faculty, especially a brash young man who had impugned the honor of the United States Air Force. To counter this, Ball, always an imaginative mediator, got the secretary of the air force, Stuart Symington, a loyal old New Dealer, to certify that the air force wasn't really mad at Galbraith anymore, although it probably still was; only Symington was not.

In the end, after President Conant allegedly threatened to resign over the matter, Wyzanski, choosing his moment carefully, managed to bring the appointment up at a meeting of the overseers where the pro-Galbraith forces present were in the majority, and he finally prevailed. On November 22, 1949, Provost Paul Buck, also a partisan, called Ken to give him the good news, and the next day his promotion was made public.

Although Ken may have secretly relished being at the center of a controversy in which he was being pilloried for his progressive views, he had been deeply distressed by the injustice of the attack on him. He responded with a memorandum in which, in his elaborate prose, he sought to set the record straight, especially vis-à-vis the Bombing Survey, and to state his own philosophy of public behavior. "It is of course possible . . . that I am unduly uncompromising in my personal and political views and in my personal relations.

"I will say that while I set the greatest store by open-mindedness — the habit of mind that learns and unlearns — in scientific and scholarly pursuits, I do believe there are times when a man must be uncompromising. Facts cannot be compromised; neither can great issues of public welfare."

Through all these travails, the person who was most constant in his support of Galbraith was his Harvard mentor, John D. Black. "My debt to John D. Black is incomparable," Ken said. "Nobody ever did so much for me at that stage of my career. He was always there advancing my case." His high regard for Black is evident, genuine, and also somewhat unexpected, for Black was far from being the kind of Harvard intellectual he usually admired. For one thing, he was not "casual," a characteristic Ken tends to look on with high approbation. Black came from a rural family in Wisconsin and was educated in that liberal state when the first La Follette was a dominant force. Not only did John D. develop a strong public interest in agricultural economics, he also demonstrated an enormous capacity for attracting federal money to this field. Harvard, which had neither a lot of money nor many students in agricultural economics, acquired both by hiring John D. Black in the fall of 1929.

So this vigorous, tenacious, and enthusiastic man was responsible for bringing Ken to Harvard in the first place, for returning him to Harvard eight years later, and finally for doing his not inconsiderable part to secure him his tenured position. As Ken has pointed out, "It was well known that when John D. Black wanted something, it might better be given to him first rather than last because he would never give up."

It is interesting to speculate about Galbraith at this point. Even as he teetered on the threshold of cherished academic acceptance, was he not still an outsider trying to make his way? Probably yes. For despite his prodigious rise to eminence as price controller, *Fortune* editor, and acknowledged expert on German wartime economy, he was, as he himself has noted, still a farm boy trying to rise above that "slight flavor of manure" that hovered about him. And agricultural economics, no matter how it was dressed up by calling it farm commodity distribution or the like, was still a mildly looked down upon field — on a par with, say, mechanical engineering — at most liberal arts institutions, and especially at Harvard.

There were other conventions quite particular to Harvard; the old saw "Yes, but what have you done for me lately?" might well be borrowed to read "Yes, but what have you done *since* coming to Harvard?" There was an instinctive refusal to be impressed by what had occurred before, especially if, as in Ken's case, it had been outside the world of academe.

The release from the University News Office announcing his appointment to full professor after one year of controversy was so bland that neither friend nor foe would have recognized the Galbraith they knew and loved — or loved to hate. "Dr. Galbraith, who has served as administrator or consultant in several governmental agencies, is a specialist in the statistical study of economic problems and has made studies particularly in the field of agricultural economics and finance." So even Ken may have felt he had his work cut out for him, making an impression on the Cambridge community he had chosen as his home base — and his future launching pad.

It had been a difficult, and ultimately would be a heartbreaking, time for the Galbraiths. First there was the matter of finding a place to live; as the start of the academic year approached nothing suitable seemed available. Fortunately, Kitty had wonderful older friends, Margaret and Willard Helburn, who had a large apartment overlooking the Charles River at 989 Memorial Drive, which they agreed to share with the Galbraith family. Although there was plenty of room for all — a bedroom with a nice river view for Ken and Kitty, a bath, a small room for Emily, and another for Alan and Douglas — it was a stopgap arrangement until they could find a house of their own. There was no place to rent, but there were a few houses to buy. Unfortunately, they could not consider doing this because, with Ken's appointment hanging fire, buying a house would have looked as if they were assuming too much. So they stayed on with the Helburns.

Luckily in this unsettling period, there was an island of peace and stability for the Galbraiths: their cherished farm, in Newfane, Vermont, which they had bought in 1947, before coming to Harvard was even at issue. At that time, when they half expected they were going to live permanently in New York City, Kitty had insisted that their second home be someplace far enough away so that there could be no question of Ken's commuting. So when their friends Janey and Charles Siepmann lent them their house in southeastern Vermont for a few weeks, they decided to look around a bit and see what

the market had to offer. In this pre-Cambridge venture it offered exactly what they were looking for. The property, eight
miles outside of Newfane, had more than two hundred acres
and a house in reasonably good condition, although without many "amenities" (the outhouse was at the end of the
woodshed). More important, the price, at five dollars an
acre — today it would be a hundred dollars — put the pur-
chase price within their reach.

The Rural Electrification Authority (REA) brought in wires
for electricity; the Galbraiths tried to use a surface well temporarily, but since this did not provide enough water for
flushing toilets, they were obliged to dig an artesian well. Both
still shudder when remembering the sound of that drilling as
it went down and down and down to the tune of seven dollars
a foot. At a depth of more than three hundred feet they finally
got water. These improvements took care of their creature
comforts so that they could be at the farm in late spring, summer, and early fall. To this day they do not have heating, although they have managed, with a huge fireplace, several
kerosene stoves, and a great deal of cheerful fortitude, to
spend a number of Christmases there.

The house is very elastic. The long, narrow living room
with fireplace is comfortable, welcoming, and has suitably
shabby furniture. At one end and at right angles to it, is the
dining room, with a kitchen, pantry, and storeroom beyond — all large, old-fashioned, plain, and homey. Numerous bedrooms of varying sizes and one complete bathroom
are tucked in, some in unlikely places, on the ground floor. Up
a steep unbanistered staircase (there are two such staircases,
both equally daunting to the visitor with suitcase) are three
large bedrooms and — a recent addition — one half-bath.
The house can and often has accommodated eight to ten
people at a time. Off the kitchen wing is a pleasant piazza
that gives onto a well-kept croquet court — Ken's single
known summer sport, and perhaps the only one at which
he excels.

Among the later additions is a dammed-up pond, the job started by cooperative beavers and completed by man and bulldozer. And while Ken was ambassador to India, he had designed and built a separate building, at some remove from the house, which is his very agreeable study.

There would appear to be a certain logic in a graduate of an agricultural college, with a doctorate in agricultural economics, a man about to be called to Harvard as director of agricultural and marketing research, buying an abandoned farm with a view to restoring it and working it profitably. Such, however, was not the case with John Kenneth Galbraith. In fact, he distinctly scorned such a practice, mocking the eager "gentleman" farmer — full of bucolic ideas and no practical experience — who earnestly believed that he could reverse what crusty natives, wise to the ways of the countryside, had given up as a bad job. "The reasons for not trying to receive an abandoned farm would seem to be fairly apparent. . . . If a particular type of agriculture is not being practiced in New England, it is roughly a hundred to one that it is because it doesn't pay. And it is at least a thousand to one that any successful new enterprise will be hit upon by some intelligent and skillful local farmer in consultation with the Extension Service, and not by a new arrival from town."[2]

Thus he neatly managed to dissociate himself from the naive gullibility of the city slickers and to align himself squarely with the earthy wisdom of the local farmers.

Ken began his second year at Harvard with his situation still unclarified. His teaching schedule had improved, however, because his colleague and friend Edward Mason had moved on to head the new Graduate School of Public Administration, and Ken inherited his course, Industrial Organization — a major offering, he noted, that required "somebody of seri-

---

2. *The Liberal Hour* (Boston: Houghton Mifflin, 1960), pp. 183–84. This book, a collection of essays, is dedicated to John D. Black and his wife.

sition" to teach. Accordingly, he had a good reason to
partly out of his directorship of Agricultural Marketing
arch, thus lessening the manure factor and strengthening
ties to the more intellectually acceptable and quintessentially
Harvard Department of Economics.

Meanwhile, Kitty had found a house to rent — small, in
poor repair, but at a very good address, 2 Willard Street
Court, just off Brattle Street. The Galbraiths were forced to
do what is repugnant to all renters — putting money into a
house they did not own in order to make it livable. As soon as
Ken's promotion became official, they started hunting for a
house to buy. But before they could accomplish that, they
found themselves facing a dreadful problem.

Douglas Galbraith, just short of seven years old, was mor-
tally ill. The first signs came on an evening when Emily and
the boys were at the movies in Harvard Square and Ken and
Kitty were out of town. As they left the University Theatre,
Douglas complained to Emily that his legs hurt and that he
didn't want to walk home. The next morning, when the normally active boy didn't want to get out of bed, Emily called
the pediatrician, Dr. Dorothea Moore, who took loving and
thoughtful care of many faculty children during these years.
She could find nothing wrong with Douglas, but when by evening he was no better, she called in a bone specialist, who told
Emily to take Douglas to Children's Hospital at nine the next
morning.

Emily did not phone the Galbraiths at that juncture because, she insists, she didn't know how sick Douglas was and
didn't want to worry them unnecessarily. Her restraint was in
part due to her reluctance to add to Kitty's already heavy burdens, since her mother was also gravely ill.

When Emily finally reached Ken, he responded with disbe-
lief and almost irritably insisted that of course Douggie
couldn't be that sick. But alas he was. At the hospital Emily
recalled the tormented look on Ken's face when, after the doctor had called him out, he came back into his son's room,

knowing that he would have to tell Kitty and Emily the truth: Douglas had leukemia.

There can be no greater anguish for parents than to watch a beloved child suffer. Although Ken is quite unable to talk about it, one can guess that, for a man who had recently begun to seem very powerful, his sudden feeling of impotence must have been nearly insupportable.

Douglas, described by his father in a brief reference in his memoirs as "intelligent, determined and variously accomplished beyond his years," lived for three months. Many gave blood to help him through his final ordeal, including every member of Ken's Industrial Organization class. Friends who came to the Galbraiths' Willard Street Court house recall Ken's carrying Douglas downstairs, his small body held rigid in a wooden frame to protect him against pain. And withal Ken still managed to joke with his little boy, to keep his tone always light, always unfrightening, always tender. He was strong for Kitty too, as she faced the loss of her son and of her mother, gently persuading her that the only solace for her — for them both — was to have another child as soon as possible.

She was pregnant in May when Douglas died, just a few weeks after his seventh birthday.

Peter Woodard Galbraith was born on December 31, 1950. Two days later the Galbraiths bought their house at 30 Francis Avenue. Finally, their roots were laid down.

If one can be said to have a symbiotic relationship with a house, they had it with 30 Francis Avenue. It is impossible to imagine one without the other. Even before they moved in, Francis Avenue had a certain panache as a street where academics — especially those with at least some outside income — chose to live, toil, and frolic. After the Galbraiths' arrival, the street took on additional éclat. (In the 1960s when it produced two ambassadors to New Delhi, the street became known as "a passage to India.") No one has enjoyed the sense of collegiality that emanates from Francis Avenue and closely parallel Irving Street more than Ken, whose habitual greeting to anyone living within the charmed circle has always been "Hi, neighbor."

Number 30 is a large, solid-looking red brick house distinguished by its pink shutters — no one remembers how that unlikely color was chosen. You enter an unprepossessing screened porch that usually has a few outdoor chairs stacked in one corner in winter and at parties a huge bulging coat rack; you see a sign over the screen door that reads Roosevelt House, which is the name of the ambassador's residence in New Delhi; you ring a bell and if no one comes you bang the door knocker. One way or another you gain admission to a wide front hall. To the left is a high-ceilinged, paneled living room that at first glance gives promise of being large and manorial and in fact isn't really either. It's an agreeable room, though, furnished comfortably but without distinction. Some of the chairs would do well in a student's room, especially the one in front of the west window where the master sits and from which he holds forth. Suitably in the professor's house there are bookshelves on every wall. One large section is filled with books by John Kenneth Galbraith; with the foreign editions — French, German, Spanish, Danish, Russian, and Japanese — they take up a good deal of room. Another section is devoted to books written and autographed to Ken and Kitty by their illustrious friends.

But in 1951 when they bought their house, they didn't have many books — none as yet had been written by Ken — and certainly not enough for all those shelves. Ever loyal and resourceful, Margaret Helburn came to Kitty's rescue with dozens of "sets" of books. Sets consisted of identically bound volumes of Dickens, Thackeray, Ruskin, and so on, which had once lined parents' or grandparents' shelves and which were doubtless as unread by them as by the succeeding generations.

As the Galbraiths' library expanded, they had no need for

those fillers, but one benefit endured from the sets: they introduced Ken to Trollope, with whom he found instant rapport. Everything about the Victorian writer pleased him: Trollope's unabashed fondness for money; his fascination with politics; his mockery of the clergy; his disdain for the self-righteous; and, of course, his skillful pen. Ken has delighted to claim him as an influence.

Ken's study, on the opposite side of the hallway, looks exactly as one may suppose, the walls above the bookcases adorned with pictures of him with various personages — John F. Kennedy, Jackie Kennedy, Adlai Stevenson, Lyndon B. Johnson, George McGovern, Angie Dickinson, Jawaharlal Nehru, Averell Harriman — along with many caricatures of his own easy-to-caricature face, and on the mantelpiece plaques and medals in silk-lined boxes, marking his many honors.

Next to the study is the dining room, presided over for twenty-five years by Emily and more recently, since Emily's retirement, by Sheela Karintikal. The food here is plain, substantial, and not the reason one looks forward to going to the Galbraiths for dinner. Other pleasures — sprightly, witty, provocative conversation, for example — provide more important sustenance.

On these occasions, as on all others, Ken has always dominated. He once noted that through the years he has steeled himself for not being universally loved. But he has never steeled himself for the possibility, however remote, of not being universally accorded center stage. His role as star player has been acknowledged, or at least more or less accepted, by the many friends who have been welcomed into his house. They, after all, have had to deal with him only sporadically. But for Kitty, who was subjected to his will at all times, it was often difficult, the more so since there was a period in their earlier Cambridge days when he was at his most overbearing with her. One friend recalls an occasion when she was sitting next to Kitty on the sofa while Ken was declaiming from his habitual seat of honor. After a bit, Kitty ventured to start a conversation of her own, perhaps aimlessly, with her friend on the couch. Ken, on hearing her voice speaking softly in the background, was not pleased. "Kitty, be quiet," he said witheringly. "*People* are talking."

The mitigating fact is that Ken, when reminded of this and similar incidents, professes to be totally unaware of any such occurrences. Either he is genuinely unconscious of them or he doesn't believe that whatever he did or said was a put-down of Kitty, since he certainly did not so intend it. Fortunately, time has noticeably softened his bouts of impatient irritability.

One of the many dividends of 30 Francis Avenue was that its back yard gave onto the back yard of Arthur and Marian Schlesinger, who lived behind them on Irving Street. Ken's friendship with Schlesinger is second only to his kinship with George Ball, and perhaps even stronger because the two men had Harvard in common, although they had come to its faculty via very different routes. Arthur M. Schlesinger, Jr., was to the manner born, the son of a revered and beloved professor of history at Harvard. Young Arthur — or "little Arthur," as he was often referred to in his earlier, more bumptious days — stepped into Harvard as naturally as a child going from kindergarten to the first grade. He justified the faith shown in him by graduating summa cum laude in 1938, and then by being chosen a member of the Society of Fellows for three years, permitting him to pursue any line of study or inquiry that the university offered. He won the Pulitzer Prize for *The Age of Jackson* in 1946, the year he became a tenured professor at Harvard.

If Ken had ever stopped to compare his own bumpy progression with Arthur's uncommonly smooth one, he might have felt a pang of envy. Certainly he would never have admitted it, nor would Arthur have even recognized such a possibility. In any case both men had, by the early 1950s, arrived at the same plateau, and it was Schlesinger who was soon to give Ken further impetus in two important new directions.

In 1952, Ken, beginning his lifelong practice of turning an article into a hardcover book, produced his first slim volume, called *A Theory of Price Control*. Economist Leonard Silk has called this book "a part of a modest tradition of apologies written by economists who have seen official service as price controllers."[3] Galbraith would doubtless dispute this, arguing that *A Theory of Price Control* was not an apology. It was a defense, an effort to convince other economists that price control should not be used only as dictated by events, but as an important tool against inflation at all times. The book was Galbraith's most technical and hence his least readable. "Five people read it," the author has said. "Maybe fifteen." Multiplied by a hundred, this is more or less par for a book published — at least in those days — by a university press (in this case Harvard) where the objective was not profit but enlightenment.

Still, Galbraith wanted both. Shortly after the tepid reception accorded to *A Theory of Price Control,* he was quoted as saying, "I made up my mind that I would never again place myself at the mercy of technical economists who had the enormous power to ignore what I had written. I set out to involve a larger community. I would involve economists by having the larger public say to them 'Where do you stand on Galbraith's idea of price control?' They would have to confront what I said."[4]

By then he had, in fact, taken the first step in his pursuit of that larger audience. Based only on his oral presentation, he had persuaded a commercial publisher — Houghton Mifflin Company of Boston — to give him a thousand-dollar advance to write a book on a new view of economics that had been rumbling around in his mind for some time. Houghton Mifflin had never made a better investment for the long term.

The book, published at almost the same time as *A Theory*

3. *The Economists* (New York: Basic Books, 1976), p. 113.
4. Quoted in Charles H. Hession, *John Kenneth Galbraith and His Critics* (New York: New American Library, 1972), p. 25.

of Price Control, was called *American Capitalism;* its subtitle, *The Concept of Countervailing Power,* encapsulated the book's astonishing thesis: competition, which among most economists was regarded as a regulator of economic activity, was being superseded by countervailing power.

Competition had been effective in the past because a large group of small independent sellers, competing for their share of the market, served to regulate prices. This safeguard, however, was changing, according to Galbraith. Now it was a *small* group of *large* sellers with a mutually recognized interest in avoiding competition which had come to dominate particular markets. And the economic power that one such group held was balanced or neutralized by the power held by an opposing group on the other side of the market. Thus, countervailing power, in Galbraith's view, provided the market regulation that had heretofore been provided by straightforward competition. The examples he cited in *American Capitalism* made the point. Powerful interest groups such as labor unions or big chain stores successfully held in check the market power of employers and manufacturers, and demonstrated that the economic system had the necessary restraints against exploitation.

The book received excellent reviews and a few scolding ones. *The Economist* aptly noted that Galbraith's "ability for lively generalization makes him peculiarly at home in the border region between economics and social analysis." But the *New York Times,* although favorable in the main, suggested that "a lot of economists will not like Mr. Galbraith's gay dismissal of most of their recent theoretical output. . . . There is still something to the idea that old fashioned price competition, blessed, if not enforced by the anti trust laws, is an essential component of economic progress, even today." Writing in the *New York Post,* Stuart Chase, a noted economist, called *American Capitalism* an important book, "perhaps a landmark in economic thinking. At the same time it is lucid, witty and untouched by the sour dogmatism which flavors so much writing in this field." Ken must have relished that line.

Still, some of those sour dogmatists were quite respectful of his thesis; others, perhaps the sourest, were dismissive or worse. Even the author has expressed considerable revisionism about what he has called the "euphoric tendency" in the text. "The idea was important," he concedes, "but I gave it too much weight. I was far too enthusiastic." Perhaps so, but the seeds of some of his greatest successes are found in this first sowing.

7

A Magic Way
with Words

IN THE 1950S the full panoply of Ken Galbraith's widely ranging achievements unfolded; so too did the rewards thereof.

Since his return to academic life, he claimed in his memoirs, he had been busy trying to make his image conform to that of a "safe and somber" scholar. Even so, he suspected, the fear persisted at Harvard that he would concern himself unduly with "political activity of a general sort at the expense of students, scholarly writing and decent academic reticence."

The fear was partly justified. During the next twenty years he was energetically involved at the top level in five presidential campaigns. Yet students apparently didn't suffer because of these doings, nor did scholarly writing, although some soreheads might question the word *scholarly*. Decent academic reticence? Well, perhaps that *was* a bit compromised, or would have been, had it ever existed.

Adlai Stevenson was the best candidate Ken could possibly have chosen for his entry-level foray into presidential politics. Furthermore, even if he had been reluctant to commit himself, which he was not, he could never have withstood the blandishments of his two best friends, George Ball and Arthur Schlesinger, Jr., both firmly positioned as right-hand men, both strongly urging him to come on board as a speech writer, once again taking advantage, he notes, of his "fatal fluency."

Ken's initial encounter with Stevenson occurred on a warm evening in August 1952 on the grounds of the governor's mansion in Springfield, Illinois. Since Galbraith was comparatively late in joining the campaign — he had not even been at the Democratic convention in Chicago when Stevenson was nominated — he was simply one of the many extremely bright, literate, mostly young liberals already feverishly at work bolstering a candidate whom they all believed to be a man of destiny.

As in any campaign anywhere, space was at a premium, and with speech writers already overflowing from the governor's mansion, quarters were rented for them — one large workroom and several smaller ones — at the Elks Club in downtown Springfield, just a few blocks away from the Leland Hotel, where many of the writers stayed, and from the governor's mansion, where they fervently hoped their man was *not* going to be staying.

Among the Elks, as they inevitably came to be called, Arthur Schlesinger was perhaps the first among equals; for one thing, he was one of the earliest Stevenson communicants and had taken leave from Harvard to sign on for the duration. For another, he was an extremely gifted speech drafter who seemed to have the knack of copying Stevenson's style, his balanced sentences, and, as Galbraith notes, "his frequent willingness to subordinate meaning to euphony," a knack Galbraith himself was quick to acquire. Other luminaries among Ken's fellow Elks were his Harvard colleague, noted American historian and writer Bernard DeVoto; Willard Wirtz, a well-known labor lawyer and activist; David Bell, an economist borrowed from President Truman's staff; Robert Tufts, an Oberlin professor; John Bartlow Martin, a *Saturday Evening Post* writer, later to produce the definitive two-volume biography of Stevenson; John Fischer, editor of *Harper's Magazine;* Herbert Agar, of the Louisville *Courier-Journal;* Eric Hodgins (*Mr. Blandings*), recruited by Galbraith;

and Sidney Hyman, a Washington writer, the only Elk to be thin-skinned about having his words rewritten.

It was a marvelous group with which to be associated. As John Bartlow Martin reports, they worked together with remarkable harmony. They also worked very hard — sometimes too hard; health breakdowns were not unusual. They would arrive at about ten in the morning and go to lunch together at two at a dingy bar called the Sazerac in order to avoid meeting the press. On the way there they would stop and peer in the window of Coe's Bookstore, looking, usually in vain, for copies of their own books. Afternoons they would slave over drafts of their assigned speeches and then at about 7:30, after stopping for a drink at the Elks Club bar, go on to dinner at Stevie's or some other out-of-the-way steak house. Then they would return to the Elks Club, to work at least until midnight, or sometimes during critical moments before a campaign trip, until two or three in the morning. Their talk during meals frequently, and often accidentally, produced policy. "One evening at dinner," Martin writes, "Galbraith said, 'It seems to me our farm policy is simple — the Democratic Party is the farmer's friend. And we're for price supports.' All agreed." Galbraith drafted a speech, as did another Elk; they put the two together to produce Stevenson's major speech on agriculture. "Obviously it was not always so casual," Martin adds. "They were serious men. They cared about the issues and believed the rhetoric."

The Elks referred to themselves as "speech researchers" because they knew that Stevenson was pained at the thought of ghost writers. He and his staff (those who worked out of the governor's mansion as opposed to the Elks Club) liked to foster the idea that this candidate wrote his own speeches. "It was a myth we deliberately created," says George Ball.

Since the Elks rarely met with the governor as a group, some of them tended to look on him as a ghost candidate; still, when he went on a campaign trip, one or two Elks usually accompanied him. Their contact with him, however, was almost entirely through top staff man Carl McGowan, although Martin notes that Schlesinger did sometimes see Stevenson alone.[1] So too did Galbraith, on at least one occasion, an occasion on which by his own admission he talked more than he listened.

According to George Ball's recollection, "Stevenson was not entirely comfortable with Ken. He thought he was a little extreme in his views. Stevenson liked him and I think they had a very pleasant relationship, but Ken was not the person Adlai would have turned to first."

Actually, as their correspondence suggests, the two men became closer after the 1952 campaign and during the 1956 one, by which time, Galbraith says, Stevenson was "less troubled by liberal heresies than he had been four years before." Yet Ken believes that the really memorable campaign was 1952, with its cheerful disregard for shopworn precedents and its exuberant bushwhacking through unfamiliar terrain. It was also the hardest to have lost.

Ken took it almost as a personal defeat. Like most Democrats, particularly Democratic insiders, he was lulled, after sixteen years of controlling the White House, into the feeling that the executive belonged to his party by divine right. The American people had rejected a brilliant, urbane, and witty candidate like Stevenson, who would surely have found a place for Galbraith in his administration, in favor of the middle-America, golf-playing, Babbitt-like Eisenhower — a military man to boot — who would not find him such a place. Ken could almost imagine that *he* had been voted out of office. He woke up the morning after the election feeling as if there were no reason on earth to get out of bed. Still, he reasoned, there was nothing unusual about that; any intelligent, right-thinking person would be feeling low on the morning of November 5, 1952.

---

1. John Bartlow Martin, *Adlai Stevenson of Illinois: The Life of Adlai E. Stevenson* (Garden City, N.Y.: Doubleday, 1976), pp. 632–40.

But instead of lessening with time, his sense of gloom deep-ened. It was true that he had been operating under a great deal of pressure; in the last two months of the campaign he had continued his full teaching schedule at Harvard and com-muted on weekends either to Illinois or occasionally to where Stevenson was campaigning, if it happened to be someplace nearer the Boston area. It was also true that he tended to be unduly worried about feeling fatigued, since fatigue was one of the symptoms that had led to the diagnosis of his incipient tuberculosis when he was a junior at Ontario Agricultural College. And finally, it was true that he found a little tempo-rary relief in a few whiskeys before dinner and was becoming more and more dependent on Seconal to give him a decent rest at night.

He was having, in other words, a real depression, so real and so painful that he was finally driven to consulting a psy-chiatrist, an action that he would normally have considered as foreign to his nature as if he had chosen to spend a summer afternoon at Fenway Park watching a Red Sox baseball game. (Who are the Red Sox? he might have asked.)

Doubtless this was not the first depression Ken had suf-fered, although possibly it was the first to be acknowledged and treated as such. Nor was it to be the last. Almost certainly the alleged cause of it — the defeat of his party's candidate for president — was not really the reason for his depression but the rationalization for it, although as such just as real to him. It is not too difficult to fathom a probable cause for his malaise. A professional sage who engages his intellect on so many fronts and who, at the same time, always demands of himself such definitive answers must now and again experi-ence inner conflict.

Ken briefly refers to his visits to a psychiatrist in *A Life in Our Times* as follows: "I learned to my surprise that I had long been subject to cycles of euphoria and depression. These had been relatively mild — not far out of the plausible range of normal reaction to good news and bad. . . . On the discovery of my disorder, I turned my mind to tracing previous cycles. Presently the cloud lifted. Thereafter when it returned, save for one occasion in India when it was evidently accentuated by hepatitis, I could recognize it for what it was."

In September 1953 Ken had a significant talk with Averell Harriman and expressed to him some concerns he had shared with Arthur Schlesinger. After both men had agreed that they were smoking too much, they turned their thoughts to the policies — or perhaps more properly the lack of policies — facing a party that was out of office.[2] Were they not in danger of lapsing into "political and mental desuetude"? And was this not a moment to make the candidate — they assumed it would be Stevenson again — more truly conversant with some of the ideas he was espousing: Social Security, trade unionism, and Keynesian economy?

A week later Ken refined his ideas in a long, rather preachy letter to Stevenson. "How can we do the most to keep the Democratic Party intellectually alert and positive during these years in the wilderness?" he asked. "We have all told ourselves that mere opposition is not enough. Yet it would be hard at the moment to say what the Democratic Party is for. On domestic matters we are for good against evil and for tidying up the unfinished business of the New Deal. . . . In fact we are still trading on the imagination and intellectual vigor of the Roosevelt era and that capital is running thin. . . . A party that has no central core of ideas is in serious danger of disunity." (It's hard to believe that he wrote these words in 1952 and not 1990.)

After quite a lot more in this vein, he went on finally to suggest that the way to formulate some sort of policy was to create a study committee attached to the Democratic National Committee, chaired by some able and thoughtful member of the party and made up of accomplished political leaders in

---

2. Ken quit smoking in the 1960s in response to the Surgeon General's warnings.

and out of office who had a strong sense of public responsibility. "As the party of the well-to-do, the Republicans do not hesitate to make use of their dough," he concluded. "As the party of the egg-heads we should similarly and proudly make use of our brains and experience."

Stevenson responded with a very warm Dear Ken letter praising him for what he termed "a perfect statement of our problem, which I have thought about for a long time. Indeed it has clarified my own thinking immensely." He was much interested in the idea of a study group; to head it, he suggested Thomas J. Finletter, a Philadelphia-born lawyer practicing in New York. Finletter came with impeccable connections and widespread international interests — he had been ambassador to NATO. "Do talk to him," Stevenson urged. "I think he might be useful what with time, intelligence and some background, but he will need somebody like yourself to help him not only to assume responsibility for specific projects but to counsel him with names, ideas, etc."[3]

In fact, Ken had already talked to Finletter, had informally agreed to act as "dean of the faculty" and to prepare a paper on agricultural policy, to be presented at the first meeting of the group, which took place at Finletter's New York apartment on October 31, 1953, just over six weeks after the original proposal had been made to Stevenson. (Herein a perfect example of Ken's ability to conceive a plan, implement it, and follow through on its execution without missing a beat.)

The Finletter Group turned out to be a distinguished brain trust; at its initial meeting, and at subsequent meetings, which were held every two weeks or so, the members ranged in alphabetical order from George Ball to Stanley Woodward, with such luminaries as Chester Bowles, Ben Cohen, Averell Harriman, Leon Keyserling, Isador Lubin, Paul Nitze, and of course Arthur Schlesinger and ten or twelve others in between.

---

3. Adlai Stevenson to Ken Galbraith, October 16, 1953.

The high point of their first season was the luncheon meeting held at 30 Francis Avenue on March 19, 1954, which Adlai Stevenson, in Cambridge to give the prestigious Godkin Lectures, attended. It was one of the few occasions at which Stevenson was to meet with the group that had been founded in large part to assist and enlighten him. Ken has noted, however, that the members were much comforted by the Stevenson assertions that he was "an avid student of the papers we debated, amended and approved." One has to wonder just how avid.

When Ken sent his initial twenty-six-page farm policy paper along to the governor, he wrote in the covering letter: "I hope you will find this paper useful, while not lacking in length. . . . If you are talking on agricultural matters in Georgia and would like some of the ideas in rough speech form, do let me know."

To this the ever courteous Stevenson replied: "I have read with the utmost interest, but superficially I am afraid [who can blame him?] the splendid memoranda. I have not yet been able to get at the Georgia speech but I shall find something useful in your formidable document I am sure."

And finally, Tom Finletter, writing to thank Ken for the most successful March 19 meeting at his house in Cambridge, added the following postscript: "You will remember that at our meeting the Governor indicated great enthusiasm for a '4 page summary by the various authors. . . .' Such being the case, could you let me have such a summary for your agricultural paper?"

Still, the raison d'être for the Finletter Group — to animate the party out of power and rescue it from intellectual torpor — is as viable and necessary today as it was thirty-odd years ago.

All the clichés about busyness seem to fit Ken Galbraith's perpetual state of being; then and now, he has his hands full, many irons in the fire, not a moment he can call his own, and other fish to fry. And like all such dynamos, he is also prone to kill two birds with one stone, so that on any given day he may be engaged in writing a book, teaching a class, giving a public lecture, polishing an op-ed piece, granting an interview, advising a statesman, entertaining a visiting dignitary, and composing a long, a short, or a smart-aleck letter to protest, mock, instigate, or commend for any one of the dozen reasons that continually occupy the attention of this world-class critic and liberal conscience.

During the early to mid-fifties, a very large idea was swirling around in his mind for a new book that would explore the causes of poverty in the United States, both in deprived rural areas such as Appalachia and in the more widely recognized and despaired-of urban settings. Preliminary work on this far-reaching theme, then titled *Why People Are Poor,* was singularly (for Ken) unproductive. Perhaps, he decided later, it was because he really didn't have a clear answer to the question his potential book was asking. By the spring of 1954 he was totally dissatisfied with the chapters he had so far written and even more stumped as to how to get himself back on track.

Fortunately, he says, he was saved from thoughts of suicide by a stroke of characteristically Galbraithian good timing. The forthcoming fall would mark the twenty-fifth anniversary of the great stock market crash of 1929, and Jack Fischer, editor of *Harper's Magazine,* asked him to do a commemorative piece. At almost the same time, Arthur Schlesinger, then at work on his monumental history of the New Deal, complained to Ken one day at the farm in Newfane that no one had ever written even a modest history about the great crash that had led to the Great Depression, and why didn't Ken undertake to fill this void? No further persuasion was needed. With evident relief, he put aside his work on poverty to engage in this divertissement. And in a flash, "frustration turned to joy."

Every aspect of *The Great Crash, 1929* was fortuitous. Ken began work in the early summer of 1954, journeying from the farm to nearby Hanover to do his initial research in the agreeable precincts of the Baker Library at Dartmouth College, fortified, as he pointed out in the 1961 reprint of the book, by a rewarding martini at the end of the day at the Hanover Inn.

By undeniably skimping somewhat on his teaching during the fall months, he was able to complete the manuscript and turn it in to Houghton Mifflin before Christmas, with a spring publication in view. Before that time, however, came an occurrence that helped to ensure a brisk sale for the forthcoming book.

In the early months of 1955, the stock market was enjoying something of a boom — boomlet, really — which seemed to many in Washington, and to the Democratic majority in the Senate in particular, reminiscent enough of 1929 to warrant a congressional hearing by Senator William Fulbright's Banking and Currency Committee. Ken, admittedly having primed the pump a bit to this end, was called upon to testify, a circumstance that he habitually found quite enjoyable.

Never one to eschew an opportunity to be looked upon as an oracle, he was slightly put out on this particular morning (March 9) to discover that John Foster Dulles was testifying in an adjacent room and was easily out-oracling him; all the press and such TV as there was at that time was with the secretary of state. Nevertheless, Ken went through his assigned task cheerfully. He had brought along proofs of *The Great Crash* and he quoted a few choice bits, of which there were many, to remind the committee of what had happened twenty-five years earlier. He urged that even-stiffer tightening of margin requirements could avoid the subsequent recurrence of the binge of unsecured speculation that had been so responsible for the disaster of 1929.

Although there was a good attendance of senators when he began his testimony, Ken knew from experience that this number would drop off substantially as the morning wore on. But after a while he began to notice to his surprise that no one was leaving and that a few senators and members of the media were actually beginning to drift into the hearing room. He also became aware of an unusual number of aides passing slips of paper or leaning over from their places behind the committee table to whisper to their principals.

What had happened was that, even as he was testifying and asserting that, yes, 1929 *could* happen again (he did not predict when), the market had taken a very sharp turn downward. Stocks on that morning lost $7 billion in value on the New York Exchange. And inevitably, although Ken was quite unaware of this occurrence, he was perceived as practically having caused it! Indeed, he was still in ignorance when the hearing ended and a CBS reporter rushed in to beg him to repeat significant parts of his testimony on camera. That he did so, and, without his senatorial audience to inhibit him, did so with a flourish that was later seen in all parts of the nation on TV, only added to the stir he had already caused.

In those days TV was still in its comparative infancy; the viewing audience was so limited that when the eminent Edward R. Murrow reached Ken the next day back at 30 Francis Avenue, he asked him to repeat his performance for Murrow's wider audience. Wisely, Ken declined. By then his phone was ringing constantly and his mail was thick with imprecations to cease and desist doing or saying anything further to disrupt the stock market. Such entreaties were mixed with the occasional threat of violence if he continued his wicked interference. To get away from it all, Ken and Kitty skipped town a few days later and went to Vermont to go skiing.

Given his general ineptitude vis-à-vis sports, it is worth pausing a moment to consider the matter of Galbraith the skier. Surely this is the athletic endeavor that demands the ultimate in grace and coordination, of which he arguably has neither. Add to that his extreme height, which puts his center of gravity inordinately far from the ground, and you have the picture of a man who should by rights be incapable of navigating even a beginner's trail or slope. But he is capable —

just. As his friend Sharon King Hoge, who has often skied with the Galbraiths, recalls, "He always looked rather like Goofy; his poles would be dangling every which way as he came down big wide slopes, not very steadily, but somehow managing to get to the bottom." Ken makes light of his ability, as evidenced by his often-enunciated first rule of skiing: "Never ski a trail you haven't skied before." But apparently, on that particular March day in Vermont, even while following this implacable rule, he fell coming down a slippery slope that he knew well and broke his leg. A few days later, hobbling, and secretly proud of his athletic badge of courage, he went to New York for a Finletter Group meeting. (His long-time friend Averell Harriman looked with mild amusement at his unlikely wound and pronounced, "It's because you don't really know how to ski." Nineteen years older than Ken, Harriman not only did know how but was so avid that he had been in large part responsible for expanding the scope of this sport in America by building the great ski area at Sun Valley, Idaho.)

Later that evening, in his room at the Plaza, Ken received a call from an aide to the ranking Republican on the Banking and Currency Committee, Senator Homer E. Capehart of Indiana. The senator had not been present on the day of Ken's testimony, but he had obviously been keeping his staff busy ever since, trying to dig up something damaging to the reputation of the radical professor who, because of his "pro-Communist bias," had rattled the stock market and caused its precipitous dip.

Full of self-righteousness, the aide called Ken to tell him that when the senator would go on a nationally televised program three days later, he would read lines written by Galbraith which amounted to a ringing endorsement of communism. He then read the offending lines to Ken, who recognized them as coming from a pamphlet he had written a few years earlier for the National Planning Association. What he had said was that he believed "the Communists had a better reputation for sincerity and determination in attacking old social grievances and that they also had found a solution to petty nationalism by asserting the higher loyalty to the workers' state." However, he had also followed this rather roundabout endorsement with a caveat in which he expressed "suspicion and distaste of communism on other grounds."[4] These words were entirely left out of what Senator Capehart was proposing to read, and did indeed read on television, on Sunday, March 20, 1955.

By that time Ken was ready for him. He had gleefully put together a rebuttal, vigorously taking the offensive by asserting that no self-respecting statesman could (1) consider it subversive to talk candidly about the stock market to a congressional committee, (2) alter a witness's testimony to make it sound more like Lenin, and (3) be so ignorant as to not know the often-stated views of said witness in the first place. He also reminded the senator that the pamphlet from which his "offensive" words were taken had originally been delivered as a speech at the University of Notre Dame, Catholic bastion of American-as-apple-pie football, in the senator's home state of Indiana, where it had been extremely well received.

All this ammunition was contained in a wordy telegram, which Kitty and the boys trundled down to the Western Union in Harvard Square to send to the wire services and the television networks. As both Galbraiths vividly recall, these messages cost them fifty dollars!

But it was well worth it since the last laugh was theirs. A frustrated Capehart backed off from his direct attack and sought help from another Galbraith nonfan, Sinclair Weeks, then Eisenhower's secretary of commerce, to enlist the FBI in trying to uncover the Harvard professor's ties to the Communists. The result, as Ken was later to find when he in-

---

4. Introduction to the second edition of *The Great Crash, 1929* (Boston: Houghton Mifflin, 1961), Sentry edition.

spected his documents under the Freedom of Information Act, was the FBI's conclusion: "Investigation favorable except conceited, egotistical and snobbish."

The Great Crash was the first of Ken's books clearly designed to appeal to a wide readership. And by all standards it did so. For the first time the general public was to meet John Kenneth Galbraith, the writer, and it appeared that they liked what they read. For one week *The Great Crash* made the *New York Times* best-seller list, and for good reason, since it's a very readable book. Lucid, compelling, and perceptive, it's an informed and spirited account of the events leading up to the disastrous days of Black Thursday, October 24, through the blackest day, Tuesday the twenty-ninth, and beyond.

The subject, of course, was propitious. Hardly anyone had not heard of the crash of 1929; those who had experienced it — often painfully — were gratified to have their recollections and suspicions confirmed; those who hadn't were glad to be enlightened and, even better, to enjoy themselves while being thus edified. Inevitably, there are dry passages that can be hard going for those neither enchanted with nor versed in high finance or arcane economics. But compensations abound.

For example, in explaining Wall Street's habit of glossing over the dangers inherent in margin accounts, the true purpose of which was to make speculation easy for the speculator, the author noted that obviously this purpose could not be confessed. If it had been, many moral men and women would have condemned it and demanded reforms. So Wall Street had to defend margin trading on the prosaic, high-minded (and also specious) grounds of greater good for the greater number of people. "Wall Street, in these matters," Galbraith wrote, "is like a lovely and accomplished woman who must wear black cotton stockings, heavy woolen underwear, and parade her knowledge as a cook because, unhappily, her supreme accomplishment is as a harlot." Or on the matter of leverage in investment trusts: "The principle of leverage is the same for an investment trust as in the game of crack-the-whip. By the application of well-known physical laws, a modest movement near the point of origin is translated into a major jolt at the extreme periphery." Or this, at the end of his chapter titled "The Twilight of Illusion," commenting on the continuation of new investment trusts, of broker's loans, and heedless speculation, despite ominous evidence of an increasing downward trend: "The end had come, but it was not yet in sight."

Many of the reviews were enough to gladden the heart of any fledgling author, which Ken, of course, was not. Stuart Chase, writing in the *New York Post,* again weighed in with a rave about the "wittiest book ever written by a professional economist." Other fellow economists — Wilson Wyatt in the *Washington Post,* A. Wilfred May in the *Commercial and Financial Chronicle,* and, to a certain extent, John Chamberlain in the *New York Times* — gave him high marks. *Business Week,* in an unsigned review, noted the "critical bombardment" resulting from the Capehart episode, but seemed to have a sneaking admiration for this man who "continues to snipe at cherished beliefs."

In London, *The Economist* was downright churlish, noting that the book "has the virtues of vulgarism . . . a desire to be popular declines into extreme bad taste." No doubt some of *The Economist*'s venom was fueled by what it considered Ken's denigration of Winston Churchill, whom he, tongue-in-cheek, professed to hold partly responsible for the Wall Street disaster because he had taken Britain off the gold standard. *The Economist* called this imputation "more irresponsible and superficial than a fine economist should be, even in his lighter moments," to which Ken shot back a sarcastic can't-you-take-a-joke response.

Coming from opposite ends of the pole, the *Chicago Tribune* and the Moscow weekly *New Times* were predictably hostile. Both reactions pleased the author. But the review that gave him, and continues to give him, the greatest satisfaction was the long (at least four thousand words) notice by literary critic Mark Van Doren, writing in the *Reporter*. The lines in his review that most delighted both Ken and Kitty (to whom *The Great Crash* is dedicated) were these: "Like any fine historian he is also a poet. He has a magic way with words and phrases, and this alone will reward many a reader of his work. His felicity, to be sure, is of the icy sort; for as a historian he belongs with Thucydides, Tacitus and Machiavelli." Heady stuff indeed, especially from such a source.

It is hard to believe that Ken had been at Harvard for seven years without having taken even one of his habitual leaves of absence. And now, according to long-time academic custom, he had earned the right to have one free — that is, without prejudice. The usual option for a sabbatical is a full year at half pay or a half year at full pay. Ken opted for the full year and made up the monetary difference by applying for and receiving a Guggenheim Fellowship. The plan was to spend the year in Switzerland, working on "Why People Are Poor." His instinct told him, and he half believed it, that the best way to think and write about a significant subject was to do nothing but think and write.

On May 26, 1955, he wrote to Adlai Stevenson: "This is, more or less, on the eve of my departure, by way of confessing my guilt about deserting our enterprise. I feel, however, that I have one more book in my system before senility intervenes [he was forty-seven years old], and obviously I must get started on it forthwith." He hastened to assure Stevenson that he would be back before zero hour in 1956, adding, perhaps with a measure of hope, that "this date can always be advanced in the interest of the Republic. Do call me if I am needed."[5]

---

5. In his response a few weeks later, Stevenson wrote, "Have a good time, and if you run into anything you don't understand, how about sending for *me?* I am sure intellectual misery must love company and I sometimes suspect that is why there are so many folks all around me these days."

Once again Ken chose to travel by water, this time loading his three sons — Alan, fourteen, Peter, four, Jamie, three — and Emily onto a freighter that took endless days (very boring days, he finally conceded) to go from Trois-Rivières on the St. Lawrence to Hamburg. Kitty, who had sensibly opted to fly, joined them there, and together they went on for the summer months to Saas Fee and Lake Maggiore.

Ken at once, and with renewed optimism, settled down to do nothing but think and write about the causes of poverty. There were some flashes of hope, he wrote, as "a few ideas emerged full and round." But the do-nothing-else policy began to collapse in the fall when the family moved to Geneva so that Alan could go to school there. Inevitably Ken was caught up in the pulse of the city and with the many people they knew who came there for one reason or another and looked them up.

A significant — in fact, a portentous — such meeting was a dinner they had with Richard Kahn, whom Ken had known in his Cambridge, England, days and who was now on his way to becoming master of King's College. The other guest that evening, described by Ken as "a tall, slender, deeply featured and powerfully self-assured Indian," was Professor Prasanta Chandra Mahalanobis, a British-educated physicist, then in his sixties and head of the government-supported, but independent, India Statistical Institute. He was in Geneva to recruit likely scholars — qualified, imaginative men and women of wide-ranging ideologies — to counsel India as she embarked on her Second Five-Year Plan. He had sought candidates from all over the world, including the United States. While in Washington, he had asked certain highly placed members of the Eisenhower administration whom they would recommend to advise on economics, and had been offered Professor Milton Friedman.

Milton Friedman, the famed monetarist from the University of Chicago, preaches a gospel that is the absolute antithesis of Ken's most cherished beliefs. Friedman is of the school of economic thought that claims the market is inviolable and will always regulate itself; therefore the government should not intervene. Ken contends that the market economy is often fallible unless bolstered by government intervention. To Ken, Friedman is a neoclassic conservative whose ideas are obsolete because they are based on what has for too long been assumed rather than on what actually exists. Ken's own deeply held convictions, he sincerely believes, are rooted in reality.

When Professor Mahalanobis told about Friedman's offer, Ken responded, after taking a moment to think up his bon mot, that "asking Milton Friedman to advise on economic planning was like asking the Holy Father to counsel on birth control." This little metaphor has become durable stock for Ken; he uses it, if he can possibly work it in, whenever Friedman's name is mentioned. On that particular evening in Geneva it pleased his listener so much that Mahalanobis promptly invited him to come to India instead! And by all means to bring Kitty along. The Galbraiths accepted with alacrity.[6]

The only condition that Professor Mahalanobis laid down was that they stay in India for at least three months, which made the logistics of leaving the children for so long complex. Kitty had been able to rent their present Geneva apartment only until January 1, so in any case they would have had to move. But move to where? Where would Emily and the boys feel most secure and content without them?

They were still mulling this over a few weeks later when Kitty and Ken went off for a weekend with no fixed destination in mind and wound up midway between Interlaken and Montreux, in a beautiful little village surrounded by low

---

6. Correspondence in the Galbraith papers at the Kennedy Library indicates that Ken had accepted a previous invitation to visit India during his sabbatical year. But he bowed out of it, in a letter written on April 11, 1955, to Austin Robinson of the International Economic Association in London, on the grounds that his broken leg and his resultant loss of weight and vigor would make coming to India during the heat of the summer too risky for him and for his Indian hosts.

mountains. Gstaad! It was love at first sight. It being November, only one hotel was open, but it was a gem, beautifully clean; the beds were just the right softness, the breakfast rolls were crisp, the waitress was charming, the view was enchanting, and they were the only guests.

In Kitty's mind the glimmer of an idea had begun to form. What a wonderfully wholesome, safe, and delightful place for Emily and the two little boys to stay. (Alan was to be a five-day boarder at a school in Geneva.) And riding on the wave of good luck they were enjoying, came an apartment — unpretentious but homey, across from the church, behind the bakery, and next to the butcher shop — with two bedrooms, one for Emily and one for Peter and Jamie, a living room with a couch for Alan to come home to on weekends, a small but cozy kitchen, and a balcony facing south. Emily was brought to Gstaad the next weekend to give her opinion. After one quick look she gleefully pronounced, "This is it."

And so with a free mind the Galbraiths, having added Gstaad to their home bases, could now set off to begin their conquest of India.

This time, however, it was not love at first sight, because the first sight was appalling. Driving from Dum Dum Airport in Calcutta to the headquarters of the Indian Statistical Institute on the evening of February 9, 1956, they had to pass what Kitty has described as "hovels of ragged refugees, many lying huddled together on charpoys or on the ground, the only light coming from oil lamps, the smoke of cow-dung patties used for cooking still heavy in the air. There were also gaunt cows, skinny dogs, rickshaws, bicycles, carts, and a few other honking cars impeding the way."[7]

Arriving at the serene Mahalanobis estate, which housed the institute, was a contrast of the sort visitors to India must

---

7. From Kitty's talk at the fifty-fifth reunion of her Smith College class of 1934, given in Northampton, Massachusetts, on May 20, 1989.

accustom themselves to as they confront the continual disparity between extreme squalor and graceful elegance. The large
stone mansion, with its terraces and balconies, was set between two rectangular green ponds and surrounded by gardens, palm trees, and fragrant shrubs.

Inside, Professor Mahalanobis and his vibrant wife, Rani,
greeted them warmly. Other Western scholars and experts
were on hand or expected. After a bit, Mahalanobis said
kindly to Kitty, "You must be tired. You will want to get to
bed." Kitty, who had been sitting with her hands folded,
raised them in assent. To her amazement, the other Indians in
the room made the same motion, raising folded hands and
holding them vertically in front of them at bosom level. Un-
wittingly she had made the Hindu gesture of greeting or parting. "How quickly you have learned the *Namaste,*" said her
host admiringly.

True to his promise, Mahalanobis soon had his visitors
traveling all over India to see for themselves the problems that
independence and the Five-Year Plan had generated. The Galbraiths were pleased to be teamed with John Strachey, a delightful Briton who was almost as tall as Ken. Strachey was a
former food minister and secretary of state for war, as well as
a former member of the Communist party, and his family had
deep roots in India. Together the three covered India from
Madras to Mahabalipuram in the south and to the Himalayas
in the north. "It was a lively, wonderful time," Ken writes.
On the Bay of Bengal the three of them visited the Black Pa-
goda at Konarak where each was struck by the superbly
carved, sexually explicit friezes covering almost the whole pa-
goda. To Ken they were "exuberantly erotic couples making
love through time"; to Kitty they were "ecstatically acrobatic
lovers"; "and to Strachey they were "a jolly good fuck."

To justify these and other pleasures, Ken felt obliged to produce a number of papers on India's Second Five-Year Plan.
These he characterizes, with unexpected modesty, as both unmemorable and sometimes even misguided. In the latter cate-

gory, he perhaps had in mind the seeds of controversy he sowed by his report on India's railway system. Travel by rail, he said, was exceedingly cheap, whereas freight movement was already at or over capacity in a country with only a single-track system.

The solution he proposed was to make travel more inconvenient — to raise fares and to schedule arrivals and departures at odd hours, for example, in the hope of discouraging what he termed "the frivolous traveller." Magisterially, the "American expert," as the press referred to him with apparent derision, recognized only four legitimate reasons for travel: health, family tragedy, livelihood, and religious motivation. For such travelers he was willing to lower fares to relieve them of their "cruel burdens."

"Recommendation unlikely to be accepted," proclaimed the *Statesman* of April 28, 1956, in a story with a New Delhi dateline. "Importing additional discomfort and inconvenience into railway travel could hardly be sustained in a democratic form of government. . . . The suggestion also appears to the Indian Railway mind as unnecessarily cruel."

Ken was stung. In a lengthy letter to the editor published the next day, he wrote, "I should not want it thought — as your story implies — that I was suggesting inconvenience for its own sake. And I was taken aback to find my own adjective 'cruel' applied to this suggestion. It must be apparent that I was searching for a solution that would work a minimum of hardship in a situation where some hardship is unhappily unavoidable."

With his "fatal fluency" and his impeccable logic, he had again managed to defuse his critics.

Ken says that every time he lands at an airport outside the United States, he experiences a distinct rush of emotion, an anticipation particular to the country where his plane has just touched down. In England he feels he is stepping into an extraordinarily civilized world; in France, a titillating, sophisticated one; in Germany he senses majestic traditions; and in Japan, a lively awareness of sharp contrasts. In India it was his aesthetic sensibilities that were aroused.

Even as a boy growing up in Ontario, Ken had always had a quickening response to moments of natural beauty as they invaded his surroundings. In India he did not have to pick and choose such moments; breathtaking, God-given natural beauty was everywhere. Of particular fascination on that first trip to India was the Vale of Kashmir and the other exquisite valleys that lie at the foothills of the Himalayan range. To Ken they exerted a compelling fascination. "Partly," he writes, "this is because of their contrast with the plains; unlike the latter, the valleys are cool and green with fresh fast streams. Partly it is the women, who are tall, clear-skinned, erect and, one senses, confidently aware of their India-wide reputation for beauty. Partly it is the mountains. All other mountains the eye associates with the earth; [the Himalayas] belong to another, more remote world related to the heavens."[8]

In India another sort of beauty caught Ken's eye, one also associated with those valleys where the Moguls had come in 1526, stayed for 331 years, and from their courts nourished a school of enchanting Indian paintings. At the Bharat Kala Bhavan, a fine museum in Benares, Ken saw his first collection of these "small, beautifully contrived works," and, as he says in his memoirs, "their aspect of amused mystery, their sometimes sophisticated, sometimes naive themes, their exquisite portraiture never thereafter left me."

Here indeed was an enthusiasm uncharacteristic for a man who, except for an occasional obligatory visit to a museum with Kitty, had never shown any such predilection. But now, truly captivated, he claimed the subject of Indian paintings as his own, learning all he could until, as he says in words that *are* characteristic, "I awoke to discover that I had both exten-

---

8. *A View from the Stands* (Boston: Houghton Mifflin, 1986), p. 155.

sive knowledge of Indian paintings and excellent judgement; indeed I was an authority on the subject."[9]

The trip was winding down. In New Delhi Ken met Nehru at a garden party and had a few moments' private talk with him, an apparently desultory conversation on economics which did not presage what lay ahead. Tea with Ambassador John Sherman Cooper and his wife, Lorraine, at the American embassy, however, did. Afterward, Ken swears, he distinctly recalls saying to Kitty, "When the Democrats get back in, I think I will get myself made ambassador to India." Kitty, however, insists he said no such thing.

Back in Gstaad, the Galbraiths were so happy to be reunited with their children that they took an apartment of their own just around the corner from the one — too small, obviously, for them all — where Emily and the boys were living. Here finally the chips fell into place and Ken was able to begin writing the book that had eluded him for so long.

He had discovered, he says, that the reason the writing had not gone well for him before was that he had been working from the wrong premise. In trying to write about poverty in America in the 1950s, he had failed to recognize that since the war poverty was the exception. Opulence (as he was calling it then) was the rule. The central theme to his mind now was that "contemporary economics changes as people get rich, and, as the urgency of wants diminishes, they become increasingly susceptible to manipulation. You can't explain to somebody why he or she wants food, but you can persuade somebody why he or she wants a Toyota automobile as against a bicycle."

As Robert Heilbroner, a percipient fellow economist, was to put it, "to discuss the problems of affluence in the vocabulary of poverty is to distort or worse to conceal the very realities with which economics must seek to come to grips." So in

9. *A Life in Our Times*, p. 334.

effect that summer in Gstaad Galbraith did come to grips; he stopped using the vocabulary of poverty to apply to the reality that was the ever growing production of wealth.

Now finally the writing flew; he began in May 1956, and, when he returned to the United States in September, he had in his luggage a completed first draft. "Why People Are Poor" was well on its way to becoming *The Affluent Society*.

8

"The Observed
of All Observers"

THE MIX OF Ken's various preoccupations was continually
shifting; old enterprises were completed or temporarily put
on hold or even occasionally sloughed off, as new interests attracted his attention and for a time dominated his thinking.

But on his return to Cambridge after his sabbatical year in
1956, an old absorption claimed his attention first. "I marvel
at the amount you accomplish in a year of 'leisure,'" Adlai
Stevenson had written to him in Gstaad. "I wonder if the time
has not come for me to unveil your conclusions in an acceptance speech in the event I am nominated. In short, if you
know what to do with the human race, I should be glad to
make the announcement, at least to the Democrats. Think
what an excellent exercise it would be to summarize your
conclusions in a reverberating speech which will have perpe-
tuity — for at least twenty four hours."

Such a challenge was irresistible, and although there is no
evidence that Ken's words played much of a part in Stevenson's speech, he was definitely back on board as a speech
writer. Most of the Elks were back too, just as cocky and as
full of themselves as they had been in 1952, although with less
reason for optimism. Their high self-esteem was further bolstered, since Stevenson's 1952 speeches had been considered

so beautifully crafted that they had been assembled in book form and had sold very well.

This time the campaign was run out of Washington, instead of Springfield, Illinois, so the weekend commute was easier, and also Ken traveled a bit more with Stevenson than he had during the first campaign. He was with him in Los Angeles at a huge rally when the candidate, in a speech that Ken had written, delivered a sharp criticism of Eisenhower for his endless golfing and general tendency to be absent or found wanting during moments of crisis, particularly in the matter of the Suez Canal. (France, Great Britain, and Israel had just moved against Nasser.) The rousing speech then went even more forcefully after Richard Nixon and his shortcomings. Stevenson had chosen Ken for this task because, Stevenson told him, "I want you to write the speeches about Nixon, Ken, because you have no tendency to be fair."

Equal to the assignment, his speech went hammer and tongs after what he called Nixonland — a place where slander, scare tactics, sly innuendo, poison-pen letters, and anonymous phone calls prevailed, all accusations that Galbraith piously maintained were "scrupulously truthful."

During the final days of the campaign Ken began to experience digestive problems that soon led to ulcerlike symptoms. A few days before the election he flew back to Boston and entered the Peter Bent Brigham Hospital. On Election Day he was still having tests and feeling so out of the loop that he didn't even turn on the television in his room to learn how badly "we" had lost. Shortly thereafter, with the doctors finding no cause for them, his symptoms disappeared.

One can only speculate about this and other psychosomatic ills — speculate because Ken himself does not, and probably cannot, provide enlightened answers. Because he hates obsolescence and is deeply suspicious of the status quo, Ken is firmly dedicated to a life of forward motion. And when that forward motion meets an obstacle and is derailed, darker moments may overtake him. His bouts of extreme fatigue at the beginning of the war, his physical collapse at the end of his OPA days, his depression after the 1952 presidential defeat, his hospitalization at the end of the 1956 campaign, and his increasingly frequent headaches during his time as ambassador to India are all manifestations of this pattern.

Early in the New Year Ken finally turned his attentions back to *The Affluent Society*. When, for the first time since Gstaad, he reread his draft, he went through the reactions familiar to all writers, first thinking his words were perfectly terrible, then, on second thought, deciding that they were quite wonderful. Still, it took him many months to reconcile these opposing notions, until at last in the autumn of 1957 he handed the manuscript over to his publisher in Boston.

He was off on a lecture tour in Poland and Yugoslavia in late May when the book made its first appearance, and he could hardly wait to get back to London to telephone Kitty in Cambridge (phone calls from behind the Iron Curtain to the West were highly unlikely in those days) and find out about the reviews.

But before he even reached her he spotted a copy of *Time* on the newsstand at his London hotel and, after looking in vain in the books section, finally found *The Affluent Society* reviewed in the business section. With sinking heart he stood, his long, lanky frame hunched over the counter, reading what his one-time colleagues at Luce publications said about it. They were, to put it charitably, patronizing in dismissing Galbraith's attempt at a searching inquiry into the U.S. economy as a "well written but vague essay with the air of worried dinner-table conversation." Here it should be noted that the last thing any of Ken's friends and admirers had heard him utter when they were breaking bread with him was anything that sounded remotely like "worried dinner-table conversation." Ironic, superior, derisive, witty, and dogmatic conversation, yes; worried, never. And what must have been even more displeasing to him was *Time*'s use of a baseball met-

aphor to describe how he never dealt with his thesis of re-
dressing social balance. "But having pointed his bat at the
bleachers," they wrote (wrongly, in fact — one does not
point the bat in the direction one plans to hit the ball), "Galbraith steps away from the plate. He never takes a full swing
at drafting the program that he implies; that the state must
take a larger role in society."[1]

Happily, *Time*'s reaction was not an augury of things to
come. Quite the reverse. When Ken reached her, Kitty was
ready for him with a stack of glowing reviews that had appeared in the country's leading newspapers on Sunday, June
1, 1958. Praise was abundant, and so too was the widespread
appreciation of his audacious challenge to cherished beliefs,
which he called — in a phrase he had carefully crafted —
the conventional wisdom. Having created that soon-to-be-
memorable phrase to express his perceptions of orthodox
economic thinking, he devoted most of his book to demonstrating the obsolescence of that orthodoxy.

The overall theme of *The Affluent Society* is that our society is in the process of being victimized by our own desire for
self-enrichment. In the eighteenth and nineteenth centuries,
when poverty was the normal state of being, the production
of goods became a goal eagerly sought to meet urgent needs.
But by the middle of the twentieth century, with affluence increasingly prevalent, we were producing far more than we
needed or wanted. It then became necessary to create the
wants artificially. In other words, we had become prey to production for production's sake, as manufacturers sought to
convince us by their advertisements that if we had one television set we surely needed another one for the bedroom and
perhaps still another for the kitchen. One car? Think of the
luxury of a two-car family. Think of bigger, faster, sleeker;
think of more! Think of cash rebates, installment buying,
credit card payment, all designed solely to make these goods

---

1. June 2, 1958, pp. 78–80.

available painlessly. Ken calls this forced creation of wants by the creator of the product to be wanted the Dependence Effect.

This Dependence Effect, stemming from an intense preoccupation with ever higher production, leads to the book's most compelling message; over and over again the author points to the terrible disparity between private wealth and public squalor. He illustrates this in many telling ways, but one paragraph over which he says he labored long and hard, and which worried him as being possibly "too patently contrived, too ripe," has become the most quoted passage in the book. His worries were perhaps justified, but so too is the unique aptness of the passage.

> The family which takes its mauve and cerise, air-conditioned, power-steered and power-braked automobile out for a tour passes through cities that are badly paved, made hideous by litter, blighted buildings, billboards and posts for wires that should long since have been put underground. They pass on to a countryside that has been rendered largely invisible by commercial art. . . . They picnic on exquisitely packaged food from a portable icebox by a polluted stream and go on to spend the night at a park which is a menace to public health and morals. Just before dozing off on an air mattress, beneath a nylon tent, amid the stench of decaying refuse, they may reflect vaguely on the curious unevenness of their blessings. Is this, indeed, the American genius?[2]

Following its fine sendoff by favorable and generally perceptive reviewers, *The Affluent Society* began almost at once to move upward, until by early summer it had found its way onto the *New York Times* best-seller list, where it was to remain for almost a year. Among academics and intellectuals in general, there was a certain snobbishness about a grouping as nonelite as a best-seller list, although this was somewhat mitigated by the fact that it was the *New York Times*. But the

---

2. *The Affluent Society*, 4th ed. (Boston: Houghton Mifflin, 1984), p. 192.

question is, Why was *The Affluent Society* on that list at all? What besides its good reviews and its notably seductive title persuaded so many people to buy such an erudite book? It could in no way be considered easy reading. Despite its many witty passages and frequent aphorisms, it is often very difficult going.

This is true particularly of the first six chapters, in which Galbraith traces in complex detail the history of economic thought from which the conventional wisdom derives. He takes us from Adam Smith (1723–1790) to David Ricardo (1772–1823) to Thomas Malthus (1766–1834) and to Alfred Marshall (1842–1924), British economists from whom our own economic ideas stem, then to American social economists from Henry George (1839–1897) to Thorstein Veblen (1857–1929) and finally to the widely opposing ideas of social Darwinism as espoused largely by Herbert Spencer (1820–1903) and Karl Marx (1818–1883). His purpose, of course, is to suggest where and when in this two-century sequence the conventional wisdom lost touch with reality.

This was compelling material and lucidly handled, even though it contained examples of what one observer has called Galbraith's "arch ponderosity." But a best seller? Yes, indeed, a *very* best seller, bought over the years by no less than 1,455,050 people. How many of these have actually read *The Affluent Society?* Enough at the very least to have made a difference in perceptions of private opulence versus public impoverishment; also enough to have seriously vexed many of America's leading economists.

Professor George Stigler of the University of Chicago grumped, "I consider it shocking that more Americans have read *The Affluent Society* than *The Wealth of Nations*" (Adam Smith's great work). Galbraith replied with obvious relish, "I am reluctant to reply to Professor Stigler, for I could seem to be urging the claims of my book against those of a very great classic. And I could conceivably be missing the deeper cause of Professor Stigler's sorrow which may be not that so many read Galbraith and so few read Smith, but that hardly anyone reads Stigler at all." This barb too has come to be very durable stock in the Galbraith store of auto-quotable phrases.[3]

The easy explanation for those economists who shared Stigler's view is that they were jealous of Galbraith's widespread success outside the profession, which they professed to scorn on the grounds that a best seller couldn't by definition be a serious book. More relevant, however, was the difficulty of fitting Galbraith into an accepted school of thought. Since he was clearly not an orthodox economist, he must be an institutionalist. Institutionalists deplore the practice of relying on mathematical models and ignoring the social and political realities. But institutionalists don't feel comfortable about claiming Galbraith as one of their own, either, and he never uses the term in describing himself.

One problem derives from the perceived fact that, apart from Veblen, Galbraith is not inclined to give credit to other, older social economists, and this leads to a wide source of unhappiness about him within the profession. He is considered very stingy with his footnotes, loath, it is argued, to attribute ideas to others writing in the same or related fields. And not to be cited makes all academics, and all nonfiction writers, for that matter, very cross. (It would make Ken cross too.)

Economist Lester Thurow, dean of the Sloan School of Management at the Massachusetts Institute of Technology and a writer with broad popular appeal, is a Galbraith supporter. He says, "At least forty percent of economists' sometimes negative reaction to Ken Galbraith can be traced to his not footnoting. Academics are egoists; when they write an article on a subject and you write an article on the same subject and don't footnote them, that makes them madder than anything. But being mature academics, they can't admit to getting

---

3. Quoted in Charles U. Hession, *John Kenneth Galbraith and His Critics* (New York: New American Library, 1972), p. 89.

mad about footnotes. So they have to be mad about something else — maybe about the way he exaggerates, stakes out a position which is probably a little stronger than reality would warrant."

Thurow also points out that another objection of economists to Galbraith is that his writings always run counter to a strong major current — mathematical economics, for example. Other economists have claimed that, besides, Ken's own ideas are never quite as original as he seeks to make them appear, and that his scholarship is often deficient or haphazard — his conclusions are asserted, not reached by logical lines of reasoning. He is also considered a showman, a self-aggrandizing personality, a journalist, a popularizer, and for all these reasons, as the anti-Galbraith segment likes to say, "He is not an economist!"

Such mutterings have surely reached Ken's ears and stung him; he is not a man to brush off criticism — even well-merited criticism — lightly. And certainly the "he is not an economist" line, still frequently cited, was not, and is not, justified, at least not according to such widely recognized economists as Thurow, Paul Samuelson, and Wassily Leontief.

If he was secretly wounded by the pettiness of some of his colleagues, he was amply compensated by the near adulation he received from both the broad-based public and the narrow-based intellectual elite. Even before the publication of *The Affluent Society* he had been looked upon as an important and influential critic of American society. Now he became a cynosure and, to quote Shakespeare, "the observed of all observers."

Once again his timing was fortuitous. Just as Ken was stepping up to his period of greatest eminence, the winds of change were blowing to bring forth a bright new political star for him to hitch his wagon to. If Adlai Stevenson had been a good fit for Ken's talents and humor, John F. Kennedy was even better. Kennedy was everything that Ken admired and probably secretly liked to think of himself as being. He was young, handsome, impatient, and rich, with an engaging candor and a fine quick intelligence; he was also casual, courageous, and full of self-deprecating wit.

Ken could not have invented him better. What's more, he had known him on and off since Kennedy's Harvard days when he was a student at Winthrop House, where Ken was a tutor. Jack came to Ken's attention first as the younger brother of Joe, Jr., but a far more easygoing and certainly much more humorous version of his overbearing older brother.

Galbraith was in touch with Kennedy from time to time during his not very distinguished career in the U.S. House of Representatives, and a little more frequently during his early years in the Senate. In 1956 when Adlai Stevenson threw open the nomination for vice-president to the floor of the convention, Jack Kennedy was narrowly defeated for the post by Estes Kefauver. As Ken tells in his memoirs, Kennedy believed, and with some justification, that his defeat was brought about by his failure to oppose fixed agricultural price supports and to favor flexible supports, as Galbraith had strongly advised him to do. After his defeat, Kennedy told Ken, "I don't want to hear about agriculture from anyone but you, Ken. And I don't much want to hear about it from you either." He also noted, rather proudly, Ken thought, "Where I grew up, we were taken out on a bus to see a cow."

The friendship ripened; often after Kennedy had moved up to the Senate and when he had to touch base with his Massachusetts constituency, he would summon Ken and Arthur Schlesinger to join him at the famous Locke-Ober in Boston for his favorite lobster stew. Together the three men would cover a wide range of burning questions, always including the one about how an Irish-Catholic politician without a notable legislative record but with a powerful and influential parent could become president of the United States. Ken found himself increasingly impressed and intrigued by Jack Kennedy, and Kennedy saw more and more ways to benefit from Ken's counsel.

Compared with much of the rest of the Eastern Establishment, many of whom continued to hanker after Adlai Stevenson, Ken rallied to Jack Kennedy's side early, as early as the autumn of 1958, when after a conclave during Kennedy's senatorial re-election campaign at which he spoke, Galbraith told Kennedy he would support his nomination for president.

A year and a half later Ken was featured prominently in an *Esquire* magazine poll (January 1960) that asked some fifty notable Americans, Republicans and Democrats, "Who should be President? What should the issues be?" Stevenson received by far the largest number in answer to the first question. Sixteen chose him — more than twice as many as those who named Nixon. Kennedy received only four votes — three besides Galbraith's. Ken himself, in the accompanying story, was accorded considerable attention as the "authoritative spokesman" of economic expansion. Many of the respondents, whether for Stevenson or Kennedy, cited Ken's famous cry of private opulence versus the poverty of public institutions and services as an overriding issue facing the country in the new decade of the sixties.

As Ken would later explain, in what appears to have been a long-overdue letter to Stevenson written on August 12, 1960, "At the time [of the *Esquire* poll] I had no notion that you would be available. But under any circumstance, I would have had problems. The Cambridge community is Jack's natural source of help. It would have implied a special lack of confidence if such help had not been forthcoming."

Stevenson's reply was restrained. He thanked Ken for his letter, which he said was hardly necessary, as he understood his position. However, he continued, "My own perplexity, indeed, is that anyone doubted my 'availability' after what happened in 1952. To have talked about it I thought would encourage a draft, and I was determined to stand aside because I thought it impertinent to seek a third nomination. It never occurred to me that anyone would doubt that I was available if wanted."

So be it, Ken concluded. Kennedy, he believed, would be a strong candidate and, if elected, a strong president. And having enunciated this thought far and wide, he went off to Switzerland, again on leave of absence, to work on the book that was now engaging his creative attentions and that he described as being concerned with "the nature of modern large-scale industrialism wherever it rears its more or less ugly head."

By then Harvard must have been well aware that with the publication of *The Affluent Society*, whether or not one agreed with his conclusions, Ken had made a notable contribution to American social thought; more than ever, he had become an academic celebrity who added luster to the university. To encourage his further pursuits, McGeorge Bundy, dean of the Faculty of Arts and Sciences, did not hesitate to grant Ken leaves of absence for the winter terms (January to May) of both 1959 and 1960. At the same time Harvard promoted him to that pinnacle of academic success, an endowed chair; he became the Paul M. Warburg Professor of Economics. To bring about this outcome, Bundy had been obliged to move the occupant of the Warburg chair, an economist named Gottfried Haberler, to another seat. (Ironically, Haberler had been the only one to vote against Galbraith's initial appointment to full professor back in 1948.)

Ken was particularly delighted with his named chair because of his high regard for the man whose memory it honored. Paul M. Warburg, a member of an eminent, philanthropic, and liberal-minded Jewish family, was a banker who had been on the very first Federal Reserve Board. In that capacity in the late 1920s, his bold, well-reasoned warning that continued unrestrained speculation would lead to a devastating market crash had won Ken's warm approval.

The Warburg family too was pleased; when Paul's son

James, who had given the money to endow the chair, came to Boston, he invited Ken and Kitty for dinner at the Ritz. "May your bottom rest comfortably on my Daddy's chair," he offered, raising his glass to toast the new occupant.

As it turned out during the next six years, Ken's bottom hardly rested there at all. He was off in Switzerland, working on what was to become *The New Industrial State* during Kennedy's state primary contests in early 1960. No great loss, Ken felt; he had also forgone the primaries in both Stevenson campaigns. But this time he did miss one stirring event: Kennedy's West Virginia speech in which the young Massachusetts senator, for the first time, forthrightly and dramatically faced the religious issue and as a result, many thought, knocked Hubert Humphrey out of the race.

Back in Cambridge in June, Ken signaled his availability to Kennedy in a letter that was flattering, although not excessively so; self-congratulatory, though within normal bounds; detached (from other eggheads) in just the right degree; and ready and willing to go to work, but with no hint of unseemly eagerness.

All reports, especially from a man like Arthur Schlesinger, who was tied to the Kennedy effort, indicate that the candidate and later the president was extremely fond of Ken and much enjoyed his witty, intellectual, and adroit counsel. Jacqueline Kennedy Onassis also confirms this, further noting that the fact that Ken came out for Kennedy "so early, when he might have been expected to be for Adlai Stevenson, was deeply appreciated and never forgotten by JFK."

Ken hadn't planned to go to the July Democratic convention in California, claiming nothing but scorn for that particular "bloated" rite of passage. But when, sitting peacefully at the farm in Vermont, he heard it announced on the radio that Kennedy had just arrived in Los Angeles, he decided to go.

At his hotel in L.A., as he recounts in *A Life in Our Times,* he found a message asking him to report at once to room 8315, the Kennedy suite and command post at the Biltmore.

It seems that either the campaign was short one delegate counter or, as Galbraith suggests, they needed someone who was not Irish, Catholic, or Jewish to marshal the troops from the great Protestant Northwest. So Ken was directed to take on this responsibility posthaste.

However, inasmuch as the nomination was all but sewn up for his candidate, most of what Ken really had to do was to jawbone his various lots of delegates — never an onerous task for him — to keep them pumped up and to ensure that there would be no defections. Meanwhile, he was a very visible figure on the convention floor and as such had to dodge a number of brickbats tossed at him by still-loyal Stevenson fans because of his perceived defection from their ranks.

Even at this point, however, Galbraith did not consider himself a true member of the Kennedy inner circle. He liked to picture himself, as always, slightly detached, standing just on the outer fringe, exactly where a true maverick should stand. To be too far inside could mean to be co-opted.

Whether for that reason or because of prior commitments, he was back in Cambridge on the night that Kennedy delivered his acceptance speech. And maybe in small part, to prove to himself that he wasn't being taken into camp by the Kennedy mystique, he promptly wrote the candidate a preachy letter, telling him exactly what he thought of the speech. He greatly approved of the content, he said, but found much wanting in the construction of the speech, which seemed to him "badly in need of editing and polishing." He was even more concerned with Kennedy's delivery.

It is evident that in straightforward exposition and argument you are superb. On the basis of your Los Angeles performances — before the caucuses and in dealing with Lyndon — I am prepared to argue that you have few masters in your time. When it comes to oratorical flights and Stevenson-type rhetoric, you give a reasonable imitation of a bird with a broken wing. You do get off the ground, but it's wearing to the audience to keep wondering if you are going to stay up.

The solution here is simple. You cannot avoid these flights

into space entirely — they are part of our political ritual. And maybe you could be less self consciously awful in their performance although personally I would be sorry if you were. But the real answer is to keep that part of speechmaking to the absolute minimum. My own guess is that people will welcome matter-of-fact and unpretentious discussion and anyhow that is what won you the primaries. In any case, I don't think you have a choice.

Kennedy apparently took all this in good humor and continued to send Ken requests for his services, and from time to time Ken sent letters and brief notes to Kennedy offering this or that possible avenue of approach. On July 29, 1960, he suggested that Nixon's claim of vast experience must be addressed promptly lest it "get away from us and keep the campaign on the defensive. I don't think it can be met by subtleties. We must hit back directly. The Throttlebottom image of the vice-presidency must be stressed."

And again on September 11, "I am here for a money-raising soiree at Henry Fonda's. I have some relaxed thoughts on the campaign and the issues which I would happily contribute. However, I want neither to break in on a needed relaxation nor thwart my ambition to be the most reticent adviser in modern political history."

He also realized this ambition — almost, but not quite. Just after the election, he wrote to the president-elect:

Dear Jack: (May I defer more seemly formality until the electoral college meets?)

There has been talk in the Boston papers, and now this morning in the *New York Times,* that I am a prospect for your Senate seat. Without suggesting that this discussion has any serious substance, may I say that I am not a candidate for anything. Might I add, what I trust you know, that I would like to number myself among those of your friends and supporters who are sufficiently rewarded by being precisely that.

In sum, Ken and Arthur Schlesinger were indeed close and doubtless valued advisers, but both were kept somewhat in the background — deliberately so by Kennedy, who, according to Schlesinger's account in *A Thousand Days,* was wary of Nixon's constant references to the Democrats as "the party of Galbraith, Schlesinger and Bowles."[4] He was also protecting the interests of his own very capable team of speech writers, led by Theodore Sorensen and assisted by Richard Goodwin and Myer Feldman, from the press accusation that they were collapsing and that Stevenson's writers were taking over.

Ken did, however, have a hand in drafting the inaugural address. Returning the speech's second draft to Kennedy, he noted in a cover letter, "This is preeminently a speech for those who read it rather than those who will hear it." And then, with what would be a sad irony, he added, "The immediate audience will not long remember it." For this reason he had made few concessions to the president-elect's speaking style (with which, as we already know, he was not entirely happy) but offered his services at smoothing out the final draft, because, he said, "The difference between a brilliant speech and a good one is what happens to it in the last half hour."

There is no evidence that this offer was accepted; nor did much of Galbraith's draft find its way into the final version. One memorable line, however, did: "We shall never negotiate out of fear. But we shall never fear to negotiate."

The Galbraiths' social schedule for the three-day inaugural celebration was glamorous and high powered. They stayed with the George Balls and put in appearances at four receptions (two for Eleanor Roosevelt). They had dinner with Marquis Child, with the David Ginsburgs, brunch with the Philip Sterns, and, along with *le tout* Washington, went to a party given by Philip and Kay Graham. All this in addition to freezing at the inauguration itself, going with thousands of others to the inaugural ball that night at the National Guard Ar-

---

4. *A Thousand Days: John F. Kennedy in the White House* (Boston: Houghton Mifflin, 1965), p. 70.

mory, and, what may have been even more fun, to the post-inaugural ball the next night in McLean, Virginia.

Now that he was at least in the Kennedy orbit, if not in the inner circle, Ken found himself with a new coterie to become the cynosure of. This clique, for want of a better term, was called the Beautiful People, and Ken's passport to it came from the set's reigning doyenne — Jackie Kennedy, ably assisted by her sister Lee Radziwill, by various Kennedy relations, by some of Hollywood's elite, and by a number of charmed writers and editors of slick magazines and liberal newspapers. Ken, along with Schlesinger and possibly Henry Kissinger, held down the academia honors. And some of his colleagues from that sector grumbled — perhaps not without reason — about how Ken was lowering his intellectual sights to embrace certain of these beautiful people toward whom he would not even have condescended had they been just ordinary people.

He would have been charmed by Jacqueline Kennedy, however, in any context, although the fact that she was who she was didn't hurt. But he exhibited a curious trait toward her; if one didn't know him better one might almost say he was deferential.

Their friendship flowered during the early weeks of the new administration. Even before the inauguration Jackie wrote to thank him for some apparently high-toned books he had sent her. "You are so thoughtful to keep giving me these marvelous books — you can't imagine how grateful I am and how lovely it will be to see you soon again. My very best to you."

Buoyed by this, Ken quickly and imaginatively began to assume the role of purveyor of books to the First Lady. Subsequent correspondence shows Mrs. Kennedy to have been responsive, eager, and striving to cling to some sort of intellectual plateau to balance the overwhelming dose of political rhetoric and other trivia to which she was being subjected. Ken was ever gallant, and if at times he was a trifle too ingratiating, who can blame him?

On March 17, he wrote to her:

Dear Jackie,

Your note came today just as I had dictated a letter to you. It was to say that I have thought of presenting myself for a visit for the past month or six weeks, but was restrained by having seen you once reading "Memoirs: duc de Saint-Simon."[5] Obviously with this background you would conclude I was currying favor in order to promote myself to high office. But now I am safely an ambassador — subject, of course, to the will of the Senate. There is nothing I need. My soul is pure. So could I stroll over and visit you one day? It would be a great joy and I make a point of seeming to be less busy than most of your husband's loyal, intelligent, but unrelenting minions.

Previously, as the Kennedy administration began to settle into place, something of a problem had arisen about what to do with John Kenneth Galbraith, both in the minds of the president and of Ken himself. He insists — perhaps protesting too much — that he had no desire to join his two far from self-effacing Harvard colleagues, Schlesinger and Bundy, on the White House staff. "I was little enchanted," he wrote in his memoirs, "by the thought of doing with slight authority what I had done with vast power twenty years ago." Indeed, he has often noted that the OPA position did seem to remain at the pinnacle of his public office career; all other posts paled beside it. And it is difficult to imagine him fitting into the relative anonymity of a staff job, even at so distinguished a Washington address.

Whether other D.C. addresses would have had more appeal is open to question. Despite his assurances to the contrary to the president, he was quite intrigued by the idea of being a senator, just as he would be about any venture he hadn't tried

---

5. Ken had given her this book. In a letter to the author (February 27, 1989) Mrs. Kennedy recalls his handing it to her at the door of their Georgetown house, where the Galbraiths had come for lunch, just before the Kennedys caught a plane to Wisconsin during the primary. Later on when she reread the book at the White House (she had previously read it in college), she saw many parallels with Saint-Simon. Since his memoirs of the court of Louis XIV are about the proximity to power, Galbraith's giving them to her at that time was, she says, fortuitous.

and thought he could do well. But in this circumstance he wasn't interested in keeping the seat warm until Ted Kennedy would be old enough to sit in it (as he would be in 1962 when he turned thirty).

Nor, as it happened, would the circumstance be right when in 1972 there was talk of his running for the other senatorial seat from Massachusetts, then held by Republican Edward Brooke. In this case he rightly decided that to run against the only black in the Senate since Reconstruction would be unseemly for a man of his liberal views.

Finally he was urged by Senator George Aiken and various others to run for the Senate from Vermont! That would, of course, have meant changing his legal residence to the farm and proving that he lived there for at least six months of the year. Such a course would have involved a number of difficult problems, not the least of which, Ken and Kitty both point out as if shocked by the very thought of such an impossible action, was that they would have had to put in a furnace.

So much for Ken and elective office, then and later. But there were a few other possibilities for him being bruited about in the early days of the Kennedy administration. His name appeared on several occasions as treasury secretary in those speculative lists that newspapers are fond of running before a cabinet is finally chosen. But Kennedy would never have put him there; ever sensitive to his narrow margin of victory, the president-elect could not take a chance, especially for treasury, with anyone perceived as being as far on the Left as Galbraith.

Kennedy probably would have sprung for the Council of Economic Advisers, but Ken scorned that post. Indeed, he likes to report that when Schlesinger proposed India to Kennedy as Ken's own preference (although perhaps not quite as his fondest heart's desire), the president seemed not displeased with the idea of having Galbraith at such a safe remove.

It turned out to be an inspired choice all around. India is

not the sort of post to which rich, socially minded, and prestige-oriented men and women aspire. Ken's predecessors, John Sherman Cooper, Chester Bowles, and Ellsworth Bunker, had all been intelligent, literate, thoughtful men, drawn to India's ageless beauty and culture and bent on addressing her vast and unique problems. Ken felt fully equal to his succession. And the whole idea of having the letters A, E, and P after his name delighted his soul. Ambassador Extraordinary and Plenipotentiary bespoke a grandeur perfectly cut to suit his larger-than-life measure.

9

U.S. Plenipotentiary

As is so often the case in moments calling for lofty thoughts, both Galbraiths were preoccupied with far from cosmic concerns as the plane carrying them from Beirut to New Delhi neared its destination. Kitty, who had agonized over what to wear for the arrival, had finally chosen a delicate apricot silk dress, graceful to wear but inclined to muss. To keep it pristine, she had hung it in the lavatory, and as they started their descent, she wondered how long she could forestall getting into it to ensure the least possible creasing.

Ken was worried about the size of their welcoming crowd — with good reason. Because he wanted to ensure a large and enthusiastic airport turnout, he had rejected a more direct flight, which would have put them into New Delhi at eleven-thirty at night. And now, this plane, scheduled to arrive at the civilized hour of 7:00 P.M. on April 8, 1961, was inconsiderately proposing to land an hour and a half early!

Ever resourceful, Ken had the Air India pilot wire this information ahead to the American embassy. Apparently chaos resulted, as aides and spouses were pulled from their Saturday afternoon siestas, from their golf games, and from under hair dryers to hurry out to the airport to greet their new ambassador.

Had Kitty not had that indoctrinating trip to India five

years earlier, she would have been considerably more apprehensive about the arrival. Even so, it was unsettling enough for her to worry how well she would perform as the ambassador's wife.

From the moment she came down the steps of the airplane she managed to look radiant yet modest, composed yet touched by the emotion of the occasion (in fact, she was fighting back tears). But her neatest trick, she recalled, was not to appear bowed down by the weight of the huge garland of flowers — the wonderfully fragrant tuberoses that had been draped around her shoulders by T. K. Menon, head of Air India and the first to board their plane after touchdown.

Behind her Ken, also garlanded, wore a suitable mien as well — proud, not quite modest, but very gracious with his elegant bearing and cheerful smile of acknowledgment. The crowd was decent if not overwhelming, large enough not to be embarrassing and small enough to constrain the ambassador from giving his prepared airport arrival speech. (Driving in to New Delhi, they passed several embassy cars going the other way, obviously on their way out to meet them.)

One of the first to greet them on the ground was C. Tyler Wood, minister of economic affairs at the embassy, by happy chance an old friend and financial adviser of Kitty's family, and a welcome sight indeed. He and Edward Maffitt, the political minister, took them off to be photographed and introduced to what is known as the Country Team, namely the heads of all Washington agencies — State Department, U.S. Information Service (USIS), Agency for International Development (AID), army, navy, air force — then stationed in India. Ken, who had been well briefed, was able to greet each person with a pleasant reference to his or her background and experience.

In due course the Galbraiths were conveyed to what would be their temporary residence on Ratendone Road. The handsome new chancery where the ambassador conducts his business, designed by the eminent American architect Edward Durell Stone, was already in use, but the new residence next door to it, also designed by Stone, was not yet completed. So Ken and Kitty were obliged to hunker down in what was euphemistically referred to as a "bungalow." (This is not quite as absurd as calling those Newport, Rhode Island, mansions "cottages," but somewhat in the same category.) The residence was the same one-story house — left over from the British Raj days — where they had first taken tea with Ambassador and Mrs. John Sherman Cooper in 1956. This too was reassuring to Kitty because the furniture, the curtains, and even the many handsomely framed mirrors on the walls were all familiar from her earlier visit.

The residence was pleasantly situated on ample grounds; a large awning-covered terrace, ringed with pots of bright petunias, overlooked a leafy garden with shrubs and fruit trees, and beyond, a border of multicolored flowers. A wall at the back separated the staff quarters, small one- or two-room houses in a clean brick yard.

The residence itself, although no squat bungalow, was quite modest, considering the splendor usually associated with our ambassadors' dwellings overseas. Besides the living room, which was of agreeable, although not very grand, proportions, and the "state" dining room, which could seat a maximum of sixteen, Kitty had a large corner bedroom and bath overlooking the garden; Ken's also quite large bedroom and bath doubled as his at-home study. The boys were to have the largest of the rooms with bath (and a small, adjoining one for Emily). The disadvantage was that this room was just off the state dining room, separated only by a pair of glass doors; the Galbraiths had lurid visions of their nine- and ten-year-old sons engaged in one of their habitually ear-splitting fights on the night that Prime Minister Nehru was a dinner guest. But since the boys were still in Cambridge, having been left behind with Emily to complete their school year, the solution to the problem could be put off for a few months. Alan, the oldest Galbraith son, was by then a sophomore at Harvard and thus not involved in this equation.

"What does an ambassador do when he arrives at his post

at seven o'clock in the evening?" Ken asked rhetorically in *Ambassador's Journal,* his lively account of his tour of duty in India.[1] "Well, I chatted briefly with Ty Wood and Maffitt and then with my personal aide, a nice young man named Gil Wing, who stands in some awe of me. Then we had a drink, had dinner and went to bed." The dinner was a disenchanting experience. The Galbraiths are accustomed to good, simple, but hardly superlative food, so neither is inclined to be picky about what is served. But Suschen, their Indian cook, stretched Ken's tolerance up to and ultimately beyond the breaking point. At that first dinner, he noted wryly, the only normal dish they had was a soup made with bouillon cubes. The rest could be described only as God-awful; the dessert, however, defied description. Suschen had outdone himself, creating, in a construct of macaroons, Nabisco wafers, whipped cream, and pale lavender ice cream, a replica of the Taj Mahal. So ended the first day as A. E. and P.

His early days as ambassador proved to be a unique experience for Ken; for almost the first time in his life he had to make a concerted effort not to be himself.

Diplomacy's basic tenets, listening patiently to what others have to say and giving inoffensive, even evasive answers, were not social habits that came naturally to this American ambassador. He is not one to make polite conversation with a total stranger by trying to draw out a few vital statistics — place of birth, educational background, present occupation, preferred leisure activity — which to him are not vital at all. Even when he gets to know someone quite well, he has no notion of where they came from or what sort of youthful traumas or successes they may have had.

Gloria Steinem comes to mind as a case in point. She met Ken, she recalls, either just before he went to India or just

---

1. *Ambassador's Journal: A Personal Account of the Kennedy Years* (Boston: Houghton Mifflin, 1969). Galbraith's quotes in this chapter, unless otherwise identified, are from this source.

after, when he came back to the United States on one of his frequent visits. "It isn't that Ken so much talks about himself," she suggests, "as he talks about external issues and interests many of which happen to be my interests too. But I don't think he ever asked about me. I suspect he doesn't know to this day about my childhood or where I came from. He just launches into his topic with whoever is present and we certainly shared an interest, a caring about India, where I had been in 1957–58."[2]

Looking back on this period, Ken reflected in an interview he gave to *Life* magazine, "It is unquestionably true that one has to be much more agreeable as an ambassador. But I would think that anyone who attempted to court popularity would . . . end up neither very popular in the country to which he was accredited, nor much trusted by the country that sent him there."

Of the two Galbraiths, Kitty was the one more completely entranced with India, more knowledgeable about its traditions and rituals. To be sure, both were sensitive to the sights, sounds, and smells; the broad avenues and flowering trees of New Delhi; the terraced tea gardens of Darjeeling; the markets lit at night by oil lamps; the vibrant colors of robes, saris, and turbans; the busy streets filled with bicycle rickshas and bullock carts; the figures sitting in the lotus position, meditating on the riverbanks; the glorious mosques, the forts, the monuments; the sounds of temple bells ringing, pipes playing, conch shells blowing, of Indians at their devotional chants; the smells of cow dung, of incense, of jasmine. Both Ken and Kitty were charmed by the gentleness and warmth of the Indian people, and of course distressed by the all too visible signs of disease and hunger and pervasive poverty.

But it was Kitty for whom the two years became truly seminal. It was Kitty who visited the tiniest, most remote villages,

---

2. Having recently graduated from Smith College, Steinem was in India at that time as a Chester Bowles Asian Scholar.

Kitty who rode in tongas instead of embassy cars with her Indian friends, Kitty who wrote a book about the nation's cultural and historical past, and Kitty who on arrival at once set about to learn Hindi. With her natural bent for languages, she was soon able to make herself understood in a sort of meat-and-potatoes Hindi, to understand a bit more than she could speak, and, even more daunting, to write the Hindi script. She could as an exercise write English in Hindi; for her teacher who came to the residence at seven in the morning to instruct her, she translated the story of George Washington and the cherry tree into Hindi. "It's simply a matter of translating English sounds into the Hindi symbols," she explains.

Ken, being a subtle man, was always very receptive to India's many nuances; but he was first and foremost the ambassador and as such ever mindful of the need to focus on the larger picture of global policy and international strategy.

Ten days after his arrival, Ken presented his credentials in a ceremony that surely gladdened his heart. First you must picture J. K. Galbraith with a good ten inches added to his height by the mandatory top hat he wore along with his cutaway coat and diplomat's striped pants. Then picture his arrival with Kitty, in an open car flanked by motorcycle escort, at the magnificently imposing Rashtrapati Bhavan (President's Palace). There he was met by a detachment of lancers on handsomely matched horses and escorted to the open courtyard, where an honor guard of beautifully turned out Sikhs was drawn up in two ranks, waiting for him to inspect them ("I found nothing seriously wrong," he reported). Then he made a quick run-through to be sure he had all his signals straight. The actual ceremony — a slow approach to the president (Dr. Rajendra Prasad), Ken's speech urging "accomplishment as distinct from conversation," the president's reply, and finally the presenting of credentials — went off with all the proper élan. After a brief private chat with the president in his study, the principals went on to a state room for the public reception, press included. And finally, as he returned to his car for the trip back to the residence, the two flags on the outfenders were unfurled for the first time and thereafter waved forevermore whenever Ken stepped into the car.

Gratifying as all this pomp was to Ken, his tone in writing about his tour of duty both in *A Life in Our Times* and *Ambassador's Journal* is ironic, and often belittling of the entire diplomatic scene, the CIA, the Pentagon, the State Department in general, and Dean Rusk in particular. (In one of his characteristically oblique phrases, written to President Kennedy, he described his extreme antipathy for the State Department thus: "I think I dislike most the uncontrollable instinct for piously reasoned inaction.")

He decried the very process that brought him to his post and the unfairness of appointing as ambassadors well-known names over career diplomats or, worse, large campaign contributors over professional foreign service officers. He made great fun of what he called the "disguised underemployment" of almost all of his fellow ambassadors, citing in particular the envoys from Argentina and Brazil, who he swears could not have put in more than a day of serious work in a month, and the more industrious Scandinavian emissaries, who may have logged as much as a day per week. Nor did he make an exception of his own efforts on the job, pointing out that he had plenty of time during his watch to write his extensive *Journal,* plus the memoir of his childhood, *The Scotch,* plus his first novel, the slight, satirical *The McLandress Dimension,* offered, so as not to blow his cover as ambassador, under the nom de plume Mark Epernay.[3]

Yet with it all he was widely regarded as an extraordinarily able ambassador. Some may have felt that he was less bent on representing the views of the United States than the views of

---

3. When one of the U.S. weekly news magazines cabled to New Delhi to ask him to confirm or deny that he was indeed Mark Epernay, Galbraith, never one to favor outright lying, cabled back the perfect nonanswer: "Who is Mark Epernay?"

John Kenneth Galbraith, but even so, they looked upon him as a very effective and influential force. He was extremely popular with the Indians, who cherished him for his intellect, his candor, and his ever present tendency to debunk received truths. Furthermore, in a country with urgent agricultural economic problems, Galbraith's expertise in that field was greatly welcomed. ("No American ambassador has brought to his job more impressive agricultural credentials than did I," he once wrote.) Also key to his success was his close relationship with Kennedy, a figure of growing popularity and trust on the Indian subcontinent.

All these virtues were perceived and lauded by the urban elite in India from the moment Ken's appointment was announced. What they could not have known was how well he was going to get along with Nehru. Ken could not have known that either, but he might have guessed, for the two had much in common. Both were men of many parts; Nehru, in addition to being prime minister and head of the Congress Party, was his own minister of foreign affairs; he was also chairman of India's Planning Commission and of the Atomic Energy Commission. Since India's independence, when he had become prime minister, his thoughts and efforts had been dedicated to bringing his country, with its age-old customs, into the present-day world. To this end he was very receptive to new ideas, new advances in science, industry, education, and health. Short, frail, and ethereal looking in his habitual garb of a white overseas cap, long brown coat, and white jodhpurs, he was impatient of delays, of apathy, of inefficiency. He also shared with the U.S. ambassador a keen eye for pretty women and a delight in wry and understated humor.

Kitty, in an affectionate tribute, wrote of her first formal introduction to Nehru, at a luncheon at the prime minister's house the day after Ken had presented his credentials. There were about a dozen guests, nearly all members of the Nehru family, including his daughter, Indira Gandhi, and his sister

Madame Pandit. When the prime minister came in, he walked over to Kitty and said, "I have heard you are shy." He then set out to put her at ease, "even to cutting my mango at dessert," she wrote, "for he knew that a mango, a very squishy fruit, can be exceedingly awkward until one learns to manage it."[4]

As always, the problem of Pakistan loomed large. From the beginning of his stewardship, Ken was at pains to try to reduce the tension between these two neighboring countries. Pakistan had been created by the British at the time of Indian independence in 1947. From the beginning, India's and Pakistan's relations had been tainted by a dispute over to which one of them the state of Kashmir, bordering on both, should belong.

At the time of partition, when the line between the countries had been drawn, the Princely States along the border — so called because they were still ruled by their Princes, or Maharajahs — had some discretion as to whether they would align with predominately Muslim Pakistan or predominately Hindu India. The Maharajah of Kashmir had wanted to remain independent, but finding that impossible and being a Hindu, he had chosen to side with India. He had then more or less abdicated, leaving his state with its enormous Muslim population vulnerable to an almost immediate border clash between Pakistan and India. As hostilities threatened to escalate into full-fledged war, the United Nations intervened and established a cease-fire line that gave the mountainous part of Kashmir to Pakistan and the valley to India. The UN also called for a plebiscite, but because neither India nor Pakistan was sure what the outcome would be, it has never been implemented.

As a footnote to the troubled history of Kashmir, Ken mentions in passing that one of the many reasons for the intensity of the dispute was that the entire Nehru family plus numerous

---

4. "Nehru: A View from the Embassy," *Harper's Magazine* (July 1965).

important members of the Indian Congress were Kashmiris.
"So," he says, "while India wanted to rule Kashmir, Kashmir
was in effect ruling India." (This conflict remains as unre-
solved in the 1990s as it was in the 1960s, and even as these
words are written the same tensions in Kashmir are again
reaching a boiling point.)

Matters were exacerbated early in Ken's tour by the Washington visit of Pakistan's president, Ayub Khan, in July 1961.
The joint Ayub-Kennedy communiqué that resulted from their
meetings referred to "extended aid," a phrase that, not unrea-
sonably, alarmed the Indians. They feared that a change in
policy, which had hitherto prohibited Pakistan from using
U.S. military aid for aggression against India, was in the making. There was further concern that the U.S. intended to step
in and try to settle once and for all the Kashmir issue.

In press conferences in both Calcutta and Madras on July
21 and 22, Ken tried most emphatically to correct this mis-
conception and to allay the supposition that "innocent words
conceal evil meanings." In typical Galbraithian language, he
was quoted in the *Madras Mail* as saying, "I would hope that
it would be possible for the U.S. to express its concern over
the issue which divides these two countries without unlimited
implications being read into it." "Nothing would be more
overwhelmingly against U.S. policy than to allow Pakistan
the use of arms against India," the *Times of India* quoted him
as "asserting." "Galbraith States if Pakistan Aggresses U.S.
Will Be India's Ally," ran the headline in the *Deccan Herald*.

These mandatory reassurances apart, Ken devoted the bur-
den of his press conferences to lecturing the Indians on the
subject of economic growth as applied to underdeveloped
countries. Urging against indiscriminate loans, he pointed out
a tendency in developing nations to lay too much emphasis on
capital equipment and technical know-how and to neglect the
human aspects of the problem. For example, in agriculture he
suggested that instead of being so preoccupied with the acqui-
sition of machinery and equipment, more attention be paid to

improving the knowledge and skills of the unemployed and underemployed in order to bring them into the ranks of productive labor. What he might have said was that many willing and needy hands could do the work of one tractor.

His warning apparently fell on receptive ears. Said the (Madras) *Hindu,* in its lead editorial and in words that Ken himself could have written, "Our advances will be much less tortuous — and certainly can be achieved at much less cost — if our planning bears a more intimate relation to economic and social realities."

Always uppermost in his mind was the importance of the United States' accepting without question India's position of nonalignment with the superpowers. He fought against what he perceived as a tendency in the State Department to think of all nations as being like Europe after World War II, and not recognizing that India, Pakistan, and Indochina were "a wholly different world where Communism was irrelevant and escape from past colonialism was all important." To Galbraith's way of thinking, the scapegoats for everything that was troublesome about U.S. relations with India were Secretary of State Dean Rusk and Assistant Secretary of State for Asian Affairs Phillips Talbot. He describes working with Phil Talbot as "like playing badminton with a marshmallow. You never could tell if he was going to stick to the racket or go over the net."

As for Dean Rusk, it is sometimes hard to believe that he was as servile and muddled in carrying out his duties as Ken likes to portray him. By all accounts he was an intelligent and a kind man, but in most regards the polar opposite of Ken: cautious, respectful of authority and of established ways and received truths, unimaginative about putting forth new ideas, and eager not to rock the boat.

Carol Laise, the widow of Ellsworth Bunker, one of Ken's predecessors in India, has been ambassador to Nepal, has wide Foggy Bottom experience, and has worked closely with Rusk and Talbot on India. Furthermore, when urgently summoned by Ken, she went back to New Delhi to be on his staff during the India-China war in 1962. She is also a good friend and neighbor of the Galbraiths in Vermont. Asked whether she considers Ken's antipathy toward Rusk justified, she says unhesitatingly, "No, I do not. In fact, I don't understand it at all and never have, and I certainly don't agree."

For his part, Rusk could not have been overjoyed by Ken's consistent refusal as ambassador to communicate with Washington through normal diplomatic channels, repeatedly bypassing the State Department to go directly to the president. George McGovern, who had become a good friend of the Galbraiths during the early days of the Kennedy administration, has this anecdote to add to Galbraithiana: "One day it seems that Rusk complained about this habit of Ken's to Kennedy, and Kennedy spoke to Ken about it and said, 'Maybe you ought to go through the State Department on things like this.' And Ken responded, 'Mr. President, trying to get a message to you through that State Department is like fornicating through a mattress.' Kennedy thought that was a worthy remark," said McGovern. "And somehow it got back to Rusk too."

A telling example of Ken's schisms with Rusk was the matter of Goa, which surfaced during Ken's first year as ambassador. Goa is a small territory on the west coast of India which was still held by the Portuguese. Although it is about half the size of Connecticut, on the map it looks like what Ken has called "the Portuguese pimple." There really was no logical reason that Goa should have remained Portuguese when, at the time of independence, both British and French India became part of the Indian Union. Thus Goa's existence as a Portuguese territory bespoke of a continued colonialism that seriously troubled the Indians.

Numerous dustups occurred during the early days of December 1961, and it appeared that the Indians were getting ready to move into Goa. In common with most liberals, Ken instinctively favored a diplomatic rather than a military approach. Since in this case it was the Indians who were about to take a bellicose action, he sought a creative solution. The Portuguese, he argued, were clearly losing their grip on their fading empire, as had already been demonstrated in Angola and Mozambique. Sooner or later the empire would fall, a process that, he suggested, could be hastened better in the UN than by an Indian military coup of Goa which was bound to be frowned on in the United States. Thus he was trying to walk a thin line, advocating that the U.S. take tough stands both on India for her threatened use of force and on Portugal for her continued reliance on colonialism. Using this rationale, he managed to delay the Indian move for a few days, but was unable to prevent it altogether, a circumstance that he blamed in large part on the home office. Even when recounting the episode years later, Ken bristles.

It appears that while Galbraith was talking as persuasively as he knew how in India, Rusk had been approached at a NATO meeting in Brussels by the Portuguese foreign minister Franco Nogieria, who urged him to provide troops to help defend Goa against an Indian incursion. But Rusk, whose passivity and reluctance to make waves was well known, placated Nogieria by saying that the U.S. had *every sympathy* with the Portuguese position; however, we simply could not spare the troops from duty in Europe to help them out. "I hardly imagined that I could be undercut in such a flaccid and incompetent way by our own management," Ken wrote. And to this day, he staunchly maintains that, given another, stronger anticolonial response from the secretary of state, the situation might have been saved — even though, as it turned out, nothing very earthshaking was lost.

When the Indians did move on Goa one morning just before Christmas 1961, the ambassador's three military attachés held a briefing in the chancery for Ken, indicating on a blown-up map of Goa just how and where two Indian columns were proceeding and where they would come together in a pincer movement. The army attaché gave the prevailing view that the operation would probably be bloody but mercifully short — perhaps as short as ten days.

Ken, speaking from his experience as a lifelong antimilitary man, shook his head knowingly. "The operation will be over by tonight," he pronounced. In fact, it was over by noon and the casualties were one man shot and one man drowned accidentally. "I was not as reckless as I sounded," Ken notes. "I did understand something of the Portuguese lack of will and their declining faith in their imperial domain. Anyway, it was the last such briefing I ever had. After that no one ever ventured to challenge my military acumen."

There were other aspects of Ken's job that, although not as frustrating as his relations with the State Department, also tried his never very large reserves of patience. He was subjected to a lot of mandatory protocol that was distasteful to him. He hated having to call upon and then receive calls back from every single ambassador or high commissioner accredited to New Delhi. "A stupid waste of time," he called it. He was also prone to be impatient with the size and in some instances the competence of his embassy staff — 300 Americans and 716 Indians — and irked by some of the other U.S. agencies in New Delhi. The USIS, in particular, seemed to rub him the wrong way.

These irritations, along with the normal stresses of his job, plus India's periods of extreme heat and uncertain food, inevitably affected his health. In *Ambassador's Journal* nearly every other entry seems to refer to another headache, dizzy spell, sinus attack, bout of insomnia, depression, or dysentery. In hindsight, Ken concedes that he may have let his natural tendency to hypochondria run away with him. He also notes that he had detailed even more instances of his physical and mental woes in the first draft of his *Journal,* but was persuaded to delete at least a third of them. The flip side of this coin was that Ken had a wonderful time being ambassador. Kitty confirms this, suggesting that despite his many headaches and other ailments, he usually appeared to function normally and with a great deal of vigor. They traveled constantly, together and separately; the embassy had its own planes and a brand-new special jet — a Convair — for domestic flights. This perk is not provided for all ambassadors, but Ken managed to justify it because of the vastness of the territories he had to cover. (India is two thousand miles north to south and eighteen hundred miles east to west.)

Life became more complete for the Galbraiths in July when Emily and the boys finally arrived. By that time Ken and Kitty, having lived in the Ratendone Road residence for three months, concluded that it was simply too small to lend itself to the lively presence of two noisy little boys (Peter was ten and Jamie nine). Fortunately, they were able to find a suitable house just down the road, at 17 Ratendone, an arrangement that did not distress the boys and gratified Emily, who loved having "her children" to herself. As the time for their arrival drew near, Kitty, having announced much earlier that she wanted at least a week absolutely free of official engagements to help settle her sons and Emily, was dismayed to learn that a conference of past and present American ambassadors to Asia was convening in New Delhi on the very night Peter, Jamie, and Emily were due to arrive. Not surprisingly, the present envoy was expected to give the first welcoming dinner party.

To amuse the boys and soften the blow of being unable to spend their first evening together, Ken suggested that they fill number 17 with a few interesting animals. Accordingly, a pair of peacocks were installed, but these proud birds adjusted so poorly to their new environment that they continually bashed their heads against the wall and had to be treated with expensive antibiotics.

Next from the New Delhi Zoo came a leopard cub. When Nehru heard of this, he threatened to have the animal "sequestered," as Ken put it; although tigers made nice pets, leopards, the prime minister insisted, were mean and unreliable. This, however, did not seem to be the case with the Galbraith leopard, who appeared docile enough and even allowed the boys to stroke his stomach to help him swallow his milk and digest his Pablum. Emily promptly set up a litter box for him, announcing firmly, as only Emily can, that she did not intend to "have leopard shit all over my house." But then, after he had been living for four weeks or so on Ratendone Road, the leopard finally showed his spots. Quite unexpectedly one day, he sank his teeth into Kitty's skirt and wouldn't let go. With admirable cool, Kitty simply slipped out of her skirt, and shortly thereafter the leopard was returned to the altogether more suitable venue of the New Delhi Zoo.

Of the two boys Peter was the greater animal lover, and also the one who had been most resistant to the whole idea of leaving his school and friends in Cambridge, Massachusetts, for the then unknown charms of India. Apparently, at one point Ken must have expressed some of Peter's misgivings to Kennedy, because, shortly after Ken's appointment as ambassador was announced, Peter received the following letter from the president.

Dear Peter:

I learn from your father that you are not very anxious to give up your school and friends for India. I think I know a little about how you feel. More than twenty years ago our family was similarly uprooted when we went to London where my father was ambassador. My younger brothers and sisters were about your age. They had, like you, to exchange old friends for new ones.

But I think you will like your new friends and your new school in India. For anyone interested, as your father says you are, in animals, India must have the most fascinating possibilities. The range is from elephants to cobras, although I gather the cobras have to be handled professionally. Indians ride and play polo so you will come back an experienced horseman.

But more important still, I think of the children of the people I am sending to other countries as my junior peace corps. You and your brothers will be helping your parents do a good job for our country and you will be helping out yourself by making many friends. I think perhaps this is what you will enjoy most of all.

The boys had two splendid years in India. When Jamie, the more stylish sportsman of the two, won second prize for horsemanship in the New Delhi horse show, he received his cup from no less a personage than Prime Minister Nehru. Jamie also distinguished himself in quite another way. Asked in his fourth-grade class at the American International School to describe what his parents did, he contributed the following: "My father is Ambassador to India, or the chief United States official here. He does many different types of work. He writes reports for the United States Government on Indian conditions. He has conferences with the Indian Government to improve diplomatic relations. And Dad makes speeches to make a little better the understanding between the U.S. and India and he represents the President on official occasions. Mother doesn't do much except arrange entertainment and administer the household."

This youthful male chauvinistic account inspired Kitty to write for the *Atlantic Monthly* a delightful piece entitled "Mother Doesn't Do Much," in which she described in pithy, eloquent detail all the things that Mother *did* do while not doing much.[5]

---

5. May 1963. Ken also put his stamp of approval on the article by reprinting it in full as an appendix in *Ambassador's Journal*.

10

Masterminding
a War

AN ASTONISHING NUMBER of the Galbraiths' friends and acquaintances found their way to New Delhi and were entertained by them during their two years there. For the most part Ken enjoyed these many visitors, especially Jackie Kennedy, who arrived for a ten-day visit in March 1962.

The plans for her visit had been many months in the making and had suffered numerous ups and downs and changes of direction. Then, at the end of February, one week before the First Lady was scheduled to arrive, Ken received a telegram from her secretary postponing her trip for a week due to what Ken felt were vaguely defined health reasons. To him it looked like "sheer disaster." In view of the thousands of hours and rupees that had gone into the planning of this event, he took, even for Ken, the bold step of tracking the president down in Palm Beach to protest. "He ticked me off in a way that would have made Dean Rusk rejoice," Ken reported ruefully. It took him four sleeping pills to get through the succeeding night, thus doubtless adding to his own vaguely defined health problems. But resilient as always, in a matter of a few days he had schedules all rearranged and bruised Indian feelings all soothed.

The residence on Ratendone Road was too small to accommodate Mrs. Kennedy. So, just as Kitty had found a small house down the road for the boys and Emily, she found another one, also down the road, for Jackie and her sister Lee Radziwill. Ken inspected it two days before the arrival date and pronounced it "very chic," an unusually trendy word for him, but, under the circumstances, suitable.

Also because of the limitations of the residence, the Galbraiths concluded that the gala farewell dinner for JBK (as she is invariably referred to in *Ambassador's Journal*) would be held at the chancery. This was no small task in a building — beautiful as it was with its magnificent central water court and its great hall — designed for business rather than social occasions; it didn't even have a proper kitchen. To make sure that all the complex logistics for this affair were in order before Mrs. Kennedy even got to India, the Galbraiths staged a full-dress rehearsal on the night before her arrival, with members of the embassy staff playing the parts of the forty-five invited guests. This was the kind of evening Ken and Kitty could pull off with panache. The tables were set out on the balcony overlooking the water gardens, with a small string orchestra installed on one of the islands. The planned menu was replicated exactly, and if the food wasn't quite as hot or the wine as cold as it would be on the "real" night, everyone had a relaxed and cheerfully nonstuffy time.

The next day they went to the airport to meet JBK, and the glittering series of events began, as chronicled by Galbraith in his *Journal* in a chapter headed "Great Fun." And so it certainly was; great fun with emphasis on ceremony; on shopping; on sightseeing; on traveling by train, plane, cart, and boat; and on parties and more parties. Everyone who came within her orbit was dazzled by the First Lady — none more so than her long-legged friend and guide, the U.S. plenipotentiary.

Here are a few of the standout occasions: On Mrs. Kennedy's second night in New Delhi, Prime Minister Nehru rounded up what Ken called "the gayer members of the community" for a magnificent large dinner followed by singing and dancing on the floodlit stage in the garden. Mrs. Kennedy, for whom Nehru had a warm affection, wore "a long dress of pale turquoise which responded brilliantly to the lights," Ken wrote, sounding a bit like a writer for *Vogue,* and then went on sounding even more so.

The scene on the Prime Minister's lawn last night would last in anyone's memory. You must imagine chairs stretching across the lawn and lit by the half moon and the reflection of stage lights. These flashed on a stunning array of saris — every woman present had chosen from many and spent hours on the choice. In front of the chairs was a little canopied area for the supreme guests, the canopy being made of flower petals. Finally before all was the stage, dancers, musicians in vivid or sometimes wild costume, the women being especially sinuous as they turned and twirled.

Of a different nature, but still with plenty of emphasis on glamor, was the next day's trip to Fatehpur Sikri, one of the seven sacred cities of the Hindus, and on to nearby Agra and the Taj Mahal. The party, consisting of Jackie and Lee, Nehru and his daughter, Indira Gandhi, and Ken and Kitty, assembled at New Delhi's VIP railroad station to board the luxurious special train that had once been the pride of the viceroy of India (and was now so of her president, who was not on board for this trip). Brilliant red on the outside, with fawn-colored trim inside, the beautifully appointed train included a sitting room, a dining room, and ample bedrooms — "unquestionably the proper way to travel," Ken noted.

Huge crowds awaited them at Agra (as indeed they did everywhere on their four-day trip to Benares, Jaipur, and Udaipur). Touring the Taj Mahal with reporters and photographers jumping out all around them was, Ken quipped, "like making love in a cage full of monkeys." After the Taj, however, Ken managed to decoy the press with an official briefing to permit JBK and her sister to go jewelry shopping.

The ambassador also spent a great deal of time during the visit trying to head off questions to the First Lady about her clothes. Mostly this was a losing battle, which he tended to blame on the inadequacies of her staff. But he staunchly maintained that although Jacqueline Kennedy may have seemed to concern herself unduly with matters of style, this apparent preoccupation often masked her "clear and penetrating intelligence."

In sum, if the Jackie Kennedy visit could not be said to have significantly improved understanding between India and the United States, it certainly did strengthen the bond between Mrs. Kennedy and Nehru. From the moment of greeting her on the tarmac at the airport, the prime minister seemed entranced by her charms, even to the point of moving her and her sister from the Ratendone Road guest house that Kitty had so carefully prepared to the viceroy's suite at his own residence.

Of more lasting significance, Nehru had instructed Ken to find and buy for the First Lady an eighteenth-century Mogul painting. This was a particularly agreeable task for him, not only because it would please Jackie Kennedy, but because, since his earlier visit in 1956 when he had first been beguiled by Indian miniature paintings, his interest and expertise had grown.

In fact, at about the time of Nehru's request he was planning (not surprisingly for him) to write a book on Indian paintings, or, more precisely, to collaborate on such a book with an Indian, highly placed in the civil service, whom he had met through official channels and who was also an expert, particularly on the Kangra paintings from the Punjab, his native area. Mohinder Singh Randhawa was very much Ken's sort of person; like Ken he could be and often was described as a Renaissance man. According to Cary Welch, the foremost authority on Islamic and later Indian paintings at Harvard's Fogg Art Museum, "both men have very bright, inquiring minds, and both have extremely large, healthy, strongly fulfilled egos."

Through Randhawa (who died in 1988) Ken met various

art dealers and other sources for acquiring paintings, from whom he built his entire collection — approximately seventy-five paintings — which he ultimately donated to the Fogg Museum. "His eye for these paintings is very good," says Welch. "It reflects his interest in life. Just as he likes to look at pictures of beautiful women, he likes pictures of things that give pleasure. He would not be at all responsive to some dark, puzzling, macabre sort of picture. He likes them to be bright and cheery. It's interesting too that such a big man likes such little pictures."

The little picture that he bought for Nehru to give to Mrs. Kennedy is on the cover of his and Randhawa's book, *Indian Painting*. And the result of Nehru's gift and Ken's persuasive enthusiasm was that Jackie herself became a collector. "It was fun to do that with him," she says, adding that Ken introduced her to Cary Welch. "One of JKG's loveliest attributes is the way he brings different friends of his together," Jacqueline Kennedy Onassis writes. "His interests, the warmth of his and Kitty's spirit and the warmth of their household make this possible. He is the hub and the spokes go out and make a wide rim of people happy."

One month later came another beauteous visitor to New Delhi — Angie Dickinson. At the time, the film star, alleged to have been one of John F. Kennedy's many dalliances, was a recent friend of Ken's. He had met her six months earlier at the White House mess during one of his official home visits and had ascertained that she was flying back to California that night. As it happened, he was also flying to California that night, but on a different airline — a situation he speedily corrected. In *Ambassador's Journal* Ken claims that by the time the two had reached Los Angeles he had "fallen deeply in love" with the winsome, sexy, and amusing Angie. He uses the phrase "deeply in love" frequently to describe his feelings toward women who delight him but with whom he has a far more platonic relationship than he would have his public believe. Teasing them about this has become a game with him.

A case in point: In an attractively bound little set of photographs sent from New Delhi at Christmas time to the 325 people on his list of closest friends is a picture of Ken lying fully clothed and asleep on a long bunk bed in what appears to be a cabin on an airplane. Next to him but separated by a wide space is a woman, also fully clothed and asleep. Her face not being clearly visible, at first glance one might think it was Kitty. But at second glance one sees that it is not Kitty but Angie Dickinson. As wicked thoughts riot through the viewer's mind, exactly as Ken intended them to, one notes but may not take in the accompanying caption: "Titus I, 15." Those with a Bible handy could appreciate the following:

> To the pure all things are pure,
> But to the corrupt and unbelieving nothing is pure.
> Their very minds and consciences are corrupt.

Kitty has taken very kindly to nearly all members of what one observer has called the WAGs (Women Adoring Galbraith). And certainly she has had far fewer worries on this score than most wives who have spent all their adult lives married to the same man.

Galbraith's first reference in his *Journal* to the incipient border conflict between China and India was in a letter to President Kennedy, written on October 16, 1962, in which he noted almost in passing that his policy "in the convenient absence of instructions" will be to express quiet sympathy and hope for a quick settlement while conveying no sense of urgency."

Three days later, the sense of urgency was forced upon him. On Friday, October 19, he flew to London where he was to give a Guildhall lecture before going on to Washington, arriving midday on the twentieth. He was awakened in the early morning of Sunday, the twenty-first, by an urgent message from the embassy saying that hostilities had broken out on two fronts of the India-China (Tibet) border in the northern-

most part of India. The front to the west was in an almost un-
inhabitable, high mountainous plateau called the Aksai Chin
in Ladakh, and the other, a thousand miles to the east, was in
an equally inhospitable mountainous territory that wasn't
even called a state but was known only as the North-East
Frontier Agency (NEFA).

There was another, even more ominous message — a "Top
Secret, Eyes Only" from President Kennedy ordering him to
return to New Delhi immediately, not, as he might have expected, because of the India-China hostilities in the Himalayas, but because of an infinitely more dangerous conflict
brewing in another part of the world. The U.S. ambassador
was being ordered back to New Delhi to explain the Cuban
missile crisis to Prime Minister Nehru and through him to the
other nonaligned nations.

That very Sunday, Ken left London and was back in New
Delhi early in the morning of the twenty-second, having spent
four consecutive days in the air between England and India.
Thus began the most hectic, arduous, responsible, and certainly the most risk-prone interval of his entire two years and
a half as ambassador.

Because Washington was completely preoccupied with the
Cuban missile crisis, Ken had been informed that the highest
official on the White House staff who had any time to deal
with his problems was his former Harvard colleague Carl
Kaysen. This suited Ken very well indeed since he and Kaysen
were substantially in agreement over the inadvisability of too
much military influence on America's foreign policy. And at
the State Department Dean Rusk, rather handsomely, as even
Ken admits, confined himself to an overall statement of support for whatever course Galbraith chose to follow in what
must at that moment have seemed very far off India. As a result, Ken says, "I had more independent authority than any
modern ambassador has enjoyed in another country in wartime."

Ken's overruling instinct was, as ever, toward a far less bellicose stance than either Nehru or Kennedy was able to assume, since both felt obliged to maintain a very tough approach toward their adversaries — Nehru toward China, Kennedy toward Russia.

Actually the border war was not going well for the Indians. On his return from London Galbraith, having quickly brought himself up to speed on the background of the two fronts, concluded that India's claim on the eastern NEFA front was valid enough to warrant U.S. moral support, which he promptly offered.

The situation to the west, at Aksai Chin, Ladakh, was another matter; for two years the Chinese had in effect been occupying the territory as they struggled to build a road through its miserable terrain to give them access to the distant northern province of Sinkiang, which bordered on the USSR. For most of that time, Galbraith believes, very few Indians were even aware of the Chinese efforts in this remote area; this seemed to him to suggest at least a "tenuous claim" for the Chinese.

However it was in the NEFA where the first serious losses for the Indians occurred. By October 26 the Chinese had taken Tawang, twenty miles south of the border; the Indians had suffered some four thousand casualties (four hundred dead, the rest missing); and Galbraith was beginning to revise his opinions about this being merely a border skirmish and to think in terms of the U.S. offering military aid when and if it was requested. The fact that at this juncture Pakistan appeared to be making pro-Chinese noises did not lessen his concerns; nor did the political tactics and exaggerated false claims of Krishna Menon, then India's defense minister, whom Ken had come to regard with antagonism. With Dean Rusk temporarily in abeyance, he was able to turn his full disapproving attentions onto Menon.

Diplomatically it seemed that a great deal rested on when, how, and by whom the United States was to be asked to provide military aid to help India in her war against the Chinese.

Ken was extremely reluctant to have Menon do the asking because he knew that if he did, he would at once present himself
as the savior, the one whose every desire was fulfilled by the
Americans. In fact Menon, who for a long time had led the
Indian delegation to the General Assembly of the UN, was
widely unpopular in the United States, and Ken feared that his
seizing the credit for obtaining U.S. military aid would have
negative consequences in Washington should further and pro-
tracted assistance be necessary. The result was a sort of Byz-
antine pas de deux in which Ken managed to forestall Menon
from speaking first and to coax Nehru, who was trying to
maintain evenhanded relations with the Russians, into doing
so instead.

By then the Cuban missile crisis had been contained ("the
other guy blinked"), and Washington, perhaps feeling a bit
remiss about having left Galbraith out on a limb during his
difficult period, was leaning over backward to comply with
his every wish. In an astonishingly prompt response, three C-
130 planes loaded with military weapons and light artillery
landed in Calcutta just four days after Ken had requested the
arms. More were to follow, and as another bonus Krishna
Menon was relieved of his duties as defense minister.

In the United States, the focus shifted from a war that was
averted to one — albeit much less dangerous and farther
away — that was not. The Pentagon arranged for fifteen or
twenty reporters to hitchhike on the planes airlifting materiel,
and before long the chancery was thick not only with members of the press, but with more offers of help from Washington than Ken and his staff could cope with. He did, however,
accept the services of another press attaché and, although
without enthusiasm, of a brigadier general standing by in
London ready to fly to New Delhi with his staff. His mission
was to scrutinize India's further military requirements, make
certain that the materiel already on hand was being put to
proper use, and to prepare for any special training programs
that might become necessary. Not surprisingly, Galbraith had

some reluctance about handing that kind of power to a military man, but he was also leery of being accused of trying to run the war by himself. "I am not fond of the role of a professor masterminding a war," he told a CBS reporter. Later he added candidly, "To be more accurate, I was fond of the role but did not want to seem so."

The war continued on the two fronts, although the Indians were always more concerned about the danger to them (and the damage to their prestige) of a setback in the NEFA than they were about reverses in the Ladakh/Aksai Chin area. Even so, they did reject an offer that the Chinese made at the end of the first week in November which proposed to keep the status quo (it favored the Chinese anyway) in Aksai Chin but to compromise in NEFA, with both sides retreating twenty kilometers. Ken thought and hoped the Indians would accept this offer, and when they didn't, he feared the Chinese might mount a new and ever more ominous push — ominous because if it happened, the U.S. might be forced to back up her military aid with American troops.

The news from the fronts seesawed: one day a disaster and the next a cocky, optimistic report of Indian success in repelling the enemy. There was always great uncertainty about ultimate Chinese intentions. But along with worry about where and when the next offensive would be, Ken had to concern himself even more diligently with the larger implications and undercurrents of this war.

With the arrival of U.S. military aid, questions arose — no doubt fostered by the Soviets — as to how the U.S. could continue to accept India's nonalignment while providing her with arms to fight a Communist enemy. Ken was continually at pains to assure everyone, up to and including the prime minister, that the United States was in no way trying to develop a military partnership or force a military alliance with India.

Still, the Indians were so sensitive on this point that their press was conscientiously playing down the U.S. airlift so as not to arouse the Russians. Such a conspiracy of silence, Ken wrote, was an absurdity. Surely the American press could and indeed should point out that U.S. aid could not be written about because the country *accepting* that aid was sensitive about the reaction of the Soviet Union. He further noted that one of the largest recipients of U.S. aid in past years had been the Soviet Union. Although such anti-Soviet talk was against his usual policy, he felt it was justified under these circumstances and, he believed, helped clear some rather murky air.

As always, the Pakistanis were another main source of trouble. Tilting toward the Chinese anyway, they were by then said to be having high-level conversations with them, with, rumor had it, a nonaggression pact being discussed. Furthermore, they were accusing the Indians of using the border war to get military aid, which they eventually planned to use against them in Kashmir. And they boldly hinted that the U.S. should give them the same number of arms and materiel as they had given to India. Ken's reaction to all this was entirely consistent; over and over he urged reconciliation.[1]

Working closely with Walter McConaughy, the U.S. ambassador to Pakistan, Ken ascertained that under proper circumstances President Ayub might be willing to offer assurances to India that there would be "no embarrassment from Pakistan" in the situation with the Chinese. Proper circumstances demanded that Nehru ask for these assurances properly — that is, not quite humbly, but with extreme cordiality.

When Galbraith broached this to Nehru, the prime minister said warily that he would have no objections to the Americans' saying the Indians would welcome such assurances from the Pakistanis. This wasn't good enough; Ken tried again. Would Nehru be willing to accept warmly? Yes, the prime

---

1. Neville Maxwell, in his book *India's China War* (London: Jonathan Cape, 1970), mentions Ken as follows: "The American Ambassador . . . [became] in effect a privy councilor of the Indian government, a role Galbraith played with zest and tact" (p. 420).

minister said, he would be willing to *have them* say that. He even added that such a gesture on the part of the Pakistanis would improve not only present but future relations between the two countries. Ken moved to press his advantage; would the prime minister himself respond to the Pakistanis' assurances? Yes, said the prime minister, he would, "at some appropriate occasion." The appropriate occasion, ventured the U.S. plenipotentiary, was now. One can imagine Nehru, small, frail, and tired as he must have been by then, looking at his lanky, vigorous, and determined younger friend and giving him his quizzical, gentle little smile of agreement.

Peace came unexpectedly, "like a thief in the night," Ken wrote. On November 22 the Chinese offered a cease-fire within twenty-four hours and a promise to withdraw completely by December 1. Why this apparent capitulation? Ken, like everyone else in Delhi, was inclined to look for the small print. Finding none, he had to assume that the offer was real, but to his dismay he soon encountered considerable sentiment among the aroused Indians for a rejection of the Chinese olive branch.

Fortunately, Nehru also found the offer genuine and believed that it had been induced in large part by the depth and speed of America's response and the tangible evidence of her military support. Predictably, Ken's advice, which he preferred to call nonadvice, was for the Indians to "keep their counsel, stay quiet, win time and be suspicious of the possibilities of air power."

In due course, at least by December 6 when he wrote to President Kennedy, Ken was able to tell him that "the immediate military phase might well be over." This, while better than open hostilities, did not seem like very much except for some pluses. The Chinese had cost Krishna Menon his job, for one. For another, Ken had the impression that the war had left the Indians with a strengthened desire for a decent reconciliation with Pakistan. And perhaps most important, he told the president that because the United States had come so strongly to India's support while never giving grounds for any suspicion of ulterior motives, "there has been a simply enormous enhancement of American prestige."

In the middle of this most arduous fortnight of his service in India, the time came for the Galbraiths to move from Ratendone Road to the newly completed residence — Roosevelt House — directly next to the chancery. This, of course, did not involve Ken in wrapping cups and saucers in newspaper, filling cartons with books, or clearing out bureau drawers. Their household staff of fourteen, plus the numerous others these regulars were prone to call in at the slightest hint of additional chores, took care of all the packing, moving, and unpacking. It is obvious that the grandeur of Roosevelt House, the whiteness, the openness — rooms set apart only by Edward Stone's famous latticed-stone screens — was not a perfect match for Ken and Kitty's taste. "It is lacking in warmth but not beauty," Ken wrote of his new residence. "A fountain runs constantly below the stairway and gives the impression everywhere of a toilet out of control." Edward Stone must have loved that homey touch. Indeed, he was quite disenchanted with everything the Galbraiths had to say about his creation in an interview they gave to *Time* magazine some months after they had moved in. "You can't have a quiet chat anywhere in the house without being overheard," Kitty was reported as saying. "When we have house guests, my husband and I talk over plans for the day in our private living room, but find it quite unnecessary to discuss them later with our guests. They've already overheard every word. It's a house for open diplomacy, openly arrived at."

The sights were almost as open as the sounds. From his bedroom Ken could look across the courtyard directly into the main guest suite. "People who live in Stone houses should undress in the dark," quipped one worthy guest. Said Edward Durell Stone in response to these Galbraith complaints, "Why are they carping about these little points? These petty features obscure the truth — they are living in a palace."

The Galbraiths of course agreed; and the boys, Peter and Jamie, found it all delightful. Living under the same roof with their parents for the first time in a year and a half, they rejoiced in various features of the palatial life that the architect had not planned — notably they loved clambering up the enormously high Stone screens. On one occasion Ken himself was said to have followed them aloft.

Not long after the move to Roosevelt House, when the war was over, and after those who had come to look into its aftermath — the press, the congressional delegation, the distinguished members of the Harriman mission — had come and gone, Ken's thoughts began to turn to the Harvard Yard and 30 Francis Avenue. Suddenly, it seemed to him time to go home.

Did he pause on the threshold before moving on to yet another break point in his life, to reflect on what his years as ambassador in India had really meant to him, on how he had been nourished by India? If not then, reflection certainly came later.

"First of all," he says, "there was the wonderful business of being between Nehru and Kennedy, two people unique in the world at that extremely interesting time in American and Indian history. And the second thing, which few people have ever articulated properly, is that India is an entirely different world. You go to Europe and you go to a different version of the American personality. Slightly different art, architecture and landscape. But when you go to India you go to a wholly different artistic personality: different art, different architecture, different music, different dance, different landscape and different ways of making a living. So the fascination with India is not with its cultural similarities but with its cultural contrast — cultural trauma you might almost call it."

Perhaps without ever articulating it properly himself at the time, Ken, more than Kitty, was ready by early 1963 for a little cultural similarity. And perhaps too his thoughts were nudged in that direction by the fact that his two years' leave of absence from Harvard was running out. Although known to be strict about that rule, even the majestic Harvard might have had trouble enforcing it and depriving the United States of a highly useful and visible ambassador. Kennedy himself volunteered to speak to President Nathan Pusey about it, but Ken urged him not to intercede, saying he would rather handle the matter himself. In truth, he probably didn't want it handled at all, because he was ready to go back to Harvard.

There are various reasons — all unstated. (Ken continues to foster the impression of a stern, unbending Pusey insisting upon his return to Cambridge.) For one thing, he had a finely honed sense of quitting the stage while the audience was still clamoring for an encore; for another, there was the problem of his many physical disorders, mostly narrowed down by then to extreme fatigue and excessive dependence on sleeping pills. But perhaps more important, there was, locked in a safe in the Cambridge Trust, the half-finished first draft of his newest book, *The New Industrial State,* a work that he confidently believed was destined to be at least as significant as *The Affluent Society,* and he hoped even more so.

There was also another growing preoccupation for Galbraith. From his vantage point on the subcontinent of Asia, he had been seeing with increasing alarm the signs of a deplorable geopolitical strategy developing in that part of the world. Because he had come to believe that an egregious error verging on insanity was in the making, he had to get home, to argue, to fight, and to scheme somehow in order to derail the dreadful conflict that he feared was about to take place in Vietnam.

11

A Combination of
Brains and Guts

PEOPLE ALWAYS SEEM to remember precisely where they were on November 22, 1963, when they heard that John F. Kennedy had been assassinated.

By then Ken was back teaching at Harvard, but on that day he had gone from Cambridge to New York to have lunch with Katharine Graham and Arthur Schlesinger. He was sitting in Mrs. Graham's *Newsweek* office, waiting for the two of them, flying up together from Washington, to join him. They came in breathlessly a few minutes late; the three good friends had just sat down at the table when an aide interrupted them to report the first appalling news from Dallas.

Ken is never one to put his most deeply felt emotional thoughts into words; instead he talks of the pain of others, most notably Jackie. Perhaps more than anyone else in her close circle, it was Ken who not only felt an acute concern for the practical considerations facing the president's widow, but who undertook to solve the most pressing of these — where Jackie and her children would live when they vacated the White House.

Recalling this period some twenty-six years later, Jacqueline Kennedy Onassis notes that she really had no place to go and that it was Ken who thought of this, Ken who asked Marie and Averell Harriman whether they would put their

Georgetown house at her disposal until she found one of her own. The Harrimans responded with characteristic generosity. Nothing, Mrs. Onassis says, could have been of greater comfort to her and her children. And, she adds, until Robert Kennedy told her, she had not even known, because he had never mentioned it, that Ken was the one who had arranged this with the Harrimans. "That," says Mrs. Onassis, "is the kind of man he is."

Partisans of John F. Kennedy have long wondered just how the Vietnam War would have developed if he hadn't been killed. For Ken, a vociferous and voluble critic of U.S. military intervention, this was a particularly vexing problem. According to the Pentagon Papers, he was credited — or as the case may be, blamed — for having at one juncture influenced President Kennedy's thinking about his course of action in Vietnam.

In November 1961 when Ken was in Washington for Nehru's state visit, Kennedy had asked him to return to India via Saigon in order to give the administration a first-hand appraisal of the situation there. The administration probably got more than it bargained for when Ken began blasting them with his nonequivocal views.

The chief object of his scorn was Ngo Dinh Diem, at that time believed by many, including the U.S. ambassador to Saigon, Frederick Nolting, to be the only leader capable of providing an effective alternative to the Vietcong. "In my completely considered view," Ken wrote to Kennedy on November 21, "Diem will not reform . . . because he cannot. It is politically naive to expect it. . . . Those who think there is hope of reform will have to be persuaded."[1]

He further stated emphatically, and surely prophetically, that "a time of crisis in our policy on South Vietnam will

---

1. *The Pentagon Papers,* Senator Gravel edition (Boston: Beacon Press, n.d.), vol. 2, pp. 121–23.

come when it becomes evident that the reforms we have asked have not come off and that our presently proffered aid is not accomplishing anything. Troops will be urged to back up Diem. . . . You will be aware of my general reluctance to move in troops. On the other hand I would note that it is those of us who have worked in the political vineyards and who have committed our hearts most strongly to the political fortunes of the New Frontier who worry most about its bright promise being sunk under the rice fields."

Once again, the time of these early warnings from Ken should be noted. November 1961 was two years before Diem's murder. (Inevitably, there were rumors that the U.S. had a hand in bringing about his death; Ken, however, denies knowledge of such a circumstance.) It was two years and nine months before the Tonkin Gulf Resolution and three years and four months before the first U.S. Marines landed in South Vietnam and before 160 U.S. planes bombed North Vietnam. And it was six years and three months before the Tet offensive.

From New Delhi on April 4, 1962, Ken sent another strongly worded memorandum for the president. Restating his fear of our growing military commitment in Vietnam, he warned that it could evolve "step by step into a major, long drawn-out, indecisive military involvement." To offset such a possibility, he again urged that we "measurably reduce our commitment to the present leadership of the government of South Vietnam, and adopt an open door policy toward a political solution. We should welcome as a solution any broad based non-Communist government that is free from external interference." There followed a number of specific suggestions as to how such a general program could be implemented.

This time, again according to the Pentagon Papers, the Galbraith memo was forwarded from the White House to the secretary of defense, who, apparently after reading it, forwarded it to the Joint Chiefs of Staff for their comment. General L. L.

Lemnitzer responded: "The Joint Chiefs of Staff are aware of the deficiencies of the present government of South Vietnam. However, the President's policy of supporting the Diem regime while applying pressure for reform appears to be the only practicable alternative at this time. . . . It is the opinion of the Joint Chiefs of Staff that the present US policy toward South Vietnam, as announced by the President, should be pursued vigorously to a successful conclusion."[2]

Already then the die was cast, demonstrating what Galbraith had often railed against — a slavish adherence to what he ironically calls "a durable" truth. All his life he had insisted that he favored a capacity to adjust one's views when the initial concept was shown to be ill-conceived or inadequate. And perhaps even more significant, from that moment on, Galbraith, the relentlessly antimilitary man, was finally tied to a popular antimilitary position.

Unlike other Kennedy insiders who could not stomach Lyndon Baines Johnson, Ken thought quite well of the new president. Perhaps it was a natural affinity between two larger-than-life men, but Galbraith promptly indicated a willingness to support and work with Johnson, especially insofar as he could help him to promulgate the ideas and policies of John F. Kennedy. Significant among these, Ken tried to convince himself, was Kennedy's instinctive resistance to a U.S. military involvement in Vietnam.

Ken recalls that at first Johnson was not as responsive as Kennedy had been to Galbraith, but he was not unsympathetic. "If you only knew how much advice I'm getting on the other side," he would tell Ken. Or, "Ken, have you any idea what [General] Curtis LeMay would be doing if I weren't here to stop him?" And as long as they could keep up this sort of dialogue, Ken hoped that his role as "insider advocate" had some chance of being effective. But gradually he began to re-

2. Ibid., pp. 670–72.

alize that he and a handful of other insiders, notably George
Ball and Arthur Schlesinger, were being hopelessly undercut in this endeavor by an overwhelming combination of the
military, the State Department establishment — led by Dean
Rusk (who continued to be Ken's favorite scapegoat) — the
cold war liberals, and the congressional Right. All these fac-
tions were pressing for a military intervention in Vietnam
because of the current domino theory, which held that if
Vietnam went to a Communist government then communism
would become a powerful, almost irresistible force that
would inevitably spread to Malaysia, Singapore, Thailand,
and Indonesia.

Ken now concedes that he cannot be sure that Kennedy too
might not have been tempted and would not ultimately have
yielded to the same strong pressures favoring involvement in
Vietnam. After all, they were being enunciated by such of his
own close and highly regarded advisers as Robert Mc-
Namara, the Bundy brothers — McGeorge and William —
Walt Rostow, and General Maxwell Taylor. It is, however,
quite impossible to imagine Ken facing the outcome with
Kennedy that he finally faced with Johnson when he decided,
however reluctantly, that insider advocacy was not working
and that he would have to break with the president altogether
and go public with his fiercely held anti-Vietnam views. Certainly it is safe to say that neither President Kennedy nor John
Kenneth Galbraith would ever have permitted such a rift to
occur — a rift that symbolized a tear in the American social
fabric.

The break did not come, however, until well after Johnson's landslide presidential victory over Senator Barry Goldwater in 1964. Ken, along with nearly all Democrats and
many Republicans, had been enthusiastically for Johnson and
against Goldwater, who was then regarded as a dangerous
saber rattler. Three months after his election, President Johnson ordered the first fierce bombing of North Vietnam, saying, "The people of South Vietnam have chosen to resist. At

their request the United States has taken its place beside them in their struggle."

The battle was thus joined, led ironically by a president who had roundly defeated his alleged cold warrior opponent largely because he was perceived as being less bellicose. One month later, as U.S. bombers continued to pound North Vietnam, 3,500 Marines landed — the first deployment of U.S. ground troops. By the end of July 1965, there were 125,000 U.S. ground troops in Vietnam and Walt Rostow, of President Johnson's staff, was quoted as saying that "the Vietcong are going to collapse within weeks. Not months but weeks." In the event, it turned out to be not months but years, and it wasn't the Vietcong who collapsed.

As the war became a reality, Galbraith found himself devoting more and more of his precious time to opposing it as effectively as he could. He decided, for example, during the ten days of Harvard's spring break in 1966 to accept every speaking engagement offered to him — and he always had a flood of these — from the state of Texas. The reason? He knew that Lyndon Johnson regularly saw the Texas newspapers, and he relished the thought of the president's reading every day about John Kenneth Galbraith blasting away against the war in Vietnam before large crowds of cheering students.

He continued his saturation speechmaking, while the atmosphere, especially in university towns, grew increasingly tense. Stormy confrontations were rampant as angry young people protested against a war they believed their country had no reason to be engaged in and as they more and more defied a draft that would compel them to fight in it. Demonstrations against college administrations, seen at least symbolically as passive warmongers, involved occupying and trashing presidents' and deans' offices, which then brought in the police and in extreme cases the National Guard — "the pigs," in student terminology — who resorted to ever more vicious tactics to quell the disturbances.

On at least three occasions, once in Texas, once in Minnesota, and once on the day Martin Luther King, Jr., was killed, in California, Ken was called in by a college administration to try to dampen down angry student protests. It appeared that these young people, because they knew that Galbraith stood with them in opposing the war, trusted him, and he was thus able to defuse serious confrontations by invoking the names of Mahatma Gandhi and Martin Luther King in persuading them not to "force a conclusion with the police."

It also happened that Ken was in California on March 31, 1968, about to give his stem-winder before a large college audience when, as he was making his way to the podium, he was handed a note telling him that Johnson had just pulled out of the upcoming 1968 presidential race. It was like driving a car through an obstacle course, he says. Every time he came to a line in his speech that no longer prevailed because of Johnson's abrupt withdrawal, he had to recast his sentence in midstream.

With his speech finished, Ken could allow himself a few moments to reflect on the not inconsiderable part he had played in Johnson's change of heart. By that time he had his own bully pulpit — Americans for Democratic Action (ADA) — a platform from which he and other vocal Vietnam opponents could speak out as peace advocates. Back in 1947 Ken, along with Arthur Schlesinger, Joseph L. Rauh, Jr., Hubert Humphrey, Chester Bowles, David Dubinsky, Reinhold Niebuhr, and a handful of other committed liberals, had joined with Eleanor Roosevelt to found Americans for Democratic Action. Although always faithful to its purposes, Ken had never been a very active ADA participant. In the mid-fifties, another political organization, the Democratic Advisory Council — an offshoot of the old Finletter Group — had claimed most of his attention. Until he went off to India, he had been chairman of the Advisory Council's domestic policy committee. Dean Acheson was chairman of the foreign policy committee, and the two men often locked gentlemanly horns, Acheson — aided by Paul Nitze — taking strongly anti-Soviet positions, Ken — backed by Averell Harriman — trying to moderate their language and urge at least some accommodation with the Soviets.

Meanwhile, the ADA had prospered: Joe Rauh, a dynamic lawyer and a dedicated civil rights advocate, had been the organization's de jure and de facto leader and its steadying influence through the years. He was also an implacable foe of the Vietnam War. On Ken's return from India, Rauh, who was a good friend, urged him to take the national chairmanship of the ADA. But Ken, with an already very full plate, had to decline. However, as the Vietnam debacle escalated, Rauh again approached him, and this time the two men agreed that in order to be effective in any way in advancing the antiwar cause, they needed an antiwar presidential candidate for 1968 — symbolic perhaps, but someone around whom the thousands of war protesters could coalesce. Through the ADA, with Ken as its chairman and Joe Rauh as its alter ego, they believed that they had a good chance of finding one.

Accordingly, as Ken writes in his memoirs, he and Rauh decided one morning in late October or early November 1967 to split up and storm the Capitol, as it were, each trying to persuade a likely candidate. Ken first went to see George McGovern, whom he looked upon, since John F. Kennedy's death, as his closest political friend. Nonetheless, McGovern said no, for the very good reason that he had his own senatorial seat to defend in 1968. Next, Ken writes, he went to see Robert Kennedy, whom he and Joe Rauh and all the other ADA people considered their strongest candidate. But Bobby Kennedy also said no, because he feared it would look as if he were simply taking out his personal antipathy on Johnson. Then much to Ken's surprise, Kennedy suggested Eugene McCarthy, whose name at that point had not surfaced at all. When Ken promptly went to see McCarthy, he got a "well, maybe" answer.

Joe Rauh's recollection of this is somewhat different. He

does not recall that he and Ken split up to work Capitol Hill; his memory (which he concedes may be faulty) is that he went alone in early August to seek a candidate and spoke to Bobby Kennedy, who turned him down, as did Senator Frank Church. Uppermost in his mind is that when he went to see George McGovern he took with him a document that he called "A Proposal for a Peace Plank." He and Ken and other leaders in the ADA had concluded that if they were unsuccessful in finding a peace candidate, their next best option was to try forcefully to inject a peace plank into the 1968 Democratic platform. And when McGovern made clear that he was not going to run for president that year, the peace plank seemed the ADA's best possible substitute action.

Both Galbraith and Rauh agree that in the summer of 1967 nobody had even thought of Eugene McCarthy, the junior senator from Minnesota, as a possible candidate. McCarthy, however, does not agree. "It's been sort of built up that I was just sitting around waiting to be persuaded," he says, "when in fact I had been openly questioning the war, and had so written about it as early as 1966. But I don't remember who it was that finally came to see me, or even if anybody did. I guess people came, but I don't think Ken did. Maybe Joe Rauh would know." Thus do great men's minds (and egos) play tricks on them about the specifics of stirring events.

Once McCarthy, by the autumn of 1967, had consented to run, both Ken Galbraith and Joe Rauh promptly endorsed him, as did the ADA at its next board meeting. And if there were a few doubting Thomases among the board members (for one thing, McCarthy's voting record was not among the ADA's most acceptable), Rauh says that Ken quickly and decisively silenced them by asserting that the organization was backing the idea and not necessarily the man.

At this point it may occur to the reader to wonder whether at any time along this route Ken, invariably on the lookout for new worlds to conquer, considered allowing his name to be put forward as the symbolic peace candidate. Yes, he

did — consider, that is. The drawback was that he had not
been born in the United States, and the Constitution expressly
specifies that presidents must be native-born. However, as
Ken pondered on how he was thus being "discriminated
against," and as Arthur Schlesinger happened to call from
New York to urge his candidacy, Ken went so far as to ask
his son Alan, a lawyer, at that time clerking for a California
Supreme Court justice, to look into whether any later consti-
tutional amendments had perhaps nullified the born-in-the-
U.S.A. bar. As his father writes, Alan wisely "expressed the
strong view that any such interpretation would be fraudu-
lent" and that Ken would at best be spending more time defending his eligibility than opposing the Vietnam War.

Far more useful than this whimsical flight of fancy was a
thoughtful, down-to-earth contribution Ken made to the
cause with the publication of his little pamphlet *How to Get
Out of Vietnam.*

The thrust of his argument relies, as his arguments so often
do, on "an official truth which has turned out to be sharply
in conflict with circumstance" (what is imagined as opposed
to what exists). What was imagined in this case was that
the United States was responding to a unified Communist
conspiracy centrally directed by the Sino-Soviet bloc against
Southeast Asia. Manifestly this was not the case, since
Chinese-Russian relations were far too contentious at that
time to permit any concerted action. What *was* true was that
the Communist threat in Vietnam was being directed by the
local command of the Vietcong in Hanoi. In other words, it
was "an indigenously motivated nationalism led by Communists." As such, we had no more reason or right to respond to
it than we would have had to respond to the fifteen years of
national communism under Marshal Tito in Yugoslavia.

From this premise Ken drew the "massive conclusion" that
"we are in a war we cannot win and, even more important,
one we should not wish to win."

So, how to get out? Here, in brief, are Galbraith's assertions: After revising our goals to make them consonant with the actuality of a nationalist war, we should stop bombing north of the thirty-ninth parallel and we should withdraw permanently from exposed positions in South Vietnam and stop the costly search-and-destroy operations. Next, we should abandon the objective of total conquest and put ourselves into a position to negotiate, starting with a cease-fire. If this means excluding from the negotiating table those who believe only in a military solution, so be it. Then if the Vietcong will not cooperate, we must be ready to provide a decent refuge for the South Vietnamese who have joined our enterprise and would be thus endangered. We should also be prepared to defend such limited secure areas by leaving in place a small security force. Finally, and perhaps most difficult, we should scale down our rhetoric, even "resorting on occasion to understatement."

Commenting on this little forty-seven-page broadside and its author, James Reston wrote in the *New York Times,* "He is just old enough and big enough and Scotch enough to turn the peace movement into a political movement . . . even Lyndon Johnson could scarcely be indifferent to such a combination of brains and guts."

On March 12, 1968, Eugene McCarthy won 42.4 percent of the vote in New Hampshire. It was an extraordinary feat made even more so by the legion of scruffy, counterculture flower children who had cut their hair, shaved their faces, washed their shirts and skirts, and appeared in staid New Hampshire "clean for Gene." Lyndon Johnson, a write-in candidate on the ballot, won 49 percent, a quite weak showing for a sitting president against an almost unknown senator from Minnesota, albeit an attractive and persuasive candidate. It was partly because of this result that Johnson withdrew from the race two and a half weeks later.

As Ken and Arthur Schlesinger sat together the next night back in Cambridge, ruminating about McCarthy's astounding "victory," the phone rang. It was Ethel Kennedy for Arthur, to tell him that Bobby was reconsidering his decision not to enter the race and asking him to lend his weight in favor of her husband's candidacy. Obviously for both Arthur and Ken an agonizing conflict was in the making, one that Schlesinger promptly resolved by jumping the McCarthy ship and going over to Kennedy's. Ken did not, a fact to which McCarthy responds with appreciative words for Ken and rather the opposite for Arthur.

But even McCarthy perhaps did not grasp one of the principal reasons that Ken did not defect. It was money — a great deal of money that he personally had raised from other strong Vietnam War objectors who were probably assuaging their guilt at not doing more. But for whatever reason, these many people had given their many dollars in good faith in response to Ken Galbraith's request. To him that seemed a binding contract that he could not break, at least not at first. What would have happened later, after Bobby's victory in California, will always remain tragically open to question.

Just a few minutes before Robert Kennedy was shot, Ken was called by Richard Goodwin (who had also switched from McCarthy) to tell him that since Bobby was obviously going to get the nomination, it was time for Ken to announce his support (as any good Kennedy man should, it was implied). Ken did not say yes or no, only that he could do nothing without first talking to Gene McCarthy.

But by the time he finally talked to McCarthy it was a few days after Bobby Kennedy's funeral (Ken did not ride on the famous New York-to-Washington funeral train). He found McCarthy listless and without any real will to continue. McCarthy had not liked Robert Kennedy, resenting his waiting until after his own New Hampshire success to commit himself, but in a way Kennedy's death had made his own effort seem to him as futile as it perhaps really was. Even Ken, persuasive as he could be, was not able to pump any fight back into his peace candidate.

It remained for Hubert Humphrey, a liberal who in his role as Johnson's loyal vice-president had remained silent on the Vietnam War, to be nominated. What is doubtless remembered most vividly from the Democratic convention of 1968 was the terrible confrontation between frustrated Vietnam protesters and vicious armed authority in Chicago's Grant Park, where Ken tried, with only moderate success this time, to calm the student participants. If Humphrey's nomination was a letdown, Richard Nixon's victory over him in the general election was a disaster, further slowing the possibility of a peace settlement. A long, bumpy road lay ahead for the liberals in the United States, one from which they have yet fully to emerge.

"He is an industry in himself," says Austin Olney, Ken's longtime editor at Houghton Mifflin. And indeed, after his return from India, between 1963 and 1969, no less than seven books by John Kenneth Galbraith appeared in bookstores.[3]

Before all of his books are published, Galbraith goes through a particular rite of passage known as contract negotiating. "It's a complicated and marvelous process," says Olney, preceded by a series of eloquent letters exchanged between Galbraith and whoever is editor in chief at the time. (For many years at Houghton Mifflin Lovell Thompson filled this role, writing in a kind of "elevated, gracious eighteenth-century manner," which Galbraith matched in his response; their stately court dance masked the tugging and pulling, as canny author and astute publisher each tried to seize the advantage.)

And when finally the two sides sit down together and the actual session begins, it is invariably marked by all manner of Galbraithian convolutions. There is, for example, the matter

---

3. *The McLandress Dimension* (1963); *Economic Development* (1964); *The Scotch* (1964); *The New Industrial State* (1967); *The Triumph* (1968); *Indian Painting* (1968); and *Ambassador's Journal* (1969).

of the advance, a sum based on the likely size of the book's total royalties. Like any author, Ken naturally tries to stretch this projected number to the highest conceivable level. Then just as a figure is about to be agreed upon, he will announce that he must now factor in what he calls the Dynamic Financial Tension (the DFT). At Houghton Mifflin, says Austin Olney, they all know that the DFT is good for at least 10 and probably 15 percent more in Ken's favor.

Of course, one of the things that drew Galbraith back from India was the thought of his half-finished manuscript that was to become *The New Industrial State,* waiting for him in a bank vault in Cambridge. Despite the time and energy he was devoting to protesting the Vietnam War, despite the demands (never overwhelming but not inconsiderable either) of his teaching load at Harvard and the dozens of other obligations of his crowded schedule, it was *The New Industrial State* that, he says, "captured all my life." The book was published in the fall of 1967.

A useful way to convey the thrust of Galbraith's thesis is to quote from the review of his book by Robert M. Solow, a widely respected liberal economist, professor at MIT, and Nobel laureate, which appeared in the fall 1967 issue of a journal called *The Public Interest.*

Put here in abbreviated and somewhat simplified form, Galbraith's book, says Solow in this straightforward account, holds the following:

1. The characteristic form of organizations in modern industrial society is not the small firm but the giant corporation.

2. With few exceptions, these huge corporations are run not by the owners — the stockholders — but by a bureaucracy organized in a series of overlapping committees, including technicians and department managers, all of whom are experts in something. Galbraith calls them the technostructure.

3. Since it is in the nature of such bureaucratically controlled organizations to avoid risk, they are unwilling to

throw themselves on the mercy of the market and must therefore integrate backward, as it were, by producing their own supply of capital and labor, by managing the consumer, and by inducing him or her through advertising to buy what they want to sell.[4]

4. Because the bureaucracy is simply managing the firm in the interests of the stockholder, there is no presumption that the firm seeks the largest possible profit. It does not. Instead, its overriding goal is survival and autonomy and the fastest possible growth of sales.

5. Since modern industry produces mainly things, it believes that an expanding production of things is the main object of national life.

6. The key resource in the modern industrial state is organized intelligence in which the government supports the system of education to provide a supply of recruits for the bureaucracy. And herein lies what Galbraith calls the "scientific and educational estate," which provides a potentially more promising source of social change and national lifestyle.

So far so good, it seems. But no, it is not so good. Solow objects quite vehemently to the Galbraith who continually reaches out for large generalities. In academic economics, Professor Solow holds, you are required to prove what you say. Reasons have to be stated; no one is allowed to claim an inch more of territory than has actually been won with solid and conclusive proof.

Although Solow's purpose in setting forth his objections is quite lethal, he wraps his jabs in such elegant prose and tinges it with such beguiling, gentle sarcasm that at times his true intent is almost blunted — almost, but not quite! "That is not an easy question to answer," Solow writes at one point, "at

---

4. This is, of course, harking back to *The Affluent Society,* and understandably so, since Galbraith views *The New Industrial State* as a continuation of the ideas expressed in his earlier book. As such, it is the second of what he had already begun to consider as a trilogy; *Economics and the Public Purpose* (1973) would be the third.

least not if you insist on evidence. Professor Galbraith offers none; perhaps that is why he states his conclusion so confidently and so often." Or this ad hominem response to Galbraith's assertion that higher living standards do not necessarily indicate social excellence: "One wonders," asks Solow, "if that paragraph were written in Gstaad where, we are told, Professor Galbraith occasionally entertains his muse."

Calling *The New Industrial State* a "book for the dinner table, not for the desk," Solow further belittles the author by suggesting that the economic profession is "not likely to be much helped or hindered by Professor Galbraith's views of Whither We Are Trending."

Ken was most unhappy. It seems that when as a courtesy he was sent an advance copy of Solow's review (which was titled "The New Industrial State or Son of Affluence"), he was so infuriated by it that he phoned Irving Kristol, editor of *The Public Interest,* to demand the right to respond. This being a not unusual request, especially among scholars, Kristol said certainly, they would run Ken's response in the next issue. That was not at all what Ken had in mind. He wanted his response to appear in the *same* issue as Solow's review. But the magazine was already locked and ready to be put to bed, protested Kristol, at which point Ken is said to have demanded that it be unlocked and agreed to pay for the costs incurred. Needless to say, there was widespread interest in that particular *Public Interest.*

While Ken should have been more than equal to the task of responding to Solow, his "A Review of a Review" is rather less successful than Galbraith true-believers might have wished, for the surprising reason that it is almost entirely lacking in wit. Although his response is probably not without merit on certain arcane economic questions, it is on the whole a defensive, self-righteous, and windy piece of work. And it does indeed seem to justify Solow's "A Rejoinder" (as the original contestant, he was allowed the last word), in which he complains that "I have always laughed at Professor Galbraith's jokes, even when they have been directed at me or my friends. So it is naturally a little disappointing that he should come on so solemn when I tease him a little."

In fairness, it should be pointed out that Professor Solow did a bit more than just "tease a little," and although today he says he really did not mean to be so deeply offensive to Ken, it is hard to see how some of his blows could have crept into his review inadvertently, without his fully meaning them to be there.

In a sense, both men's positions were about equally supported in the widespread reviews that followed the publication of *The New Industrial State.* "The economic event of the year," proclaimed *The Economist.* "Professor Galbraith is so scintillating in his prose style, so devastating in his wit, so balanced in his cynicism. . . . But . . . one is still left heretically doubting how much really lies behind the bubbly."

"Galbraith's model is important and original," wrote Robert Heilbroner in the *New York Review of Books.* "But his grand outline is weakened by an unwillingness to press home his analysis to its bitter conclusion." R. J. Saulnier, in a *New York Times* review that came closest to mirroring Solow's opinion, said, "The critical question is whether Galbraith's building-blocks are sufficiently strong to support his structure. This reader thinks they are not. It is not that what he says on specific issues is completely wrong. Rather, what he says is just true enough to be plausible, but not true enough to make a convincing case. . . . Nevertheless, his considerable intellectual achievement . . . deserves the widest possible attention and discussion."

And a review that must have been particularly sweet to Ken was written for the *Saturday Review of Literature* by Adolph A. Berle, Jr., from whose work, Solow implied, Ken had borrowed heavily with only scant credit. Galbraith vigorously denied this, and Berle certainly bore no grudge, for his review was almost unqualifiedly favorable.

Also to gladden Ken's heart, this book, which he regards as his most important ("I have written *The New Industrial State* and several other books," he once said), sold hundreds of thousands of copies, was reprinted in four new editions, was translated into every conceivable foreign language, and very promptly found its way onto the *New York Times* best-seller list, where it remained (for the first four weeks in the number one place) from July 16, 1967, until March 10, 1968. Then on April 28, 1968, came another Galbraith entry on the best-seller list, this time in the fiction column — *The Triumph*.

So now we meet John Kenneth Galbraith the novelist. Surprisingly, it was Ken himself who best summed up his role in that capacity in his little foreword — "An Explanation," he calls it — to *The Triumph*. "This is a story I have tried to tell before in articles and lectures. But it has occurred to me that maybe there are truths that best emerge from fiction. I did hesitate to describe this small fable as a novel; there is, as the reader will discover, too much attempted instruction by the author. Perhaps Truman Capote would wish to call it a non-novel novel."

Perhaps a good many other readers may wish to do the same. For despite his fluency and his talent for apt descriptive passages, Ken just isn't a novelist. Primarily it is his characters: they are mere puppets, or to borrow his own phrase, "caricatures of their stereotype," put on the page solely to make a point — in this case a satirical point that the author wishes to make. One can argue that is why all fictional characters are on the page, but the trick is to make the characters seem like flesh-and-blood people with wills and points of view of their own. And this, as many reviewers pointed out, is what Galbraith fails to do in *The Triumph*.

The story concerns a mythical Latin American republic called Puerto Santos, which is ruled by a thieving dunce of a dictator whom the U.S. State Department of course supports as the bulwark against communism. A coup d'état engineered by an able and progressive young liberal strikes fear in the heart of Assistant Secretary of State Worth Campbell. After a series of complex machinations, Campbell agrees to elevate the crooked dictator's favorite son, bringing him back from his harmless life as a student at the University of Michigan to run this banana republic. To everyone's surprise, the young man shows some spirit of his own. (This was written before Grenada and, of course, before Panama.)

"It is all quite devastating," said the *New Republic*, "but in spite of the author's detailed knowledge of the scene somewhat tedious and not altogether convincing. . . . What works against one's enjoyment of this clever book is the tone in which the enterprise is conducted. It is all loftily condescending and relentlessly witty." Anthony Burgess, writing in the *Saturday Review*, said, "None of the characters engages our love or hate or sympathy as in a real novel. . . . I prefer to see this as the sort of thing a man of exceptional literary talent, not to mention cerebral power and personal sophistication, might throw off lightheartedly as a relief from what he must consider more important matters."

Ken, however, was not willing to settle for any such justification. He persists in calling *The Triumph* one of his best books, although when he protests too vigorously it is often the sign of a put-on. But in this case he backs his contention with a reference to cold cash figures. "The earnings of *The Triumph*," he points out with some irony, "were roughly the same as my earnings in my first fifteen years as a professor at Harvard."

1972: Once again back in the thick of a presidential campaign, once again on the losing side. However, during George McGovern's candidacy in that year, Ken was no longer in the role of mere speech writer, but of elder statesman (much as he may have disliked the thought that made him sound like Bernard Baruch). Clearly he was especially valued by McGovern, who says, "I've gotten more laughs and more good ideas and more stimulus out of Ken than anyone else I can think of. I discussed everything with him in '72, from the Vietnam War to farm price supports to feeding the hungry to cutting military expenditures — in fact, to converting military expenditures to civilian alternatives, literally beating swords into plowshares."

At the 1972 Democratic convention, held in Miami, Ken was a member of McGovern's Massachusetts delegation, and as such, he ruefully admits, he contributed marginally to McGovern's misfortunes and even to his later defeat. All this was quite inadvertent and came about as Ken, playing a part not in keeping with his usual practices, turned out to be a king un-maker.

One of the more obvious weaknesses of our presidential nomination ritual is the necessity it forces on our newly selected candidate to name his vice-president with almost the first words he utters after his acceptance speech. And because communications at the huge nomination conventions frequently bog down, not everyone who should be consulted about this decision always is. In this instance as McGovern, quite out of the blue, was about to name the two-time mayor of Boston, Kevin White, to be his running mate, Ken, who as a member of the Massachusetts delegation certainly should have been informed, was not; nor were any of the other members of the Massachusetts delegation. All were thunderstruck. When Ken called Father Robert Drinan, also a prominent Massachusetts delegate, to tell him the news, Father Drinan was unbelieving. "Kevin White," he quipped, "why that's the same name as the mayor of Boston."

As McGovern recalls it, "I was sitting in my hotel room when I got a call from Ken saying he thought this would be disastrous and that it was quite possible the whole Massachusetts delegation would walk out if I selected Kevin White. His objections and theirs were based in part on the fact that Kevin had been very active in Ed Muskie's campaign for the nomination, and those primary things get pretty bitter."

Also, White was by no means universally admired in his

own city, where some of his campaign practices were considered highhanded, to put it charitably, by a number of his constituents. "Teddy Kennedy was unhappy about it too," McGovern conceded, "but in the end he said, 'Well, if that's what you want, why don't you go ahead and pick Kevin and I'll bring him down to Miami on my plane?' So he was willing to go along. But I never saw any relenting on the part of Ken or any other members of the delegation."

Ken prevailed and McGovern was obliged to turn to Thomas Eagleton, senator from Missouri. Although Eagleton was well qualified — probably better so than Kevin White — he was fated to become a hapless footnote in history.[5]

With yet a third vice-presidential candidate, Sargent Shriver, McGovern lost the general election to Richard Milhous Nixon, carrying only Massachusetts and the District of Columbia.

Although he did not go into the same sort of depression he had suffered after Stevenson's two defeats, Ken still felt quite conscience stricken about the part he had played in the downfall of his good friend George McGovern, to say nothing of Kevin White, with whom he also claimed a friendship. He was therefore constrained to do something he does quite gracefully (and more often than his detractors suppose); he was forced to admit he had been wrong. He wrote Kevin White a note to that effect, which the agreeable and personable mayor of Boston graciously accepted. Six years later, when White ran for mayor again, Ken, perhaps still feeling pangs of guilt, enthusiastically endorsed him. "You don't have to live in Boston to vote for Kevin White," he wrote in a

---

5. For the benefit of younger readers, Eagleton, after having assured McGovern that there were no skeletons in his closet, was found to have years previously had a brief bout of depression for which he was given shock treatment. As McGovern points out today, had Lithium been discovered by then, the results might have been quite different. But after having firmly stated that he was for Tom Eagleton 1,000 percent, McGovern was ultimately forced to yield to public pressure and release him.

statement for attribution. Fortunately, someone in the White campaign had the wit to change that to "You don't have to live in Boston to *be* for Kevin White."

With the defeat of George McGovern, Ken's active participation in presidential politics came to an end. (Carter is barely mentioned in his memoirs, and Mondale is not even in the index.) But certainly no other facet of his indefatigable life even slowed down. In fact, by then he was only at the midway point of his writing career. By 1972, John Kenneth Galbraith had published thirteen books. Since 1972, he has published fifteen more, and counting.

12

No Swan Song

A NEW ROLE emerged for Ken at the 1972 Democratic and Republican conventions, both of which were held in Miami Beach that year. Along with William F. Buckley, Jr., he became an instant TV commentator; every morning the two friendly antagonists appeared on the *Today* show to give their slanted, blasé, and waggish views of what had been or was about to be played out at this quadrennial political rite of passage.

Ken may be arrogant, but he doesn't look arrogant, whereas Buckley manages to look positively haughty. On the *Today* program, Ken at least seemed a benign, languorous rustic. In contrast, Buckley somehow always contrived to tilt his head in such a way that he appeared to be looking down at whomever he was addressing his spate of polysyllabic words to — not easy when that happened to be J. K. Galbraith. But no matter. They were a smash hit, and their early-morning debates were full of the kind of sharp, quick parrying that best showed off each man's humor. As one columnist writing in the Memphis *Commercial Appeal* noted, "Buckley just might be the right wing's only true wit. Galbraith, a John-of-all-trades, is equipped to handle anything Buckley serves up."

"Everyone wanted to know most whether I had enjoyed debating Buckley at the two conventions in Miami," wrote Galbraith. "I said I did, which is so. Bill Buckley is the ideal opponent — pleasant, quick in response, invulnerable to insult and invariably wrong."[1]

"Where else, except in Galbraith, can you find someone who is at once president of the American Economic Association, past president of Americans for Democratic Action, author of the best-known economic treatises since John Maynard Keynes, and principal dispenser of the kind of snake oil they have been drinking here in Miami Beach."[2]

The good fellowship and humor that flowed between these two men of polar opposite political views was in notable contrast to the acrimonious debates between Buckley and Gore Vidal held at the previous, 1968 Democratic convention. This pairing had resulted in a near-slugging match after Vidal called Buckley a crypto-Nazi and Buckley responded furiously with "Now listen, you queer. Stop calling me a crypto-Nazi or I'll sock you in your goddamn face."

Galbraith and Buckley had first met six years earlier at Truman Capote's Black and White Ball, an event that conferred on them both, as on the five hundred other guests (Gore Vidal included), a certain modish distinction. But their unlikely friendship might never have flowered if it had not been for Gstaad, where both spent considerable time each winter and where the two men, among other pastimes such as skiing, soon developed the arch bantering style that continues to mark their relationship. You may wonder if they have ever ventured beyond this obvious piquancy. Have they sat down together and discussed their profoundly held differing views of society? "Only," says Buckley, "if there's a third person present who raises a question and wants to hear Galbraith and me on it. Then it becomes a political conversation, but that's very rare."

---

1. John Kenneth Galbraith, *A China Passage* (Boston: Houghton Mifflin, 1973), p. 7.
2. Washington Star Syndicate, 444 Madison Ave., New York, July 15–16, 1972.

All this seems to say that they perform rather than really communicate, a constraint that may be endemic to both. But they genuinely like each other, and their ideological incompatibility is mutually stimulating. Their zeal to top one another is unending.

To wit, a piece Buckley wrote from Gstaad for his syndicated column, "On the Right." It seems that another Gstaad celebrity, David Niven, a great favorite of both Ken's and Buckley's — and of practically everyone else who ever encountered him — had written a best seller called *The Moon Is a Balloon*, which was prominently displayed in the window of Madame Cadonau's much patronized little bookstore cum variety shop. "I felt no resentment at all against the display of his book," wrote Buckley. "But just next to it was another book by a famous local resident. 'War, Economics and Laughter,' by John Kenneth Galbraith [*Economics, Peace and Laughter*]. Bad enough, I thought, to pollute this unspoiled Alpine retreat by displaying a book by Mr. Galbraith, but altogether intolerable in the light of the fact that a chapter in it is devoted to the disparagement of a classic on municipal government written by a third distinguished writer-in-residence of the area, to wit, me."

From there on the nimble Buckley takes off; every display of one of his own books is bested by another one of Galbraith's, as Madame Cadonau "dutifully shoehorns" each new entry into her overcrowded window. She is finally forced to retire *Everything You Always Wanted to Know About Sex* to make room for Ken's 1934 Ph.D. thesis and Buckley's response — the original copy of a letter he wrote when he was sixteen years old to King George VI at Buckingham Palace.

Would that all of Ken's encounters with those holding opposing views — this includes a sizable number of mainstream economists — were so full of merriment. While Ken at least pretends to disparage these naysayers and to treat them dismissively, they seem to fall all over themselves to justify their disapproval of him. Numerous articles and even a few books have been written by orthodox economists, defensively trying to spell out and solve what one has called "Das Galbraith-problem." (Although the exact purpose of putting the question in German is obscure, it should in fairness be pointed out that Professor John Adams, the author of this particular article, did succeed in giving a very balanced picture of Galbraith the man.)[3]

Milton Friedman, the biggest name among anti-Galbraithians, has written a book (a paperback pamphlet, really) unambiguously titled *Friedman on Galbraith*. To make sure that no one misses the point, the cover of this publication is adorned with two inverted triangles one on top of the other, joined at their points. In the larger, upper triangle is the name Friedman in bold, clear, and strong black letters on a white background. Below, in the smaller triangle, is the name Galbraith in wavery, quavery white letters on a black background. Such heavy-handed symbolism sets the tone for a rehash of all the usual Galbraith-as-noneconomist shortcomings: unrealistic ideas, many of which derive from the uncredited and better-realized work of others, and insufficient evidence to sustain boldly articulated generalities, or, to quote Friedman exactly, "the reconciliation of the factual inadequacy of the Galbraithian view and the dogmatic confidence with which he asserts it."

Imagine how Milton Friedman and his disciples must have reacted when Galbraith's name was proposed in 1971 as president of the sacrosanct American Economic Association.

The traditional meeting of the AEA's nominating committee at which the next president is chosen to serve a one-year term is usually a cut-and-dried, noncontentious affair. In 1971, however, the introduction of John Kenneth Galbraith's name evoked a vociferous response from the Friedman/

---

3. John Adams, "Galbraith on Economic Development," *Journal of Post Keynesian Economics* (Fall 1984). Most of this issue was devoted to a Galbraith symposium. His son James K., a professor of economics at the University of Texas, and Arthur Schlesinger also contributed articles.

Chicago/monetarist clique. Doubtless such words as *mounte-
bank, popularizer,* and — almost worse — *journalist* were
being bandied about, but this time the conservatives over-
played their hand. The more they were disdainful about Galbraith, the more the others on the committee were determined
to have him.

Both Samuelson and Thurow, fair-minded adherents, suggest that although anywhere from a third to half of all AEA
members are not Galbraith fans, he did (and does) have his
share of strong backers. Otherwise he would never have
prevailed to become president of the association, an honor
that, Samuelson points out, was denied to Thorstein Veblen.
Solow, perhaps not in the same category vis-à-vis Galbraith as
his two MIT colleagues, suggests that Ken in the 1970s was
enjoying a wave of popularity, especially among the younger
members of the AEA, because of his vigorous stand against
the war in Vietnam.

Another economist who played a part in all this maneuvering was Wassily Leontief, a onetime professor of economics at
Harvard and later at New York University. He won the Nobel
Prize in 1973; the phrase "input-output analysis" is forever
linked to his name. "It is me who saw to it that Ken one year
became president of the American Economic Association,"
he says in his Russian-accented English. "I was president of
the association at the time and I could more or less just say I
want him. Obviously Ken was not a greatly rounded classical
theorist, so it was not too easy, but I did it."

Ken was phoned in Gstaad to ask if he would be president
of the AEA. Ken said yes, he would be, and in fact he was very
pleased. Here at least was one way to stick it to the he-is-not-
an-economist crowd.

Let no one be deluded into believing that Ken Galbraith has
ever taken lightly or in stride all the slings and arrows that
have come his way from the economics fraternity. By his own
admission he is thin-skinned about criticism directed at him,
particularly when he feels it is hidebound, as criticism of him

often is. He especially resents the implication that the reason he operates outside the economics mainstream is that he didn't have the ability to make the grade inside. Clearly, he knows this isn't true. He never lacked ability, but made a conscious choice not to be a card-carrying economist and not to squander his mind and resources on assembling elaborate statistics to support trivial propositions.

"Suppose that I had decided to write *The Affluent Society* as a rigidly technical book," he reflected once. "This is 1990. So by now it would have been forgotten for thirty-two years. Only it wouldn't have been called *The Affluent Society*. It would have been called — well, probably it would have been called something like 'Theoretical Aspects of Income Deprivation.'"

The job of being president of the American Economic Association is really not much of a job at all. Its only duty is to plan the program for the next annual meeting at Christmas, and one year later to give a presidential address. Ken did not flinch from this task; his speech was called "Power and the Useful Economist," and if it had been delivered by an unseen presence over a loudspeaker with no author identified, any reasonably perspicacious listener would have recognized pure Galbraith. Having first established that neoclassical economics (even when it is called neo-Keynesian) has become a pejorative phrase, he sets out to scold its practitioners.

> In eliding power — in making economics a nonpolitical subject — neoclassical theory destroys the relation of economics to the real world. In that world, power is decisive in what happens. And the problems of that world are increasing both in number and in the depth of their social affliction. In consequence, neoclassical and neo-Keynesian economics relegates its players to the social sidelines. They either call no plays or urge the wrong ones. To change the metaphor, they manipulate levers to which no machinery is attached.

Like many successful people, Ken is often very lucky. If there is a last plane to get out of Paris before a massive strike shuts the city down, Ken is on that plane. If there is a dramatic confrontation between two opinionated celebrities at a party, Ken is right on hand to referee the fight and even to reap some of the benefits accruing to the winner. And if he is in Germany giving a lecture, the Berlin Wall comes down practically before his very eyes.

So it was that in September 1972 when it was arranged for the two past presidents of the American Economic Association (Leontief and Yale's James Tobin) and for the current president to be invited to China to assess that country's economic status, Ken happened to be the current president. Out of this trip in September 1972 came *A China Passage,* his brief and vivid "visitor's view" of what he saw, heard, thought, and remembered on his eighteen-day journey.

There was something rather different about Ken's writing in this book — it seemed a less complex and more direct communication from author to reader. And because it appeared so to one discerning observer, *A China Passage* was, at least in part, responsible for another sea change in Ken and Kitty's life.

As before when Ken has said these "break points" happened to him out of the blue, it later developed that he had given just a little shove. This, however, was not the case when Adrian Malone called from the BBC in London in the summer of 1973. The two men had never met and Ken hadn't even heard of Adrian Malone, who introduced himself as the person who had produced the celebrated Jacob Bronowski television series, *The Ascent of Man;* he had also been involved in Kenneth Clark's highly acclaimed *Civilization.* Malone had been casting about for another series and had tentatively concluded that economics, a discipline he considered to be in a state of flux in the early 1970s, might be a good subject, particularly if it were done by someone who "had a sense of wholeness and who could cut across intellectual boundaries."

Such criteria led him directly to Galbraith, most of whose books he had read and much admired even though he says he had not always fully understood their economic subtleties.

But it was *A China Passage* that had tipped the scales for him. "Television is a blunt instrument," Malone says. "It needs a person who can make a reductionist statement and who can do so with authority." The first was demonstrated by *A China Passage*. The authority is present in all of Galbraith's books.

Even Ken, shock proof as he always seems to be, was somewhat taken aback by the unexpectedness of Malone's suggestion. How long would it take, he wondered, from conception to completion of such a series? Two to three years, Malone told him. So certainly Ken couldn't undertake such a project while continuing his teaching at Harvard, and just as certainly he couldn't ask for a leave of absence for two years to make a television series, even for the prestigious BBC. Furthermore, he would be sixty-five in a few months and eligible for retirement, although Harvard was just about to change its mandatory retirement age and Ken knew he would be urged to stay on and teach until he was seventy. But did he want to? No, he did not. He was actually quite glad for a way to get out of further teaching obligations so gracefully, and he agreed with some enthusiasm to consider Malone's offer.

It was not that he found his teaching chores onerous (especially as he often managed to use his lectures as a testing ground, trying out on his classes chapters from whatever book he happened to be writing at the time). It was just that his teaching was really number 3 on his priority list, with his writing a runaway first and his outside lectures and his political/public service activities numbers 2a and 2b.

Galbraith is quite undefensive about his preferences; he has acknowledged his order of things on numerous occasions. In his Class Day "Recessional," delivered in the Harvard Yard in the spring of his last year of teaching, he said, "Harvard has always had two kinds of professors, the inside people and the outside people. The insiders make their lives within the university community; the outsiders are only associated with it. The outside men — most of us, alas, have been men — are the best known; the insiders are the most useful. They serve on the committees, help in the administration, know the students, attend at the Houses, see the university as the embodiment of their own lives."[4] Then, having patted "these truly unselfish scholars" gently on the back, he launched into what by then had become his familiar anti–ivory tower speech. Although milder in tone than his American Economic Association presidential address, he still managed to rebuke those scholars who, albeit truly unselfishly, "retreated from involvement with public issues and opted instead for the hassle-free comforts of academic routines."

How effective a teacher was Galbraith? As far as graduate students go, he concedes he never had a coterie of students writing their doctoral theses under him. This may have been because he felt some psychological conflict between what he was doing and what he would be advising them to do. He was doubtless thinking of the large disparity between his own writing and the impeccably scholarly, earnest, and unreadable style and content of most Ph.D. theses, with which he had so little empathy.

At the undergraduate level where he usually lectured to large numbers of students, he was generally quite successful, although he played to mixed reviews. Here are a few from the *Confi[dential] Guide,* the student publication that for many years has, more or less fairly, evaluated Harvard's instructors. In the early days when Ken was still teaching the large survey course Ec 1, the *Confi Guide* of 1953 found that "the best lectures were by Galbraith and Baldwin who drew accolades for strikingly well organized material and rapid fire delivery." By 1955 it was Galbraith and Dunlop whose lectures "gave us a chance to hear some of the department's best people," and by 1958 "students found the lectures worthless. . . . Only Galbraith and Samuelson received any praise."

Ken considers the course he instituted on economic ad-

---

4. Reprinted in *A View from the Stands* (Boston: Houghton Mifflin, 1986), pp. 129–36.

vancement in underdeveloped countries (Ec 169) his most significant contribution as a Harvard professor, particularly after his return from India. The students agree, sort of. "A course with JKG is always enjoyable and informative and this is probably his best. . . . [His] emphasis on the social and political problems facing the underdeveloped nations infuriated orthodox Ec majors, but the uninitiated found themselves delighted with the broad perspectives gained."

His largest course — around 250 students — was Soc. Sci. 134, the Modern Industrial Society, about which the *Confi Guide* noted, "More or less a summary of JKG's most recent book, *The New Industrial State*. JKG has failed in all his past courses to demonstrate either economic vigor or an interest in undergraduates. And this new course will probably be no different. It will draw freshmen, awed by the name and reputation and seniors by JKG's extemporaneous witticisms about past and present government officials. But undergraduates could absorb the subject matter more quickly and easily by reading JKG's book and then inviting the great man to dinner." And one year later came an opposing view: "Galbraith is a man who knows an awful lot and whose mouth relates with a great deal of clarity the ideas of his mind. He would, if our country decided such matters on these merits, make an excellent President."

As to Galbraith's lack of interest in undergraduates, Ken agrees that he has a "less benevolent" view of his students than some of his popular Harvard insider colleagues. On the other hand, he has shown some kindnesses toward students that others may have considered very benevolent indeed, had they even known about them. For many years he gave an annual prize to the professor who was voted by a committee of graduate students in economics to be their best teacher. Not only did the winner receive a five-thousand-dollar honorarium, but the students got a fee for serving on the selection committee.

Most notable was his Affluent Society fund. Established in

1967 with all the royalties from the second edition of that book, it specified that funds be available to students who were facing an unexpected crisis in their lives. (Quite naturally, this most often involved unexpected pregnancies, as Ken had been well aware it would.) The reason he had chosen *The Affluent Society* as the source of revenue for his fund was that it had always bothered him that in 1956 he had received a Guggenheim Fellowship to work in Switzerland on what was then being called "Why People Are Poor." Then, as the success of the book became evident, he worried that he was in effect being paid twice for the same job. But because he couldn't quite see repaying the well-endowed Guggenheim Foundation with the money that poured in from *The Affluent Society,* he hit on this way of fulfilling what only a man like Ken would have thought of as a moral obligation. On several other occasions he has made similarly imaginative gifts to Harvard.

One has to understand about Ken and money. He can be tightfisted about paying his own airfare, or close to rapacious about squeezing out the last penny in a book contract. But two other of his characteristics provide the "countervailing balance." First is his sense of propriety. The man who wouldn't be paid twice for the same work, who couldn't leave the McCarthy campaign because people had given money to it at his urging, also refused to accept a check for five hundred dollars from the *Saturday Evening Post* for an article on the case for the Democrats that he wrote at the behest of the Stevenson campaign. He made the check over to the Volunteers for Stevenson because, he said, "while I suppose ghostwriting is inevitable in our time, the role of a paid ghostwriter somehow does not appeal to me."

Second, and never to be underestimated, is Ken's natural instinct to help people who need a boost, or who have done something worthy of reward or recognition. This applies to institutions as well as individuals, to colleagues, to junior faculty, to young friends, to children of old friends, to relatives. One niece has kept a letter she cherished, written to her by her

Uncle Kenneth at the time of her divorce. "It is perfectly normal," he assured her. "The very best people have them. . . . For my part I never attend weddings, only divorces. In that way I know that I will be encountering people who are certain to be happier than before." Then on to the "basic reason" for his letter. "If you find the problems associated with separation involving a financial grind, let me know. That is what relatives of the more affectionate sort are meant to be for. This includes very specifically an offer to help should you want at some future time to exploit your new independence and go back to school, launch some new career or whatever." This, too, is pure Galbraith.

Given the relative inconsequentiality of classroom teaching in Ken's grand scheme of things, his official retirement from Harvard in the summer of 1974 has made little or no dent on his way of life in Cambridge. He continues to occupy his two-room office in Littauer Center, presided over by his devoted assistant, editor, friend, and alter ego, Andrea Williams, along with whoever occupies the other desk as her assistant, secretary, scheduler, and general expediter. Through this office, which takes on the coloration of the cheerful and extraordinarily resourceful Andrea, flows an incredible amount of mail and a constant stream of telephone calls, always including one — at noon each day when he is out of town, which he is more often than not — from the boss himself.

Other aspects of his lifestyle remain unchanged by the addition of the word *Emeritus,* after his Paul M. Warburg Professor of Economics title. He continues to enjoy his lunches at the long table in the Harvard Faculty Club, where faculty and staff who happen to be lunching alone forgather to exchange prophetic insights, dazzling erudition, and brilliant badinage, as befits their profession. Ken takes such pleasure in these encounters that he devoted the three opening pages of his most recent fictional offering, *A Tenured Professor,* to re-creating the long table scene.

He and Kitty also continue to give their celebrated "Champagne in the Garden" party on the afternoon of commencement. Professor Henry Rosovsky, in "The Most Famous Professor at Harvard," a tribute to Ken, writes of this festivity attended by *le tout* Cambridge.

> It is one of the main social attractions of the season; nearly all recipients of honorary degrees are regularly in attendance and available for close inspection; the more glamorous members of the Harvard faculty are also present; so are assorted ambassadors, foreign statesmen, journalists and occasional jet-setters. Even a few students manage to get an invitation. Over the babble of voices and tongues, one tall figure floats from group to group extending a hand, bending down to pat a back while smiling in a slightly detached way at the hundreds of guests. It is a pleasant enough gathering, but even if one views cocktail parties with loathing, not to be invited would be a hellish comment on one's position in Harvard society.[5]

In sum, every advantage that his long association with Harvard had netted him remained intact as he embarked on his new career as a television star. Little did he know, despite all warnings, what was in store for him, how much he would have to learn, unlearn, and relearn.

A dry-run filming was held in Cambridge in the senior common room of Winthrop House to indoctrinate Ken and to see how he would perform on camera. As Kitty tells it, the star did not shine brightly on this occasion. Naturally, he had been off giving a lecture at some distant place, and had got home late the night before. So he was tired to begin with and much more so after having shot eight or nine takes of the same paragraph (the subject was Keynes), each time with slightly different moves or gestures; in the end the first take was considered the best. Thereafter, Adrian Malone decreed,

---

5. Samuel Bowles, Richard Edwards, and William G. Shepherd, eds., *Unconventional Wisdom: Essays on Economics in Honor of John Kenneth Galbraith* (Boston: Houghton Mifflin, 1989), pp. 327–28.

Ken was never to appear on camera when he was tired; there was always to be a day of rest before each shoot, and there were to be no outside commitments during any of the filming periods.

Eventually, there would also be another prohibition — no skiing. Lloyds of London, which had insured the series, warned that if anything happened to incapacitate Ken it would mean a loss of more than a million pounds, a large enough catastrophe to set off the Lutine Bell, which traditionally rang at Lloyds only for such disasters as a ship lost at sea.

Patience, never one of Ken's strongest virtues, was strained on every shot as he waited for camera crews to set up, for the sun to come back from behind a cloud, as an airplane above ruined one take, a pigeon flying in front of the camera another, his own misstep yet another, as lines had to be said, and said again, and again, and again, until even his own words, which he was reciting, became meaningless.

He believed that his style was to underplay, that his slightly detached air provided the best setting for his wry and ironic humor. He was quite right, that was his style, but he had to discover how to project it for television, how to make it play believably on the small screen in people's living rooms. To master this he had to trust producer Adrian Malone, director Richard Gilling, and associate directors Mick Jackson and David Kennard. He soon did; he respected these sage young professionals and held them in high esteem. He also greatly enjoyed them, as he came to enjoy nearly everything about this intriguing new adventure. "It was a very happy series," says Adrian Malone.

Early in 1974 Ken sat down with these four young men in London to plot the series — they soon agreed on its title, *The Age of Uncertainty* — and to decide what material would fall into which of the thirteen projected programs. Fortunately for posterity and future biographers, Kitty, always the literate, perceptive diary keeper, wrote a vivid account of the goings-on before and behind the screens for *American Film*, in which she spelled out the overall purpose and meaning of the series:

[The programs] would start with classical capitalism — Adam
Smith, David Ricardo, Thomas Malthus and their relevance to
the Industrial Revolution. . . . The second program, more
lighthearted (for the "dismal science" has its lunacies too)
would deal with social Darwinism, the survival of the fittest, as
typified by the more rapacious entrepreneurs of the latter nineteenth century. The dissenting doctrine would, of course, come
from Karl Marx. . . . The program on Lenin would also stress
the breakdown of the old social order, the end of the traditional ruling class, which took place in World War I. Mid-
twentieth century economic policy would focus on John Maynard Keynes.

Other programs would treat colonialism and the problems
of the Third World — the cold war, the military-industrial
complex, and the arms race. Most were sketched out by mid-
1974, and my husband wrote an essay on each. In the process,
one topic, a history of money, grew into a complete book
[*Money: Whence It Came, Where It Went*] by itself.[6]

Their operational base was London. The Galbraiths took a
flat on Hill Street just off Berkeley Square, and Andrea soon
joined them in England to see to many of the administrative
details with the BBC that otherwise Ken would have had to
do himself, and in general, to grease the wheels as only she
could.

At the BBC studios — Kensington House in Ealing — a
mammoth blackboard mapped the logistics of each program.
Where would the location shots be (usually there were at least
ten in different parts of the world for each program)? Which
of the two camera crews would be on location and which
would stay with Ken? How many of the location shots was
Ken in, doing what in TV parlance is called his "stand-up" on
camera? And how many of the location shots requiring his
presence on camera would be in Paris, for instance, thus en-
abling them to shoot the Paris scenes for all the programs at
the same time?

Sequential shooting, although easier and more logical, was

6. *American Film*, February 1977.

far too expensive to contemplate for a series whose budget was already stretched to almost 2 million pounds. But nonsequential shooting meant that a careful check had to be made before each shoot of exactly how Ken looked. What was he wearing? And what had he been wearing when the previous chronological shot in that particular program had been made in, say, Northfield, Minnesota (birthplace of Veblen)? How long was his hair? Did he have his glasses on or off?

Ken solved the clothes problem by ordering two identical gray-flannel suits from his London tailor and by buying a number of identical blue shirts and two or three dark blue knit ties, so that no matter where he was, he was always wearing the same thing. The hair length was not quite so easy. As Kitty records, the BBC provided a stylist to shape and cut his hair initially, then to photograph it from all angles. Thereafter at regular intervals, she would come to his flat and trim his hair to accord with the master photo. He was under strict orders to let no one else touch his locks. He did his best, but occasionally during the year and a half of filming when he was at home in Cambridge and far from his stylist, he would slip furtively into his Harvard Square barbershop for a trim and an update on all the latest Harvard gossip. The eyeglass problem was the simplest; he kept taking them off and putting them back on during shoots to read the cue cards, so there wasn't any continuity on that score anyway.

Ken had already written the essays that formed the basis of each program, but he still had to write a working script that covered his stand-ups and his voice-overs. (He also selected the quotations read by the actors playing the parts of various key figures, such as Marx, Keynes, and so on.) Here Malone and his associates had to do some tactful editing, or, as Andrea puts it, "see that the script didn't get lost in verbiage."

"There wasn't a sentence that didn't have three or four ideas in it," says Malone. "Sometimes they got so dense that the viewer would miss the point. He can be prolix, yes, but this is a man with a very considerable mind."

The initial filming (for program number three, "Karl Marx: The Massive Dissent") took place in Paris at the Luxembourg Gardens on April 14, 1975. Shot one, take one, of thirteen hours of programs had Ken leaning over the balustrade, facing the pond and the Palais de Luxembourg. He looked quizzical; actually, his teeth were chattering from the raw, biting cold, a cold that only Paris seems able to produce in mid-April.

His first words did not sound particularly prolix: "All revolutions have a geographical center," he said in clear, firm tones. "The French Revolution had its great center on the Place de la Bastille. And the Revolution of 1848 for a Marxist was centered here in the Luxembourg Gardens. It was an unlikely setting for a revolution. A bit like having a revolution in Regent's Park [and here the camera pans to show the Palais and adjoining courtyard gardens] or even on the Boston Common."

Having thus launched the series, he goes on in his next stand-up to talk about the nature of revolutions — a quite literate account. "Three conditions are absolutely essential: Revolutions must have determined leaders who know exactly what they want; they must have disciplined followers who will accept orders and who don't think for themselves. It is my impression that this is inconsistent with the revolutionary tendency. People who participate in revolutions want to think for themselves. Well, that can't be allowed. And finally the other side must be weak."

"It was all tightly worded and well written," recalls Malone, "but very woodenly spoken. Everyone was trying to relax him and he was getting more and more annoyed with everybody, but mostly with himself. And I said, 'Look, let's try to ease this out. Just tell me about revolutions.'

" 'What the hell do you think I've just been saying?'

" 'No,' I said, 'Don't *write* to me about it. Just tell me.'

" 'Well damn it,' he shouted. By then he was really furious. 'Damn it. Revolutions are the kicking in of a rotten door.'

" 'Ah, marvelous,' I said. 'Marvelous.' "

That's how Galbraith finally ended his stand-up about the nature of revolutions — and with gestures. George Mc-Govern has noticed and commented on a rather droll thing about Ken's gestures. When he is especially intent on getting an idea across, he will extend his oversize hands forward, palm up, and if he wishes to enumerate a point he will grip, say, the index finger of his left hand and bend it far backward. Point a. Then quite randomly at point b he will bend back another finger, never the next one in order, say the little finger this time, then maybe the third finger for point c. Thus did he illustrate the three conditions that make for a good revolution.

He was perhaps a little more polished on later programs; his gestures were more controlled, and the unruly hank of hair that often falls over his forehead was neatly combed back and sprayed firmly into place. But he always managed to sound quite like himself, if at times just a bit more avuncular than he does in real life.

The series is laced with familiar and somehow reassuring little Galbraith homilies: "Money differs from a mistress, an automobile, or cancer in being equally important to those who have it and those who don't." Or, "Some speak of service and public responsibility, and if men speak often enough of those virtues, they may persuade themselves at least a little of their practice." Or, "World War II was the last great battle of World War I."

The last program of the series was filmed at the Galbraith farm in Newfane. A dozen luminaries (Galbraith included), over half from foreign lands, traveled to Vermont to sit in a circle on white wooden Adirondack chairs and expound, some looking a bit uncomfortable in this insistently rural setting.[7] They talked during their day and a half of sessions

---

7. They included: Dr. Gyorgy Arbatov, Prof. Ralf Dahrendorf, Mrs. Katharine Graham, Rt. Hon. Edward Heath, Mr. Jack Jones, Dr. Henry Kissinger, Hon. M. R. Kukrit Pramoj, Prof. Arthur Schlesinger, Dr. Hans Selye, Rt. Hon. Shirley Williams, and Thomas Winship.

of such matters as participatory democracy, individuals in a mass society, Third World concerns, the influence of the press, arms control and new weapons, secrecy and nuclear diplomacy.

The program was notable for many reasons, not the least of which being that Ken listened much more than he talked. But the last word, as indeed it should have been, was his. "This was a discussion, not an argument," he told his listeners. "You will have sensed our shared feelings of urgency. I would be happy as I end this program if some of this same sense of urgency remained with you, my long-suffering audience, and, as I hope I may call you, my friends."

The Age of Uncertainty (needless to say it was made into a book of the same title) was not universally well received. Many accused the series of being overproduced, even gimmicky. But this did not apply either to Ken's writing, which came across well, or to his performance, which did too. However, in a way he was at least indirectly responsible for the lukewarm reception of *The Age*. At the time of its release both in America and in England, the social tide was turning to some extent conservative, creating a less friendly atmosphere for a liberal like Galbraith to be elaborating on the mass media — even on the relatively elite mass medium of public television.

Now the tide may be turning the other way; at least it is turning back toward Ken Galbraith. Invitations to speak, which had declined during the late 1970s and early 1980s to a level that would still have overwhelmed an average mortal, are now back to a level that might even overwhelm Ken if he were an average mortal, but do not, because he is not.

Moreover, he delights in his almost absurdly complicated daily schedule, his gigantic correspondence, his morning writing stint, his mass of friends, greats, near-greats, and no-greats included. He takes as much pride in his family — his wife, his three sons, and his six grandchildren — as he does in his endless string of accomplishments.

Honors, especially honorary degrees, pour in. Kitty loves to tell about the time they learned that Ken was to receive his very first honorary degree, from Bard College. Although they were supposed to keep this great news secret, Kitty could not resist a bit of bragging about it to her friend and neighbor Marian Schlesinger, then Arthur's wife.

"Is this Ken's first?" Marian Schlesinger asked. Kitty nodded proudly. "Arthur has two," Marian replied.

Ever since, "Arthur has two" has come to be a Galbraith-family rallying cry whenever the subject of honorary degrees arises. But no one, certainly not Ken, and neither Kitty nor Andrea — both stern-minded record keepers — can remember how many such degrees Ken actually does have (circa forty-five is the consensus), let alone which institutions they are from and in which year they were awarded. Some, of course, are standouts. Moscow University and the University of Paris (the Sorbonne) were two such, as was the University of California for sentimental reasons and also for the same reason Smith College, the year of Kitty's fifty-fifth reunion. And most sentimental of all and what at the time seemed the ultimate in honorary degrees was Harvard in 1988. But even that was topped by Oxford University in 1990. (Arthur had received this honor the previous year.)

Oxford calls the occasion at which the university-wide honorary degrees are conferred the Encaenia (pronounced *en-see-nia*). The ceremony is held in the seventeenth-century Sheldonian Theatre, designed by Christopher Wren (at that time an Oxford professor of astronomy). Inspired, we are told, by the Roman theater of Marcellus, the Sheldonian is semicircular at one end, with a magnificent painted ceiling, a riot of flying Cupids.

In attendance at this colorful and prestigious affair are Oxford's High Steward; the Heads of Houses; Doctors of Divinity, Civil Law, Medicine, Letters, Science, and Music; the Proctors; the Assessor; The Public Orator; the Registrar; the Chancellor with his trainbearer; and various respective spouses.

Also present is a small but prominently displayed claque of Galbraith admirers (wife, sister, granddaughter, assistant-editor, biographer, and biographer's granddaughter). At a given moment, with the organ music swelling to a nice crescendo, the big rear doors swing open and the seven honorands enter, wearing their splendid red robes, their velvet tam-o'-shanters tucked under their arms, among them the giant Galbraith and the diminutive Bishop Desmond Tutu. They line up in the aisle leading to the stage; The Public Orator steps forward and begins, first for Bishop Tutu, his lengthy Latin citation (English translation provided).

Ken comes third. He is to receive a Doctor of Civil Law, which The Public Orator tells us might equally have been a Doctor of Literature, because "verba enim elegantissime componit lectorisque arbitrio consulit." Ken several times looks down over the Orator's shoulder, as if reading what he is saying, but more probably to try to guess how much more there is still to go.

When finally it is finished, one of the seven distinguished-looking stewards, dressed in elegant black and carrying a mace, steps down from the stage, goes down the aisle, bows to Galbraith, and escorts him back onto the apron of the stage to stand looking up the steps to where the Chancellor — Lord (Roy) Jenkins, a good friend of Ken's — waits to read, also in Latin, the admission.

Ken looks well groomed, well poised, his face quite beautifully serene, although his eyes do take in the unexpected sight of his little claque sitting on the stage in front of him. One imagines the barest twinkle. "Economist extraordinary," reads the Chancellor (his Latin not quite as polished as that of The Public Orator), "who by the lucidity of your phrases have illuminated many obscurities, and brought hope and sustenance to needy people and poor countries. I admit you by my own authority and that of the whole University to the honorary degree of Doctor of Civil Law."

One award that has eluded Ken is the Nobel Prize in economics. Many respected intellectuals who are not economists vehemently believe that he truly deserves this honor. Within the economics profession are those who say that a strong case can and should be made for him as a creative artist who generates economic ideas much as did Swedish economist Gunnar Myrdal, laureate in 1974. Galbraith and Myrdal have much in common; like Ken, Myrdal's early experiences on his family's farm in Sweden are said to have sharply influenced his economic and political philosophy. Like Ken, his interest in pure economic theory was not paramount. *An American Dilemma: The Negro Problem and Modern Democracy* is far more in the spirit and intent of *The Affluent Society* than in the mold of a mathematical economist who might win the prize for something like "The Least Squares Regression Method of Quantifying Linear Relationships."

Some consider it even more unjust that Ken has never won a Pulitzer Prize or a National Book Award, as indeed his literary skills would strongly suggest he might have done. But who is to say that these laurels might not still come his way? Or that he might not tomorrow or the next day or next month or next year be awarded a $300,000 MacArthur Fellowship, be invited to be a visiting professor at Kyoto University, be appointed head of a Canadian agricultural mission to the USSR or economic adviser to a newly elected Democratic president of the United States? Or, at the very least, as this determined overachiever continues at the age of eighty-two to achieve, to publish his twenty-eighth and twenty-ninth books?

Given such an infinite range of possibilities, and such a vibrant embrace of life, how can one close a book about John Kenneth Galbraith? Perhaps only by quoting his own words one more time: "The end has come, but it is not yet in sight."

Index